THE FATHER

THE FATHER

Contemporary
Jungian Perspectives

Edited and with an Introduction by
ANDREW SAMUELS

New York University Press
Washington Square, New York

First published in the United States of America 1986
by New York University Press
Washington Square
New York, NY 10003

First published in Great Britain 1985 by
Free Association Books

Library of Congress Cataloging-in-Publication Data

Main entry under title:

The Father: contemporary Jungian perspectives.
   Bibliography: p.
   Includes index.
   1. Father and child—Addresses, essays, lectures.
2. Psychoanalysis—Addresses, essays, lectures.
3. Jung, C. G. (Carl Gustav), 1875-1961—Addresses,
essays, lectures.   I. Samuels, Andrew.

BF723.F35F37   1986   155.9′24   85-25918

ISBN 0–8147–7853–4

Typeset by Grassroots Typeset, London

Printed in Great Britain
by Short Run Press Ltd, Exeter

CONTENTS

ACKNOWLEDGEMENTS

Acknowledgements are due to the Editor of *The Journal of Analytical Psychology* for permission to publish the following papers:
Allenby, A. (1955). 'The father archetype in feminine psychology', 1 (1), pp. 79-92.
Beebe, J. (1984). 'The father's anima as a clinical and as a symbolic problem', 29 (3), pp. 227-87.
Dieckmann, H. (1976). 'Some aspects of the development of authority', 22 (3), pp. 230-42.
Greenfield, B. (1983). 'The archetypal masculine: its manifestation in myth, and its significance for women', 28 (1), pp. 33-50.
Kay, D. (1981). 'Paternal psychopathology and the emerging ego', 26 (3), pp. 203-19.
Samuels, A. (1982). 'The image of the parents in bed', 27 (4), pp. 323-39.
Seligman, E. (1982). 'The half-alive ones', 27 (1), pp. 1-20.

Acknowledgements are due to the International Association for Analytical Psychology and Verlag Adolf Bonz for permission to publish 'The concealed body language of anorexia nervosa' by Bani Shorter, which first appeared in *Money, Food, Drink, and Fashion, and Analytical Training: Depth Dimensions of Physical Existence* (The Proceedings of the Eighth International Congress for Analytical Psychology) ed. Beebe, J. (1983).

Acknowledgements are due to the Editor and publishers of the *International Journal of Psycho-Analysis* for permission to publish 'In search of a loving father' by W. Ralph Layland (1981). 62 (2), pp. 215-24.

Grateful thanks are due to Routledge & Kegan Paul, London and Boston, and Princeton University Press for permission to publish 'The significance of the father in the destiny of the individual', taken from Vol. 4 of the *Collected Works of C. G. Jung*.

Editor's acknowledgements
I should like to thank Kenneth Lambert for his helpful comments on a draft of the Introduction. Karl Figlio of Free Association

Books, Rosie Parker and John Beebe also made constructive suggestions. Responsibility for the ideas expressed in the Introduction, the introductory remarks before each paper, and the selection of papers is, of course, mine. Catherine Graham-Harrison deserves special gratitude; much of the work for this book was done in her spare time.

NOTES ON BIBLIOGRAPHY AND CONVENTIONS

Citations of the Works of C.G. Jung
Except where indicated, reference to Jung's writings is by volume and paragraph number of the *Collected Works of C.G. Jung*, published by Routledge & Kegan Paul, London and Boston, and Princeton University Press. Edited by H. Read, M. Fordham and G. Adler. Translated mainly by R. Hull.

Note on spelling
The convention has evolved, especially in Britain, of using the spelling 'phantasy' as opposed to 'fantasy' when it is intended to refer to whatever activity lies under and behind thought and feeling. 'Fantasy' is restricted to daydreaming and mental activity of a similar nature of which the subject is aware. The contributors to this book, coming, as they do, from diverse backgrounds, do not display a uniformity of style. Editorial policy has been to let each writer retain his/her original usage. The Editor's present personal preference is to use 'fantasy' in all circumstances, relying on context to make the meaning clear. This was not the case in 1982 when his paper was written, however.

CONTRIBUTORS

AMY ALLENBY, Ph D, D Phil. Training Analyst of the Association of Jungian Analysts (Alternative Training); Professional Member, Society of Analytical Psychology, London. In private practice, Oxford. Author of numerous papers on analytical psychology. C.G. Jung's *Introduction* to her doctoral thesis is in *CW* 18, pp. 656-9.

JOHN BEEBE, M D. Member of the C.G. Jung Institute, San Francisco. Editor, with P. Rosenbaum, of *Psychiatric Treatment: Crisis, Clinic and Consultation*. Editor of *Money, Food, Drink, and Fashion, and Analytical Training: Depth Dimensions of Physical Existence*. Author of several papers on analytical psychology and Editor of *The San Francisco Jung Institute Library Journal*.

HANS DIECKMANN, M D. Member and former President of the German Society for Analytical Psychology. President of the International Association for Analytical Psychology. Editor of the *Zeitschrift für Analytische Psychologie*. Author of numerous books and papers on analytical psychology. In private practice, Berlin.

BARBARA GREENFIELD, B A. Teaching Assistant, Dept. of Psychology, University of Michigan. Editor, with J. Landman, of *Social Psychology: Many Voices* (forthcoming). Author of several papers on culture and psychology. Doctoral thesis on father-daughter attachments.

DAVID KAY, M B, Ch B. Professional Member, Society of Analytical Psychology, London. In private practice. General physician 1961-83. Author of 'Foetal psychology and the analytic process', (1984). *Journal of Analytical Psychology*, 29 (4).

W. RALPH LAYLAND, M D, D P M, M R C Psych. Full Member, British Psycho-Analytical Society. Former Consultant Psychotherapist, Napsbury Hospital, nr. St. Albans.

FRED PLAUT, M B, B Chir, F R C Psych. Training Analyst of

the Society of Analytical Psychology, London. Former Editor of *The Journal of Analytical Psychology*. Author of many papers on analytical psychology, and also on the making of maps. Co-author of *A Critical Dictionary of Jungian Analysis* (forthcoming, 1986). Responsible for entries on analytical psychology in the *Glossary* of the American Psychoanalytic Association.

ANDREW SAMUELS. Professional Member, Society of Analytical Psychology, London. Author of *Jung and the Post-Jungians*. Co-author of *A Critical Dictionary of Jungian Analysis* (forthcoming, 1986). Has written many papers on analytical psychology and was responsible for the section in the *Yale Handbook of the History of Psychiatry* and entries on analytical psychology in the *Glossary* of the American Psychoanalytic Association.

EVA SELIGMAN. Training Analyst, Society of Analytical Psychology, London. Formerly Senior Staff Member, Institute of Marital Studies, London. Co-author of *Marriage: Studies in Emotional Conflict and Growth* and several papers on analytical psychology.

BANI SHORTER, M A. Diploma in Analytical Psychology, C.G. Jung Institute, Zürich. In practice in London. Co-author of *A Critical Dictionary of Jungian Analysis* (forthcoming, 1986). Responsible for entries on analytical psychology in the *Glossary* of the American Psychoanalytic Association. Her book *Woman and Her Initiation* will be published by Routledge & Kegan Paul in 1986.

Introduction

ANDREW SAMUELS

1

I N THE INTRODUCTION I want to explain how the book came into being, to say something about the relevance and importance of the theme of 'the father' and to suggest why it is significant that this is a book of Jungian papers. To lay a foundation for the papers that follow, I also want to outline some of the areas of disagreement or difference of emphasis between psychoanalysis and analytical psychology (the term for Jungian psychology); to give a brief account of the main features of analytical psychology in relation to the psyche and to analytical treatment (focusing in some detail on questions of gender, sex and man-woman relations); and finally to introduce at some length a spectrum of ideas concerning the father.

In 1983 I was writing a chapter on the development of personality when I happened to notice that several papers on the subject of the father, written by Jungian analysts, had been published in the late 1970s and 1980s. It was clear that these writers were quite consciously attempting to redress what they perceived as an imbalance in their professional interest in the mother and mother-child relations—a major area of psychoanalytic attention in recent years—in order not to overlook the rôle of the father in psychological maturation, nor to fail to acknowledge 'him' as a powerful inner agent in the emotional life of a person.

Around the same time, several friends were having babies. They talked about their plans, hopes and fantasies for parenthood in a way that signalled commitment to a true marital partnership. That is to say, the man's part in the rearing of the child was mentioned no less than the woman's. Several men commented that a problem for them was that their intentions were so radically different from their experiences of their own father in childhood that they would be flying blind. Sometimes, we looked at the books on pregnancy and childhood, and, without exception, all commented on the importance of the father at this time, adding that this was a relatively recent phenomenon.

When I reviewed my analytical practice, I could see that issues concerning the father figured just as prominently as those to do with the mother; the patient's perception of his or her parents' marriage often emerged as a central psychological factor. And yet, following the head of steam generated by Freud's concentration on castration and frustration, the father seemed to have faded from the analytic scene—or at least from analytic writing.

It is clear that a change is in the air. It is a change in the way things are 'seen' and experienced as much as a change in conscious attitudes or behaviour, though there are intellectual components. The Women's Movement has obviously played a part, together with a rethink, at least in some sectors of society, about traditional male patterns. If feminist consciousness leads to awareness of patriarchy then the patriarch emerges from the shadows and no perceptive man can avoid locating him in his soul or fail to consider what growing gender uncertainty might mean. Such introspection has its influence on the women in his life and the cycle starts again.

It must be acknowledged that these social and cultural changes have brought enormous emotional difficulties in their wake. We can observe a painful divorce from a lengthy cultural tradition. Sometimes, reappraisal of what it means to be a man has gone beyond questions concerning 'masculinity'. Then we see a takeover of mothering by the father, an overdetermined and hence spurious assumption of traditionally 'feminine' qualities such as gentleness and, above all, a profound confusion about interaction between the sexes.

Analysts are beginning to meet a new kind of man. He is a loving and attentive father to his children, a sensitive and committed marital partner, concerned with world peace and the state of the environment; he may be vegetarian. Often, he will announce himself as a feminist. He is, in fact, a wholly laudable person. But he is not happy—and bids fair to stay miserable until either the world adjusts to him or he manages truly to *integrate* his behavioural and rôle changes at a level of psychological depth. Otherwise this man, casualty of a basically positive and fruitful shift in consciousness, will stay a mother's boy. He is a mother's boy because he is doing what he does to please Woman.

Mention of psychology leads to a consideration of why it has been analytical psychologists who have been prominent in publishing their ideas and findings concerning the father. It is a fundamental tenet of analytical psychology that imbalances in conscious attitude tend to produce a compensatory unconscious

3

movement. The psyche is conceived of as 'wanting' to rest in balance. If that is applied to the question of the father, then it is more understandable why analytical psychologists have demonstrated an interest (though, as Layland's paper shows, psychoanalysis seems to be moving in a similar direction). Perhaps it is a case of analysts responding to a wider need for papers to be written rather than simply writing them for the sake of it.

There are two specific reasons why analytical psychology may present this responsiveness in such a marked way. The first has to do with the establishment of analytical psychology as a clinical discipline in its own right, practised with professionalism and restraint. From a pragmatic point of view, it is obviously attractive to enter relatively uncharted areas. Interest in Jung's work focuses, these days, on its psychotherapeutic dimension as much as on his approach to transcendence and transformation. Actually, it would be more accurate to speak of attempts to heal the split in analytical psychology between so-called 'mysticism' and an overtly clinical ethos (Stein, 1982; Schwartz-Salant, 1984; Samuels, 1985). The papers in the book may be read in the context of this process.

The second special factor which has led analytical psychology to focus on the father just as these cultural changes have been happening is the interest Jungians have in the collective aspects of man's nature. Several of the papers in this book, notably the one by Jung himself (published outside the *Collected Works* for the first time), make explicit use of collective material (myth, legend, typical pattern) in addition to the kind of history we expect to find in a case illustration.

It is necessary for an introduction to a volume of papers to delineate the scope of the book. This is to avoid disappointment as much as anything so that there are no false promises between writers and readers.

The reader will not find a sociological analysis of patriarchal society, nor more than an oblique integration of feminist ideas. And some of the assumptions used may seem old-fashioned (a point which is discussed more fully below). On the other hand, the psychological perspective, which is common to all these papers, even those with a collective or cultural concern, is just

4

what is missing from contemporary debates on sexuality, gender and parenthood. By 'psychological perspective' I mean much more than autobiography; children writing of fathers is not uncommon. What is implied is a distillation of deep, emotional experiences and the subsequent offering of such a distillation in an organized and thought-through form. Clinically informed readers will already be familiar with this style of writing; my concern is that those of a more sociological/cultural outlook, or those whose interest in consciousness is in its mass aspect, should be able to refer to the analytical ideas expressed here as at least one undercurrent to their interests. In particular, what analysts have to say about the daughter-father relationship, in health and pathology, represents a new perspective on the subject (see below).

If the ground covered is familiar to some readers, the comprehensiveness of this initial survey of what is relevant to 'the father' nonetheless has its own value; breadth may generate its own depth. For those whose knowledge of archetypal theory is sketchy or non-existent, an orientation is likely to be a must. Similarly, not all those versed in Jungian ideas are *au fait* with developments in psychoanalysis; this introduction is for them as well. Indeed, I have included a psychoanalytic paper with this end in mind. Though there are numerous case studies and vignettes in the book, there is also a variety of conceptual threads which need discriminating without anticipating the content of the papers to too great an extent.

Jung and Freud: 1906-1913

There will be few readers completely unacquainted with the factual bones of the Freud-Jung relationship: that Jung read *The Interpretation of Dreams* in 1900 and re-read it in 1903; that Jung sent Freud a copy of his *Studies in Word Association (CW 2)* in 1906 and a correspondence began; that this speedily became of great importance to both men; that they met in 1907 and talked for thirteen hours; that Freud saw Jung as the Crown Prince of the psychoanalytic kingdom (Freud was the elder by nineteen years); that Jung's non-Jewishness was a boon to Freud, who feared psychoanalysis would become a 'Jewish science'; that they visited the USA together in 1909; that personal tensions and conceptual disputes crept in; that relations were sour by 1912, when Jung published *Wandlungen und Symbole der Libido* (later *Symbols of Transformation; CW 5*); and that a final break took place in 1913. Following this break, Jung designated his psychology 'Analytical Psychology'.

The two men gave each other something. Freud gave Jung the father of strong conviction and moral courage he had lacked and also the status of the one on whom the mantle was laid. Further, Freud's influence on Jung as a long-distance supervisor of his clinical work, and particularly of difficulties therein, was immense. In addition to those personal factors, Jung gave to Freud a first empirical validation of the idea of the unconscious by the word association test. What Jung did was to analyse responses given by subjects to certain stimulus words in terms of speed of response, hesitation, no response, repetition, and so on. If the list of words were administered again, discrepancies were noted. Tension and anxiety around the key words gave a profile of an individual's problems. The results were impressively consistent. The test is no longer used clinically by analytical psychologists nor is the psychogalvanometer which was introduced later to measure physiological changes such as skin conductivity. The test has fallen out of use largely because, when the clinician has the basic concept of complex with which to work, he can ascertain what the matter is by ordinary therapeutic interaction.

A *complex*, which is what the test reveals, results from the blend of an archetypal core (see below and glossary) and human experience, particularly in the early years of life. Jung referred to the complex as a 'feeling-toned group of representations'. He meant that we feel according to our complexes. Regarded dynamically, the complex may be in conflict with what we consider reality to be or with what we may see as ideal—so that psychic activity is interfered with.

Returning to the Freud-Jung break, assessments of this vary greatly. Some, including staunch adherents of one side or the other, believe the break preserved the purity of each man's ideas. Other writers regard what happened as catastrophic, seeing Freud and Jung as exerting a balancing influence on each other which was thereby lost. Similarly, there have been many theories as to why the break took place (and here psychobiography has had a field day): homoerotic problems, son-father dynamics, Jung's inability to cope with sexuality, Freud's power complex, the different psychological type of the two men (see glossary). Sometimes Freud and Jung are recognized as writing within two quite different world-views: 'For Freud, a *Weltanschauung* exists as an external social set of beliefs... A *Weltanschauung*, according to Jung, is an individual construction... Freud has characteristically stressed the external, while Jung has emphasized the internal' (Steele, 1982, p.316).

Before considering the substance of the break, there are some contextual observations I should like to make. Freud and Jung were allies. *Inter alia*, this required an enemy or enemies against which to pit the partnership. Such enemies could be found in the opponents of psychoanalysis, though Freud greatly exaggerated such opposition and Jones, his biographer, perpetuated the fable. Even more satisfying to both men was the demolition job they carried out on many of their friends and colleagues in their correspondence. We may now understand this as a projection of their unconscious mutual antipathy, but there is an additional ramification. Psychoanalysis and analytical psychology evolved defensively, in a mirror relationship with criticism. Thus, although there was the natural and important wish to correct errors in previous attempts to capture the essence of things, some of the early momentum of psychoanalytic development derived from the fantasy of being attacked (see Freud, 1926, wherein he invents an imaginary opponent with whom to argue). This habit of mind never left Jung; right to the end he complained of being misunderstood.

A further observation concerns the norms then in existence for scientific intercourse. These stressed what seems to the modern ear an unrealistic politeness, in public at least. Thus, differences of opinion were thrust into the background. Pioneers such as Freud and Jung, whatever the emotional aspects of their difficulties, lacked a social context within which to debate and dispute. While it may be contended that present-day intellectuals are in the same dilemma, the differences become clearer when we realize that Freud and Jung never really discussed the book which Jung insisted on publishing and whose publication was intolerable for Freud (*CW* 5).

The siege mentality clouds over the historical situation and exaggerates the specialness of psychoanalysis. The early psychoanalysts were not the only group of individuals engaged on matters of moment in the early twentieth century. The Frankfurt School of Sociology and, in the world of the arts, the Bloomsbury Group, the Surrealists and the team assembled by Diaghilev for his ballet company—all these radiate something of the same mixture of excitement, cross-fertilization and an ever-present competitive tension. In that sense, psychoanalysis was hardly an isolated and defended bastion of intellectual and cultural brilliance in a hostile and lethargic sea of reactionaries.

Returning to the break between Freud and Jung, and concentrating now on Jung's evolving ideas, we can note six key conceptual disputes. *First*, Jung could not agree with what he saw as Freud's exclusively sexual interpretation of human motivation, preferring to see a symbolic meaning in what might look like simple sexual material. Unlike Freud, Jung did not regard the incest impulse in a literal manner, though he could not avoid remarking on the concrete way children express this. (Jung's ideas on incest are detailed in the section on father and daughter, below.)

Jung's approach to incest also involved him in modifying Freud's concept of libido. Jung applied it to more than sexuality, and eventually he developed a theory of psychic energy which could take any one of a number of paths—biological, spiritual, moral. The direction of flow of this energy could alter. Incest fantasy demonstrates just such an alteration in the direction of energy, in that the taboo on physical enactment turns it into another, more spiritual pathway.

The *second* of Jung's main disagreements with Freud revolved around his inability to agree with Freud's approach to the psyche, which was, in Jung's view, mechanistic and causal. Jung argued that human beings do not live according to laws analogous to physical or mechanical principles. Jung was more interested in where a patient's life was leading him (the final or prospective viewpoint) than in the causes of his situation (the reductive viewpoint). Sometimes Jung described his preferred orientation as *synthetic*, with the implication that it was whatever emerged from the starting-point that was of primary importance. This ideology of Jung's is shared in several quarters of contemporary psychoanalysis (Rycroft, 1968; Schafer, 1976). In general terms causality, as a principle of explanation, is under fire nowadays (and not only in psychology). It must be emphasized that Jung never eschewed the analysis of infancy and childhood as such—he regarded this as essential in some cases, though limited in scope.

Jung argued that certain 'primal fantasies' originated in man's phylogeny (i.e. were part of the entire biological inheritance) rather than in specific personal experiences or conscious perceptions. The latter were the *expressions* of primal fantasy. We know now that, eventually, Freud had to come round to this point of view (Laplanche and Pontalis, 1980, p. 332). The existence of primal fantasies, coupled with the abandonment by Freud of the trauma theory, implies that what a patient might tell the analyst may derive from his innate tendencies, fears and wishes. Clinical material should not be regarded as historically true but as subjectively so and, hence, meaningful. Here depth psychology makes a contribution to philosophical debates about the nature of reality.

The *third* criticism Jung had of Freud was that there was too great a distinction made between 'hallucination' and 'reality'. Throughout his writings Jung's concern is for psychological reality as experienced by the individual as opposed to what Freud termed 'actual reality'. In this context, the unconscious is not to be seen as an enemy but rather as something potentially creative and helpful. A modern psychoanalytic parallel would be Winnicott's insistence on the same point. Dreams, for instance, cease to be regarded, in Jung's perspective, as somehow deceitful, requiring decoding. Instead, dreams are claimed to reveal the unconscious situation in the psyche just as it is; quite often the opposite of what pertains in consciousness—for example, the over-assertive man who dreams of a little girl or of being a little girl.

Against Freud's concept of wish-fulfilment, Jung set his own of *compensation* to explain a main function of dreams. There are two aspects to this. First, Jung states that 'the dream is a spontaneous self-portrayal, in symbolic form, of the actual situation in the unconscious' (*CW* 8, para. 505). Second, 'every process that goes too far immediately and inevitably calls forth compensation... The theory of compensation [is] a basic law of psychic behaviour... When we set out to interpret a dream, it is always helpful to ask: What conscious attitude does it compensate?' (*CW* 16, para. 330).

Post-Freudian dream theory does seem to have moved away from Freud's starting-point to a position closer to that of Jung's. Rycroft (1979) agrees with Jung that a dream is not a deception and hence with Jung's claim that Freud's manifest-latent content division is unhelpful. Similar positions are present, according to Gill, in the work of such diverse psychoanalytic writers as Masud Khan, Pontalis and Lacan (Gill, 1982).

Lying behind these differences over dreams is a different approach to symbols (though here Jung's version of Freud is somewhat biased). Jung felt that Freud operated within the confines of a relatively limited symbolic vocabulary. 'Freudian' symbols, according to Jung, are not symbols at all—they are signs. This is because they refer only to what is known, whereas true symbols refer to what is not known and are unique ways of expressing something, perhaps a bringing together of hitherto irreconcilable attitudes. For example, Christ, as a symbol, brings together the ethereal and the corporeal, the human and the divine, the fulfilled and the cut-off-in-his-prime. A patient of mine dreamt of a skyscraper. This turned out to refer to his problems in relating his 'higher' values and his spirituality to concrete achievements in the external world. The Freud whom Jung knew would have said 'penis'—or so Jung assumed.

What is specific to Jung's approach to symbols is the part played by pairs of opposites. 'The opposites' are the lifeblood of the psyche, according to Jung, and the interplay between them actually creates psychic energy. For, when two opposites meet, they may combine to form a new psychological product, a third option which may supersede or transcend the previous either /or situation. This model of psychological growth owed something to Hegel's thesis-antithesis-synthesis formulation. What is accentuated is the role of symbolic experience and the capacity of the psyche to develop and change through its 'transcendent function' (*CW* 8). The items transcended are the differences encapsulated in the opposites (for my patient, spirit and achievement) and the rigid divide between consciousness and the unconscious. Though the transcendent function is an expression of the working of the self (see glossary), much depends on the capacity of the ego, first to discriminate the opposites, then to allow their interaction to happen and, finally, to protect whatever new product or position might emerge.

The *fourth* area of disagreement concerned the balance of innate (constitutional) factors and the environment in the formation of personality. This balance was perceived differently by each man. Jung was later to refine his interest in the innate (see archetypes, below, and glossary), but it is interesting to speculate what might have happened had Freud continued to develop the possibility that some elements in the unconscious have never been conscious, a point which would perhaps have led to a concept such as 'archetype'. Instead, both before and after his major theoretical revision of 1923, Freud emphasized the unconscious as a repository of repressed but once-conscious material. Though the id was stated to be, in part, hereditary and innate, this idea was not fleshed out until Melanie Klein's work fourteen years later. Similarly, early references in Freud to 'primal phantasies' as a 'phylogenetic endowment' tend to be muted in subsequent expositions of his thought.

Fifth, there was a difference of emphasis regarding the origin of conscience and morality. For Freud, the super-ego was the psychical agency that corresponded to these, and it was derived from the introjection of images of the prohibiting parent of the same sex in the Oedipus complex. Jung tended to see morality as innate, as the moral channel for libido referred to earlier, and this orientation aligns Jung once more with Klein and her theory of the very early genesis of the super-ego, and also with Winnicott's stress on innate morality. From within analytical psychology, Hillman has pointed up the differences between an externally located prohibition and innate inhibitions, which do not have to be learnt at all (Hillman's example is the 'masturbation inhibition'). Ethological material on the co-operativeness of animals adds additional weight to the argument for innate morality which becomes more relevant when we look at Jung's concept of the self later.

The *sixth* and final key area of disagreement concerned the nodal status of the Oedipus complex. Jung's approach to the development of personality highlighted the earlier relationship of infant and mother. Jung's interest in pre-Oedipal dynamics and his introduction of various terms to describe early psychological states anticipated the findings of later psychoanalytic object relations theorists (who have had their own battles with their classical colleagues). For example, Jung's concept of *participation mystique* may be compared with projective identification: a part of the personality is placed into and experienced as if it were in the object. The term was derived from anthropology, but was adopted by Jung to illustrate this particular relation between subject and object; the anthropological reference was to the tribe's placing something of their group psychology in a totem or cult object. Similarly, Jung wrote in 1921 of a state of identity, in which subject and object are one, psychologically speaking. When applied to early development in infancy, the concept resembles the American research psychoanalyst Mahler's later formulation of 'normal autism'. In general, as Roazen noted, Jung was arguing that neurosis was not just a matter of fixation 'years before the rise of ego psychology' (Roazen, 1976, p. 272).

Jung before Freud: 1896-1905

It might help our assessment of the creative tension between analytical psychology and psychoanalysis if we step back from the split between Jung and Freud and get a sense of Jung's own philosophical and psychological interests before he met Freud. The recent publication (1983) of the papers Jung gave to a student discussion group at Basle University (the Zofingia Club) has thrown open the question of Freud's influence on Jung for reassessment. At that time, Jung had never heard of Freud. Prior to a thorough study of these lectures, analytical psychology's roots were assumed to lie solely within psychoanalysis. It turns out, however, that many of Jung's later interests found expression in these early lectures and we can also take from them the clearest possible picture of the conceptual background to Jung's work, remembering that he was twenty one years old when the first paper was delivered to his peers.

In 1897 Jung read a paper entitled 'Some Thoughts on Psychology'. Here, after setting the scene with quotations from Kant and Schopenhauer, he discusses the existence of 'spirits' beyond the body and 'in another world'. The ideas are remarkably similar to those which later appear as the theory of the autonomous psychic complex (see glossary). In the lecture, this leads on to the suggestion of a life-principle; this is the 'soul', which is greater than our consciousness. Later in Jung's development, these seeds blossom into the theory of psychic energy and the concept of the self (see glossary). In sum, as von Franz writes in her introduction to the *Zofingia Lectures,* 'here Jung first mentions indirectly the idea of an unconscious psyche'. What is more, the 'unconscious' is stated to be purposeful in its behaviour and outside of space-time logic. Jung then introduces the fields of spiritualistic and telepathic phenomena to underpin what he would later call 'psychic reality'. The lecture concludes with a plea for morality in science (on this occasion a condemnation of vivisection) and for an approach to religion which allows for its irrational aspects. Again, these are both crucial topics for the mature Jung.

The Psyche

Moving from the historical account of the differences between Freud and Jung, it might be useful to summarize briefly Jung's views on the structure and dynamics of the psyche. By his basic definition of the psyche as the 'totality of all psychic processes, conscious as well as unconscious' (*CW* 6, para. 797), Jung intended to delineate the area of interest for analytical psychology. This would be something different from philosophy, biology, theology and a psychology limited to the study of either instinct or behaviour. The somewhat tautological nature of the definition emphasizes a particular problem with psychological exploration: the overlap of subjective and objective interest. Jung makes reference to the 'personal equation', the impact that the personality and context of the observer (the analyst) makes on his observations.

This concept of psyche can also be seen as requiring a special

13

perspective on phenomena, which is characterized by an attention to depth and intensity and, hence, to the difference between a mere event and an experience. Here the word 'soul' becomes relevant, and it is in connection with such a depth perspective that Jung usually uses it rather than in a conventionally Christian manner. Finally, a truly psychological perspective contains intimations of pattern and meaning, not to the extent of a fixed predestination but, nevertheless, discernible by the individual.

This leads us to a consideration of the structure of the psyche. The tendency to organize his thought in terms of opposites, which was noted earlier, led Jung to map psyche in a way that seems somewhat too pat for the modern eye. However, a systemic arrangement of psychic components enables us to see how developments at one point send ripples throughout the entire system. If we take this systemic and cybernetic aspect of Jung's thought together with its structuralist cast, we can see Jung as more in the mainstream of twentieth century thought than is usually regarded as being the case. *Figure 1* should be read in conjunction with the glossary; it should not be taken literally, but the reader may find it useful to refer back to it.

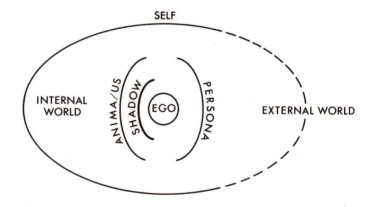

Figure 1

In Jung's description of it, the psyche is an entity made for movement, growth, change and transformation. He refers to these capacities of the human psyche as its distinguishing characteristics. A degree of evolution towards self-realization is therefore embedded in all psychic processes. This idea brings its own problems: Is man to be seen as developing out of some original, unconscious state of wholeness, realizing more and more of his potential? Or as moving with greater or lesser regularity towards a goal that is, as it were, marked out for him—the 'person he was intended to be'? Or as proceeding in an anarchic manner from crisis to crisis, struggling to make sense of what is happening to him? To say that all three possibilities are intermingled is simple. But each has its own psychological tone and flavour, and the weighting given to each plays a crucial part in understanding clinical material.

The psyche, like most natural systems such as the body, struggles to keep itself in balance. It will do this even when the attempt throws up unpleasant symptoms, frightening dreams or seemingly insoluble life problems. If a person's development has been one-sided, the psyche contains within it whatever is necessary to rectify or compensate for this. Over-optimism or blind faith must be avoided here; keeping in balance requires work, and painful or difficult choices often have to be made.

Jung's speculations on the nature of the psyche led him to consider it as a force in the universe. The psychological takes its place as a separate realm in addition to the biological and spiritual dimensions of existence. What is important is the relationship between these dimensions, which comes into being in the psyche. Jung's ideas on the relationship of psyche and body do not involve the psyche as based on, derived from, analogous to, or correlated with the body but as a true partner with it. A similar relationship is proposed with the non-organic world (the theory of synchronicity; *CW* 8).

Jung's view of analysis and psychotherapy

Jung's view of analysis, expressed in many of his writings, is that of an interactive process. Analyst and patient are equally 'in' the treatment. The analyst's personality and development are as important as theory or technique and, above all, both participants may be affected or even transformed by what happens between them:

> For two personalities to meet is like mixing two different chemical substances: if there is any combination at all, both are transformed. In any effective psychological treatment the [analyst] is bound to influence the patient; but his influence can only take place if the patient has a reciprocal influence on the [analyst]. You can exert no influence if you are not subject to influence. It is futile for the [analyst] to shield himself with a smokescreen of fatherly and professional authority. By so doing he only denies himself the use of a highly important organ of information. (*CW* 16, para. 163)

That passage was written in 1929. Jung may therefore be seen as a pioneer of the use of countertransference affects by the analyst and of understanding these as unconscious communications from the patient. *Figure 2* demonstrates this. It is based on a diagram of Jung's (*CW* 16, p.221).

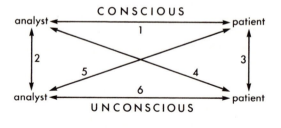

Figure 2

The double headed arrows indicate two-way relatedness: '1' indicates the conscious relationship between analyst and patient, the level of their rapport and, ultimately, the therapeutic alliance; '2' indicates the analyst's connection to his own unconscious, aided by his training analysis and, it should be added, containing whatever it is that makes him a 'wounded healer'; '3' indicates the patient's relation to his unconscious, his resistance, conflicts, compulsions, obsessions, needs, shadow, etc; '4' indicates the analyst's attempt to understand the patient's unconscious situation and also the influence of the patient on the analyst's ego—what he knows he is learning from the patient; '5' indicates the analyst's use of empathy and intuition to deepen his relation to the patient, and also what the analyst has unconsciously gained or lost from his contact with the patient; '6' indicates connection between the two unconscious systems of patient and analyst. There are two additional relations that should not be forgotten, though they would complicate the diagram (much as they cause complications in a real analysis): the relation of analyst and of patient to his or her apparent outer world (family, friends, job).

How does a relationship between two people lead to internal change in one or both? How does internal change affect relationships? To answer these questions, Jung made use of alchemy—understood as a metaphor both for psychological growth and the events of the analytical process. Many alchemical terms illuminated analytical happenings. For example, the *vas* or alchemical vessel could be compared to the containing analytical relationship. (There are very many technical links which may be made and the reader is referred to Lambert, 1981, pp. 243-6, and Samuels, 1985, pp. 178-82.)

The important thing to note about the alchemical metaphor is that the human body finds a use as a symbol of psychological phenomena. Without the body of another person, or the differing bodies of the two sexes, the psyche would be deprived of anything onto which to project its contents.

The alchemists tended to work in actual or fantasied relation to a *soror mystica,* a mystical sister. This stress on the other, whether bodily real or imaginary, suggests a parallel with one of the central themes of contemporary psychoanalysis: the experience of oneself in a relationship with another person. Lacan noted this in connection with mother and infant and referred to the mirror phase of development (1949). Winnicott also wrote of the same phenomenon (1967). It is not always recognized that the analytical psychologist Neumann was on the same track with his assertion (written in 1959) that the mother 'carries' the infant's self. There is always an other, even an Other, in the sense of a significant other. This can be the unconscious itself, the analyst, the patient, the *soror,* the blank page for the writer, his audience

17

for the lecturer, God for the mystic. The alchemists anticipated Lacan, who wrote of the Other in analysis as 'the locus in which is constituted the I who speaks with him who hears' (Lemaire, 1977, p. 157). In a sense, the analytic dialogue is itself the Other, at the point where the internal worlds of patient and analyst overlap. Or one may imagine an Other in relation to the entire analysis, a sort of guarantor of good faith; in Lemaire's phrase, a 'third-party witness'.

Post-Jungian analytical psychology

It is important to note that not all Jungian analysts think alike. Though formally constituted schools do not exist, there are broad groupings within analytical psychology, groupings whose foundations are located in disputes about the relative weight that should be granted to Jung's original concepts and the extent to which these should be modified or extended. For instance, there is a considerable variation in the importance given to 'historical' material from the past of the patient, the way this appears in the analytical relationship and the meaning given to it. While none of these writers adopts causality as a guiding principle, some are more concerned with historical facts than others. Analysts who do not deal in terms of a *person's* history adopt what might be called a macrohistorical perspective; the history of human culture and its development form the backdrop in this instance. Other theoretical distinctions will receive comment *en passant* (and see Samuels, 1985).

Gender, sex and psyche

We return at this juncture to the questions asked earlier: why *now* for the father? What's going on? The idea of the father raises questions about the nature of sexuality and gender identity, about which there has been a profound shift in collective perception. Freud's emphasis was on the omnipresence of sex; Jung's on its symbolic significance. And in the last quarter of the century the focus seems to be more on behaviour than on biology or symbolism. This concentration on what people do, rather than on what they have previously been presumed to be, underpins the

18

important distinction that is made currently between sex and gender: the first referring to anatomy, reproduction and the biological substratum to behaviour (should there be one); the second, on the other hand, covering rôle, attitude and expectation. The difference is between our speaking of male and female or of masculine and feminine. The operative part of that distinction is that, because masculine and feminine possess the fluid characteristics of psychological entities, they may be regarded as much more than indices of behaviour. They refer to an internal psychological state, even to an internal balance (see below).

The relation between sex and gender is an issue that captivates. It is a conundrum that constantly engages people in argument about what is 'really' feminine or 'naturally' masculine—with the implication that a woman or a man may be expected to demonstrate the qualities under examination. Such assertions are simplistic in that they assume a *direct* equation between anatomy and psychology; a man, for instance, must be an assertive, penetrative creature *because* he has a penis (thought to behave in such a manner), or a woman is more likely to be receptive to the needs of others *because* of the shape and function of her womb and breasts. The argument against this kind of thinking is that it is culture and not anatomy which plays the decisive part in determining gender rôle and hence our expectations; biology's influence is indirect and difficult to identify (Sayers, 1982).

It would, however, be erroneous to conclude from this argument that women were identical with men. Clearly, in our culture, and perhaps in all cultures, there are differences in expectation, rôle, behaviour. In fact, all that seems clear about men and women is that culture depends on there being a difference. But are men and women really different in the way and to the extent that our culture seems to emphasize?

There is a view that men and women are complementary to each other, such complementarity being psychological as well as biological (for reproduction). In other words, there are essential, invariable and, above all, different psychological characteristics which pertain to men and women respectively. This view, apparently reasonable and certainly convenient, presents us with a number of problems. Certainly, as far as

19

way in which an individual's values and attitudes may shift even within an oppressive system. It should be noted that this does not suggest a woman obtaining access to a 'male' world. Rather, she is construed as having access to all psychological possibilities.

Similarly, Jung's concepts of Eros and Logos also radiate a sense of universal potentiality. Eros and Logos are archetypal principles of psychological functioning; that is, both are built into all of us. It has been suggested that they are discernible in the different functioning of the two cerebral hemispheres (Rossi, 1977). Eros speaks of connectedness, relatedness, harmony, a holistic perspective, and is named for the lover of Psyche and son of Aphrodite. Logos covers rationality, logic, intellect, an analytical perspective; it means 'the word'. Clearly, human life requires both of these great principles and all persons, male and female, demonstrate their access both to Eros and to Logos each and every day. But sometimes Jung eschews this attitude. Then Eros and Logos are-tagged 'feminine' and 'masculine' respectively. This in itself need not present a problem (though it is confusing) for, as we have seen, a woman can behave in a culturally 'masculine' way quite easily. But it is when men and women are described as if they were exclusively Logos or Eros creatures that the weakness in analytical psychology becomes marked. Nevertheless, when Jung writes that 'it is the function of Eros to unite what Logos has sundered' (*CW* 10, para. 275) and numerous other similarly balanced statements, his ideas acquire the new use I have been sketching.

We need a more neutral language, and one which permits greater flexibility. Maybe Bion's use of 'container/contained' would suffice. It might be better, though, to exert the discipline of not using gender terminology unless absolutely necessary.

These remarks, which are a suggestion as to how Jung may be read (that is, a deconstruction of Jung), should serve as an antidote to the image of Jung and, by association, analytical psychologists, as biased or prejudiced. Jung *was* a man of his era but he also had a vision of individuation (see glossary) that went beyond conventional restrictions on gender potentialities.

This overview has a relevance for our consideration of the father. What does masculine-feminine complementarity mean for him? Is there a 'feminine' aspect to fathering which might be highlighted? Our image of father, the behaviour of our father, our functioning as father—all can be seen from an innate (archetypal) or from a personal perspective, or from a combination of these. And there is both an internal and an external aspect— the real father as we know him in the outside world and then the presence of an image of father in us (and combinations of these). It is to the first pair (personal and archetypal father) that we now turn our attention.

The archetypal father

The mention of the archetypal father is in contrast with a vision restricted to personal experience. The idea is that, behind the personal father whom we know and to whom we relate, lies an innate psychological structure which influences the way we experience him. This structure functions as a blueprint or expectation of certain features in the environment; it is a predisposition which leads us to experience life in a patterned way; the psychological equivalent of an instinct. Whatever the salient features of fatherhood may be, and whether or not a male figure has to be their executor, those features are not the result of accident or coincidence. The perception of our personal father is an end product resting on an archetypal substructure. Both halves of this formulation need each other: no archetype, no pattern or consistency within 'father'; no personal embodiment of the archetype, no human life. When we relate to the father, we relate also to our expectation of him. He is strong or weak, castrating or facilitating, depending on how he does or does not fit in with the expectation. This may not be the same as a culturally determined precondition demanded of a man who is to be a father, but a case may be made for holding that the cultural preconditions themselves derive from parts of the archetype (Shorter's and Greenfield's papers in this book).

Analytical psychologists are usually careful to separate the notion of the archetypal structure or pattern from the archetypal *image* of the father. This is because, though the structure may be innate or inherited, the image is influenced by individual and cultural experiences. The theoretical point has another use: to underline that one's images of father are a combination of the

23

archetypally and culturally determined expectations just mentioned and the personal, historical experience of the idiosyncrasies of a particular man. The flavour of one's image of 'father' depends upon the personal father's mediation of the archetypal father.

The actual father may therefore be characterized as archetypal to some degree or other; the problem then is to demonstrate how the image of father acquires its humanly manageable dimension. For the more archetypal the image of father and the more extreme and primitive it becomes, the more difficult it will be for a person to achieve a human connection with his personal father. We can formulate this as follows: the degree of humanness in the image of the father and the ease with which the image can be related to by a child depends upon the success of the personal father in humanizing the archetypal images. If we return to the two spectra mentioned above (strong-weak and castrating-facilitating), the task of the personal father in his relationships with his children is to avoid being hooked up at one end of the spectrum so that all other positions are lost. Extreme positions cause the child to be faced with a father image that is too exaggerated and one-sided for a satisfactory relationship with the real father to become possible.

As ever in psychopathology, the problem is at the same time one of there being too much and one of there being too little. Too much of a strong father quells the child's independent spirit. Too little strength (too much weakness) leaves him or her unprotected and unstimulated. An all-facilitating father is not a good introduction to life. But an all-harsh, critical, castrating father wreaks havoc in the psychosexual and social functioning of his offspring. Given an excess or a serious lack of simple emotional qualities in the personal father, the individual can only relate to a heavily archetypal image of father.

The internal father

So far we have been discussing the blend of personal and archetypal factors in our perception of our actual father; that is, the father outside us to whom we relate. He is 'outside' even when coloured by projections from within. But what of the father image inside, a *symbol* of certain emotional capacities or psychological functions? That, too, will be a blend of the introjected personal characteristics of the actual father and the structural (i.e. archetypal) father of the unconscious. But, crucially, he is now a part of the individual's own psyche. There are four main themes which can be picked out in which the internal father plays a prime part. These are: (1) the question of personal and social authority; (2) the evolution of ideals and values; (3) the development of sexuality and psychosexual identity; and (4) social and cultural rôle. I propose briefly to discuss these four themes relating to the internal father and then to examine a number of specific emotional relationships in which the father as a whole is involved: father and mother, father and daughter, father and son, and so forth.

Inasmuch as our culture has given to men more opportunity to exercise authority, mobility and power than to women, the internal father symbolizes an individual's relationship to authority and also the capacity to be authoritative. Qualities such as decisiveness, courage and forcefulness may, in this symbolic approach, be regarded as attached to either a boy's or a girl's internal image of father. In more negative form, these traits appear as moral rigidity, authoritarianism and obsessive thought or action. Over the course of a lifetime, the centre of authority in a developing person seems to shift. At first, introjections of parental prohibitions and internalizations of parental disapproval form a base for self-esteem and for relations with others. Gradually, then, a form of inner voice with its own specific authority emerges, something like a gravity forms, an impression of being rooted, grounded, capable of independent judgement. The movement from super-ego dominance to this independence depends on an optimal space being created between the individual and his or her internal authority/father. Too little space and over-rigid boundaries, and a sense of authority rooted in the self will not evolve. Too much space and a lack of boundary, and what authority may exist will be too easily won, hence spurious and likely to appear either as dogmatism or, conversely, as perpetually requiring the support of others (see Dieckmann's paper in this book).

The second symbolic theme was the linkage of the internal

father image to the development of ideals and values. Jung was interested in the father as a representative of the spiritual world as opposed to the earthiness encapsulated in symbolic images of the mother. Remember, he is not saying 'fathers are spiritual, mothers earthy'. The following passage shows that he is talking about the archetypes of the mother and father:

> The archetype of the mother is the most immediate one for the child. But with the development of consciousness the father also enters his field of vision, and activates an archetype whose nature is in many respects opposed to that of the mother. Just as the mother archetype corresponds to the Chinese *yin*, so the father archetype corresponds to the *yang*. It determines our relation to man, to the law and the state, to reason and the spirit, and the dynamism of nature. 'Fatherland' implies boundaries, a definite localization in space, whereas the land itself is Mother Earth, quiescent and fruitful. The father...represents authority, hence also law and the state. He is...the creative wind-breath—the spirit, pneuma, *atman*. (*CW* 10, para. 65)

Some support for Jung's coupling of the internal father image with 'spirit' can be found in Kohut's work in psychoanalysis. Kohut's version of early development is that the personality evolves around two poles (Kohut, 1971, 1977). The first of these is concerned with actual achievements: at first the milestones of infant development, walking, talking, toilet training. The second pole has to do with values and one's attitude towards achievement. The first pole arises out of the mother's 'mirroring' of the child's omnipotence. She permits an illusion of his grandiosity and omnipotence to flourish and then facilitates a gradual deflation leading to an acceptance of his immaturity and vulnerability. Only then can genuine achievement take place. The second pole (values) is facilitated by the father who, in normal development, is idealized by the growing child, whether male or female (perhaps 'admired' would be a better word), and then 'emulated'. It is interesting that it is not the father's achievements upon which Kohut focuses but rather his attitude to achievement, i.e. that aspect of his personality and how the child feels about him. Taking the two poles together, the child's sense of self and of having a self gradually form.

The rôle of the father in the development of sexuality does vary according to the sex of the child (this was our third theme). In general terms, and from a developmental perspective, both the attitude of the father to erotic life and his behaviour in this regard have an impact. It is his relationship to his wife as well as to the children that needs to be considered. In our culture, the boy usually sees a rôle model, the girl a love object (see section on father and mother, below, for a fuller discussion). As far as psychosexuality is concerned, the father's relationship with and perception of his own parents become central. It was the negative reaction of son to father that was noted by Freud. Similarly, the father appears in much psychoanalytic writing as fundamentally opposed to his son's sexual desire. Instances when that negative image has been a personal reality (and the opposite case for the daughter, the over-erotic father) are also more fully discussed below in the sections on father and daughter, and father and son.

Our fourth and final theme involved the father's impact upon his children in terms of their perceptions of their cultural and social rôle. Here, even when we are talking of the internal father image, there are bound to be enormous differences for boys and girls. It might help to consider what differences in developmental experience there actually are for male and female children.

A boy does not have to switch his love object as he moves from two-person to three-person relating: the feeding mother and the Oedipal mother are the same person. In Western culture, a girl will have to make a switch. Different problems are presented to a boy in developing his gender identity from those presented to a girl. The relationship of boy and mother makes a feminine identification a distinct possibility, and one to be overcome; a girl does not have to surmount her relationship to her mother in quite the same way. It is true that she does have to distinguish between woman as mother and various other possibilities (sexual woman, career woman, etc.), and it is not always easy to discriminate these alternatives. Nevertheless, the notion that a boy has a different kind of difficulty in separating from his mother seems reasonable.

While it may be true, as Eichenbaum and Orbach suggest (1982, p.31), that women learn about their place in the world

27

from their mothers, less attention has been paid to what happens within the daughter-father relationship, his attitude towards her, and what he inspires or extinguishes in her. As I worked on the papers for this book, I became aware that what they say about this particular relationship is of the greatest significance.

The father and his relationships

FATHER AND MOTHER. I have chosen to discuss this first because an opportunity is offered to consider the chronology of the father's appearance in the psychological life of the child. One problem is that demonstration of recognition of father as 'father' may postdate an emotional recognition that is unexpressed behaviourally and, hence, unobservable. The father's presence may be experienced first as an interruption of the mother-infant relationship. It has been observed that an actual recognition can be seen as early as the fourth or fifth months (Abelin, 1975; Harris, 1975; Main and Weston, 1981). If this is so, then the father has a part to play in the process of empathic mirroring that has usually been regarded as the mother's province. Such mirroring is crucial to the infant's experience and acceptance of himself as a whole person. But it is not clear that this very early mirroring father is experienced as more than a part or an extension of an essentially maternal mirroring environment.

The early recognition of father implies that discrimination of the parents into two entities takes place at the same time as attachment and separation processes in relation to the mother. The father has to be active and insert himself between mother and baby as a reminder of the world outside their relationship. So the important move from two-person to three-person functioning has to be envisioned as a very early phenomenon. Indeed, in my paper in this book, I suggest that the images of mother-infant interaction in the infant's psyche and the image an infant has of his parents (joined or separate) play into each other. Both sets of imagery provide foundations for subsequent movements within the psyche. How the infant perceives his parents' relationship affects his relationship with both mother and father in addition to his subsequent sexual relationships. Then there is the attitude he develops towards his inner world, where images of persons symbolize parts of the infant's own personality. We are concerned with the level of sexual satisfaction actually experienced by the parents and communicated to or picked up by the child, and also with the child's fantasies about this.

In this introduction, I would like to mention one aspect of the father-mother relationship explored much more fully by Kay in this book. This is the rivalry between the parents, engendered or simply fuelled by their baby (later, we look at rivalry between parent and baby). Such rivalry is, when in proportion, the inevitable darker side of parental joy. But sometimes the identity of a parent becomes tangled up with a worry that they might not be the 'special' parent of their baby. What has happened is that images of the parents of the parent become projected into the infant, who acquires a power quite different from his healthy, infantile fantasies of omnipotence, and who then turns his parents' marriage upside down. The rivalrous parent of such an infant is expressing an unmet need to feel special, stemming from his or her own childhood. Nowadays, and in our culture, fathers may still have to accept that there are things they cannot do for their babies. As mores shift, the list becomes shorter and more biologically orientated, but that compounds the problem from a clinical point of view. It is sometimes extremely difficult to ascertain whether an involved father is motivated by love and interest or by envious rivalries arising out of his unresolved childhood conflicts (as in Kay's case history, below).

FATHER AND DAUGHTER. To appreciate analytical psychology's slant on this relationship, it is necessary to make a brief excursion into Jung's ideas about incest. As previously noted, Jung, unlike Freud, did not regard the impulse in a literal manner, though he did not deny children's sexual feelings towards parents, and vice versa. Rather, he saw incest fantasy as a complicated metaphor for a path of psychological growth and development. When a *child* experiences incestuous feelings or fantasies, he can be seen as unconsciously attempting to add enriching layers of experience to his personality by his contact with the parent. The sexual aspect of the incestuous impulse ensures that the encounter is deep and meaningful. The incest taboo prevents physical expression and, as we shall see in a moment, has its own psychological purpose.

When an *adult* regresses in an incestuous manner, he can be seen as attempting, by linking with his roots, to recharge his batteries, to regenerate himself spiritually and psychologically. Regression has, therefore, to be valued as something more than an ego defence. For an adult, incestuous regression need not necessarily be towards a particular figure or image, though it often is. The state in which a person finds him or herself also signals such regression: serene, floating, dreamy, nostalgic, at one. This is the state of creative reverie which those who study the processes of artists have noted. Out of the temporary giving up of adult ego-ic behaviour comes a new and refreshing encounter with what lies within and with the grounds of being. For the child (and for the adult, particularly if a specific image of a person inaugurates the regression), the sexual element, whether in consciousness or not, is a symbolic entry to such a state and its rewards. Unpacking the symbolism, the two bodies which might engage in the sex act represent different parts of the psyche which are not, as yet, integrated. Intercourse symbolizes such an integration and the baby which might result symbolizes new growth and regeneration.

Sometimes incestuous regression becomes a search for a different kind of oneness—power and control over others (Samuels, 1980). Jung stressed that it was vital to emerge from this state whether as a developmental task or, for an adult, as a return to ordinary living. A re-emergence has its unpleasant aspects, for being merged with a great parent figure does do away with the need to make decisions and think for oneself. So re-emergence is often a heroic struggle against one side of oneself. Luckily, the merged state may also seem dangerously devouring and unending and there is, therefore, also an incentive to get out of it by struggle with one or both parents, who are fantasized as attempting to prolong the incestuousness. (Those interested in following up this brief summary of Jung's thought should read Volume 5 of the *Collected Works,* entitled *Symbols of Transformation*.)

Jung developed these ideas about incest from a man's point of view in terms of incestuous entanglement with, or regression to the mother. There is no reason why the model should not apply to the daughter's relationship with her father. For a girl, this implies that she needs to experience a deep connection to her father that has its erotic tone. For the adult woman, it means that her experiences of oneness can arise out of regression to an early relation to her father. But what if this eroticized relation fails to take place? Then a father cannot, as it were, initiate his daughter into the next stage in her development, for she will be too distant from him for their relationship to have a profound effect on her. The point is that the erotic element *guarantees* the significance of the relationship which then cannot be avoided. The father could not be more different from his daughter; he is male and from another generation. That is what gives him his potential to stimulate an expansion and deepening of her personality. But he is also part of the same family as his daughter; that should make him 'safe' as regards physical expression of this necessary sexuality and also provides a reason for his own emotional investment.

Many fathers and daughters fail to achieve this link. Some mothers and sons do, as well, but my clinical experience is that this is more of a problem for the father-daughter relationship. This is because men tend to be extremely cautious about becoming erotically involved with their daughters (even in fantasy), whereas a mother has experienced a closer and earlier physical bond with all her children and hence is less anxious at her own incestuous impulses. The father's failure to participate in a mutual attraction and mutual, painful renunciation of erotic fulfilment with his daughter deprives her of psychological enhancement. This can take many forms: mockery of her sexuality, over-strictness, indifference—and, if the *symbolic* dimension is savagely repressed, actual incest. It should also be remembered, as Allenby points out in her paper in this book, that too close an incestuous tie produces its own problems. In both instances—the absence of eros or its excess—the daughter loses sight of herself as a sexually viable adult, with disastrous consequences.

Another way of conceptualizing what a 'good enough' father does for his daughter is to regard him as the harbinger for her of an alternative image of femininity to the maternal one. Until the processes just described have taken place (say by the third

31

or fourth year), femininity has equalled femaleness has equalled mother. Paradoxically, a woman's capacity to go beyond the rôle of 'mother', to which our society may have assigned her, depends in part on her release by her father from an imaginary confinement to one possibility only: maternity. It may seem strange to some readers, but an image of herself as an erotic being is the liberating factor. I would not want to minimize other features, more to do with the daughter-mother relationship, such as the mother's capacity to envision herself as an erotic being and the success with which she has carved her own place in society as something in addition to being a mother; but this is a book about the father.

Lest these insights into the symbolic aspects of incest be considered Jungian fancies, we should note the psychoanalyst Searles' suggestion that acknowledgement of attraction between father and daughter (or mother and son) and then a regretful renunciation by both individuals is at least as important a factor in the resolution of the Oedipus complex as identification with the same sex parent. The implication of this movement beyond Freud, anticipated by Jung, is that one's viability as a person rests on the working out of the incest theme (Searles, 1959).

Two points arising from these arguments need to be picked up. The first concerns the positive place given to regression. For Freud, regression was nearly always a pathological phenomenon whereas Jung stated that therapy might have to support a regression even to a pre-birth level (*CW* 5, para. 264). Contemporary psychoanalysis has modified Freud's strict attitude so that the watchword (and goal, perhaps) is now 'regression of ego in the service of ego' (Kris, 1952); or a distinction is made between malign and benign regression (Balint, 1968). Here, as in so many areas, Jung's version has proved somewhat more prescient than Freud's.

The second point concerns the incest taboo, which was stated to have a specifically psychological value and function. It is a mistake to see the incest impulse as somehow animal, hence natural, and the incest taboo as a later societal or super-ego prohibition. The incest impulse and the incest taboo are as 'natural' as each other. To stress the taboo, but ignore the impulse, suggests to us a frustration-based boost to conciousness—but this will be spurious, desiccated, intellectual. To stress the impulse, but not the taboo, leads to our focusing on short lived pleasure and the exploitation of the child's vulnerability by the parent or, conversely, the child's capitalizing on his or her more than special relationship to a powerful figure. We might add that it is one function of the incest taboo to force an individual to consider with whom from outside the proscribed family members he may mate. He has, therefore, to regard a potential partner *as an individual*. The moment choice is limited, choice becomes highlighted (and this is true even in a system of arranged marriages). The incest taboo, thought of like this, underpins I-Thou relating just as much as it promotes a movement from instinctuality to spirituality (see below).

FATHER AND SON. There are two quite distinct but compatible ways to view this relationship: in terms of intergenerational conflict or in terms of intergenerational alliance. It is the peculiar genius of Freud's Oedipal theory that, in it, such a dual viewpoint exists. Unfortunately, as the emphasis in psychoanalysis has been almost exclusively upon the prohibitive, castrating father, until recently we have heard little about the alliance with his son—save as a somewhat desperate way out of the Oedipal jungle. Yet the interplay of alliance and conflict is crucial to any kind of organic cultural development. Conflict and competition between father and son is not always negative, for it indicates change, improvement, progress, vitality and a healthy check on permanent revolution. The overt alliance provides a frame within which this can all happen. There is also a connection between past and present, for the father-son link is nothing if not historical and the image of the elder telling all he knows to the younger is a compelling one.

Freud's proposal of identification as the mechanism for Oedipal resolution should not be completely discarded, however, in favour of Searles' thesis. It is as if father and son strike a bargain: if the son gives up his claim on the mother, he will receive help and facilitation with his life tasks. Only when it is used in an excessively defensive way does identification lead to a submergence of the boy's individuality in the image of his father. Nor should the castrating father of Freud's vision be ignored. For the incest taboo to be effective (and this has to be the case lest all culture and progress sink into a familial miasma), the older generation has to be well muscled. This is not the place to discuss castration anxiety or the castration complex in depth, for this is a huge debate within psychoanalysis. Nevertheless, Jones's concept of 'aphanisis' is relevant (Jones, 1927). This means the removal, presumably by the same-sex parent, not only of the means to express sexual desire, but also of the capacity to feel such desire itself. It is an attempt to verbalize what it is that the Oedipal child is frightened of and, hence, what gives the prohibition its power. Jones's idea resonates with Klein's views on early envy, which do not concentrate on the primacy of the phallus (penis envy). Klein's conception is much more general; one envies what one has not and what is fantasized as good and rich (Klein, 1957). We can speak, then, of breast or womb envy (and see my remarks on rivalry between father and mother, above).

The reader will recall that one theme of this introduction is the dynamic between the external and the internal father. For the son, the internal father functions both as a figure suggesting conscience and as a connection to values and ideals. Jung makes a fascinating point about this. The father may well be the representative of spirituality. Then his function in relation to the son is to turn incestuous libido away from sexual expression and into new directions so that the psychological enrichment arising from incestuous involvement with the mother finds its way into outer life. But the father expresses his opposition to instinctual incest in the most virulent instinctual form—castration or other terrible punishment of the son. The castrating, powerful father may be represented in myth as a bull, a creature whose potency and virility mingle with its other terrifying and violent features. Instinct serving spirit is being used to drive out or, rather, transform instinct serving physical incest. The spirit is also 'instinctual' as it were. This paradox suggests that, in terms of the son's internal father image, we must face the reality that a degree of emotion or passion is necessary alongside spirit. Many male patients complain that this is what their otherwise unobjectionable fathers lacked and it is part of the 'missing father' syndrome (see Seligman's paper in this book). A passionately spiritual father is different from one whose dry concentration is on conformity; the whole flavour of prohibition varies. Similarly, the passionately spiritual father is not the same as a bully, a father whose self-image rests on the defeat of his son.

To conclude the section on the father-son relationship, I should like to add a few comments on homosexuality. So far we have spoken of sexuality exclusively as heterosexuality. Freud taught that humans are born bisexual or, more accurately, *sexual* and develop *hetero*sexuality because of cultural and reproductive pressures. Jung felt that males and females are born with an innate expectation of each other but he also referred to the earliest sexuality as having a 'polyvalent germinal disposition' out of which heterosexuality could later emerge (*CW* 17, p.5). From this, it follows that homosexuality is therefore to some degree a constant and not an aberration. Of course, we distinguish homosexual genital sex from homoerotic involvements, but psychosexual life must have something of a homosexual element. The homosexual constant enables us to talk of a 'homosexual Oedipus complex'; for a boy, there are feelings of love and attraction for his father and a desire to eliminate his mother. This gets mixed in with the boy's identification with his father arising from the 'heterosexual Oedipus complex'. The same kind of thinking can be applied to Jung's incest model. The boy is not only regeneratively regressing to the image of mother but also, in parallel, to an incestuous relation to his father. The internal father also functions as an incestuous, personality-enriching agent for his son, though, in a predominantly heterosexual culture, less emphatically than for his daughter.

The external-internal division, never more than a convenient approximation to how things are, breaks down when we consider the question of homosexual sex. If a boy fantasizes his father as strong and admirable *and* his mother as vastly inferior and unlovable, then what may transpire in adult life is an over-valuation or idealization of all that is summed up by 'penis'. This would not be a symbol of the passionately spiritual father, rather more a lifebelt or panacea upon which to depend. For some homosexuals, this is their internal situation. For others, the penis is not a penis but rather a breast-substitute for an earlier deprivation.

This last point may also apply to some heterosexuals, the theme of 'penis-as-symbol' is relevant to the father-daughter relationship, to which we return for a moment. If there is serious maternal deprivation, then a girl may look to her father to make up the lack. In adult life, the penis of her sex partner may also be experienced in fantasy as a breast; she will manifest a separation anxiety more appropriate to her relation to the early, feeding mother. Sexual penetration may be unconsciously linked with an invasive, penetrative breast, and hence be unenjoyable. Taking all these ideas together, we can see just how rich a symbol the penis, the father's penis, may be.

FATHER AND HIS FATHER. How a father approaches his task of fathering depends to some extent on how he perceived and experienced his own father, consciously and unconsciously. The working through of the various Oedipal themes may be important. Though it may once again seem somewhat academic, I would suggest that whatever it is that distinguishes the technical terms 'identification', 'introjection', and 'internalization' may illuminate this area. We have already seen that identification is a normal defence of the ego; in the Oedipal situation this is against anxiety engendered by fear of terrible punishment for illicit impulses. As a man grows up, the fear should lessen and hence the intensity of the identification. He can be more his own man.

Introjection is also a defence and refers to the way in which parts of the external world are fantasized as being contained in the inner world for the twin purposes of enjoying their value and controlling them. Thus the father or a part of the father may be introjected by the son. Later on, the introject may be re-projected as a man's base for a *modus vivendi* with his own son, influencing how he treats him. It follows that it is rather important just what the balance of positive features (introjected for their worth and for pleasure) and negative features (introjected for control) might be.

Internalization differs from introjection in one crucial respect. What is internalized is not a person or a part of a person but an image of the subject's relationship with a person or object (Laplanche and Pontalis, p.226). A son internalizes a picture

36

of himself and his father together in their relationship. Later on, when he is a father, the positive or negative internalization will be utilized in much the same way as an introjection—as a foundation for his own functioning as father. But if the relationship between father and son has felt non-existent, then what is there to internalize? I touch on this question in a later passage.

Pulling these thoughts together, and remembering that we are concerned just now with the father's relationship with his own father, we are looking for a lessening of identification, an ascendancy of positive over negative introjects, and a positive relationship which is capable of being internalized.

This schema can be used as a yardstick. Take the simple example of the father's experiencing of his own father as tyrannical and domineering. Identification will be high because a separate way of living may have seemed prohibited and hence not found. The son may attempt to be like his father or, equally likely, the identification will remain unconscious and the son will constantly be comparing himself with his father to his own detriment, again unconsciously. In this example, introjections will be negative, smacking of powerlessness and despair. The impact on fathering could be either to produce a total lack of confidence or a false competence, all too easily punctured by a confident, growing son—who may reincarnate the powerful father of his father. As for internalization, if one has been excessively dominated, it is difficult to conduct relationships outside of a sado-masochistic mode and this will creep out of the first into the second father-son relationship. Or, it could be argued, being dominated is not a relationship at all. Then we may be observing another facet of the emotionally missing father.

The example comes from the pathological end of the spectrum and everything that has been said could be applied in a more positive way. The relationships of very many men with their fathers are not based on excessive identification, do include positive introjects, and what is internalized is, on balance, productive and satisfying.

FATHER AND HIS MOTHER. The fluidity of the psyche means that anyone can stand as a symbol for anyone else. We have already seen how a baby can represent a parent figure for its parents when stimulating a rivalry between them. If a father has not had a satisfying primal relationship with his own mother, then this rivalry becomes more likely. Tensions often enter a marriage when, after the birth of a baby, the father feels somewhat displaced and cut off from his wife. This is unavoidable but, for some men, is exacerbated by an earlier, unresolved separation anxiety. Then the new mother (wife) is emotionally reminiscent of the old. Another possibility is that the anxiety generated when a baby is born may be of an Oedipal nature; the man's wife is lost to him in the way he lost his own mother to his father.

If the father has had a negative and hostile relationship with his mother, then unconsciously he may employ the defence of identification with the aggressor. If one places oneself in the shoes of a person who may do one harm, then the threat is defeated because there is nobody there to be damaged. This placing of oneself in the aggressor's position may lead to a taking over of the aggression and a self-presentation reminiscent of the aggressor's. By 'aggressor' is meant anything or anybody experienced as a threat. So a cold, indifferent mother may provoke in her son cold and indifferent behaviour towards others (wife, son, daughter). How often analysts hear a patient sadly reflect that they have behaved in some way exactly like the problematic parent they felt they had and were *consciously* trying to escape. Identification with the aggressor may be what lies behind the baby-battering father. Not only might he be jealously resentful that the baby is getting his wife's (mother's) attention; his actions towards the baby are a concrete re-enactment of the mother he experienced in his own infancy, perhaps, but not necessarily, in fantasy.

Returning to a more positive perspective, the father's image of his mother may be that which helps him to make a direct, physical, earthy, non-squeamish relationship with all his children—by internalization, as discussed earlier.

FATHER AND ANIMA-ANIMUS. In a number of the papers, references are made to the father as his daughter's animus. Remembering our earlier discussion about animus and anima, this would invoke him as a symbolic representative of her

psychological potential and, possibly, as standing for an identity and rôle not easily accessible to her in societal terms. That
is, if she wants to be a different kind of woman from her mother,
her father/animus facilitates this. One interesting discussion point
is whether we should state that it is the pre-existing (archetypal)
animus that is projected by the daughter onto her father or
whether a more accurate version is that the personal father fills
out and colours the daughter's innate animus structure. If the
latter, then her father's actual personality is crucial to a possible expression in her life of unconscious potentials; her animus
is limited by his limitations. If the former, then the daughter's
image of her father is created by archetypal projections and his
actual personality will have less influence. An interaction is the
most likely conclusion and, anyway, from the clinical standpoint,
personal material concerning the daughter's father will always
have its hidden, symbolic dimension.

Similarly, the father's own anima may be projected into his
daughter. In that case she becomes the vehicle for *his*
psychological development. His wife, too, may be the recipient
of anima projections which may have heavily underscored their
initial attraction for each other, working in conjunction with her
animus projections. In his paper in this book, Beebe takes a
rather different look at the father's anima by stressing 'anima'
as an attitude which a man may assume in relation to the world.
This theoretical shift requires explanation.

As we have been discussing them, anima and animus, while
represented by symbolic personages, are more accurately used
as value systems or internal paradigms or ideologies. It is
therefore possible to conceive of anima and animus as the two
poles of a spectrum; such a spectrum would, by definition, cover
the widest range of psychological possibilities. The father will
have a relationship to this entire conglomerate. For instance,
animus may refer to focused consciousness and systematic
thought, anima to creative fantasy and play. In this way anima
and animus lose their 'contra' nature. The spectrum is envisioned
as available to males and females though culture will determine
which set of values is the more problematic. When he relates
to the whole spectrum, the central issue for the father is his
tolerance of and attitude to change: change in his children as

they grow up, change in himself as he matures, change in his marital relationship over time and changes in the culture in which he lives. For a spectrum of potentialities has little use if changes do not flow from a confrontation with it.

NOT RELATING TO FATHER. The father who is actually or emotionally missing and the subsequent negative impact of this on the children are extensively dealt with in Seligman's paper. Two further facets may be mentioned here. First, the existence and operation within a child of the archetypal father means that some form of internal image may develop even when no external man is present; the origin of the image may not be known to the child's consciousness, nor will there necessarily be an external object. Sometimes, though, when there is no father in a family, attachments are formed with adult males to flesh out the imagery: teachers, milkmen and so forth. Sometimes a fantasy figure such as Superman or a rock star fills the gap. What I am trying to convey is that an imaginative experience of 'father' can be available to some extent to a child who grows up in a home which has no father in it. This is not to minimize the problems of growing up in Western culture in a single-parent family. In 1984, more than 1 in 8 British families were headed by one parent—one million families and one and a half million children (ten per cent of single parents are men). During the last ten years, the proportion of single-parent families has risen from eight to thirteen per cent. Significantly, such families experience enormous economic and social disadvantage, particularly if their state is long-term.

From the psychological point of view, for some single mothers, having a child or children seems more agreeable than a permanent relationship with a man which, for emotional reasons, may be too much to handle. This may lead a woman, consciously or unconsciously, to terminate the relationship with the father of her children. She may be in the grip of an 'androgynous' fantasy (Samuels, 1976). This missing father, as he crops up in clinical material, may in some cases be the outcome of androgynous fantasy in the patient's mother and not an example of fecklessness or immaturity on the part of the patient's father.

The phenomenon of the *single father* should also be approached with caution. A fantasy-parent is not the same as one of flesh-and-blood. However, given a flexible attitude, a father who is reasonably strong and conscientious, and some luck, the outcome may be satisfactory.

In general, the long-term psychological stresses placed upon members of single-parent families need to be distinguished from ensuing social and environmental difficulties. However, we must accept that there is likely to be an interaction between the material and the emotional.

Analysis and the father

This section will be brief because reflections on analysis of and around the father form the main theme of many of the papers in this book. In analysis, images of father are projected by the patient onto the analyst in the transference relationship. Though the real sex and age of the analyst may play a part at first, troublesome (or enriching) material can eventually be projected into a younger, female analyst. The analyst may become the recipient of archetypal images of the internal father in a case where the external father was 'missing', or of positive imagery when reality was completely negative. Then he or she performs the function of humanizing such images, entering the patient's internal family in the process. If a patient has had a very poor emotional experience of fathering (one confirming the archetypally negative father image), the analyst may receive an intense transference projection as a bad father. Or he may be invested with archetypal goodness, and idealized out of all proportion in the patient's unconscious hope for a rectification of the earlier extreme, negative experience. In either case, the hope is that the therapeutic relationship mediates the extreme imagery. As far as I can tell, it has never been suggested that working with paternal material requires an alteration of technique. If the analyst is more aware of certain depths in his patient's father imagery—say after reading this book—then the tone of the work will alter, but not its essential nature. Because of this, it seemed sensible to conclude this introduction with a summary of the main thematic polarities on which we have touched. These are the polarities of transference and countertransference images of the father. Of course, not all these pairs will be active at the same time, nor is work in an analysis ever quite so neat:

having a father/being a father
archetypal father/personal father
internal father/external father
castrating father/facilitating father
strong father/weak father
erotic father/inhibited father
spiritual father/incestuous father

The papers which follow explore a range of issues to do with the father. Some address archetypal themes; others explore the personal father. Several specifically set out to bridge that divide. The reader will find that, in these papers, written for professional purposes, many Jungian ideas are taken for granted. That is one reason for the introduction—to explain some of the basic tenets of analytical psychology. The glossary should also be helpful in this respect. The specific conceptual background needs to be borne in mind even when the clinical process resembles psychoanalysis. What the book shows is that differentiation from, and rapprochement with psychoanalysis are both features of analytical psychology today.

References

Abelin, E. (1975). 'Some further observations and comments on the earliest rôle of the father', *Int. J. Psychoanal.,* 56 (3).

Balint, M. (1968). *The Basic Fault: Therapeutic Aspects of Regression.* London, Tavistock.

Eichenbaum, L., Orbach, S. (1982). *Outside In ... Inside Out: Women's Psychology: A Feminist Psychoanalytic Approach.* Harmondsworth, Penguin.

Freud, S. (1926). 'The Question of Lay Analysis', *Standard Edition of the Complete Psychological Works of Sigmund Freud.* London, Hogarth Press, vol. 20.

Gill, H. (1982). 'The life-context of the dreamer and the setting of dreaming', *Int. J. Psychoanal.,* 63 (4).

Harris, M. (1975). *Thinking about Infants and Young Children.* Strath Tay, Perthshire, Clunie Press.

Hillman, J. (1975). *Loose Ends.* Dallas, Spring Publications.

Jones, E. (1927). 'Early development of female sexuality', in *Papers on Psychoanalysis*. London, Baillière, Tindall & Cox, 1950.

Jung, C.G. (1896-9). *The Zofingia Lectures*. Supplementary Vol. A, *The Collected Works of C.G. Jung*. London, Routledge & Kegan Paul; Princeton University Press, 1983.

Klein, M. (1957). *Envy and Gratitude*. London, Tavistock.

Kohut, H. (1971). *The Analysis of the Self*. New York, Int. Univs. Press.

Kohut, H. (1977). *The Restoration of the Self*. New York, Int. Univs. Press.

Kris, E. (1952). *Explorations in Art*. New York, Int. Univs. Press.

Lacan, J. (1949). 'The mirror stage as formative of the function of the I as revealed in psychoanalytic experience', in *Ecrits*, trans. Sheridan, A., London, Tavistock, 1977.

Lambert, K. (1981). 'Comment on "The riddle of the *vas bent clausam*" by Newman, K., *J. Analyt. Psychol.*, 26(3).

Laplanche, J., Pontalis, J.-B. (1980). *The Language of Psychoanalysis*. London, Hogarth Press.

Lemaire, A. (1977). *Jacques Lacan*. London, Routledge & Kegan Paul.

Main, M., Weston, D. (1981). 'Security of attachment to mother and father related to conflict behaviour and the readiness to form new relationships', *Child Development*, 52.

Neumann, E. (1973). *The Child*. London, Hodder & Stoughton.

Roazen, P. (1976). *Freud and his Followers*. Harmondsworth, Penguin.

Rossi, E. (1977). 'The cerebral hemispheres in analytical psychology', *J. Analyt. Psychol.*, 22 (1).

Rycroft, C. (1968). *A Critical Dictionary of Psychoanalysis*. London, Nelson.

Rycroft, C. (1979). *The Innocence of Dreams*. London, Hogarth Press.

Samuels, A. (1976). 'The psychology of the single parent'. Unpublished research carried out for the Family Welfare Association, London.

Samuels, A. (1980). 'Incest and omnipotence in the internal family', *J. Analyt. Psychol.*, 25 (1).

Samuels, A. (1985). *Jung and the Post-Jungians*. London and Boston, Routledge & Kegan Paul.

Sayers, J. (1982). *Biological Politics: Feminist and Anti-Feminist Perspectives*. London, Tavistock.

Schafer, R. (1976). *A New Language for Psychoanalysis*. New Haven, Yale University Press.

Schwartz-Salant, N. (1984). 'Archetypal factors underlying sexual acting-out in the transference-countertransference process', *Chiron*.

Searles, H. (1959). 'Oedipal love in the transference', in *Collected Papers on Schizophrenia and Related Subjects*. London, Hogarth Press, 1968.

43

Steele, R. (1982). *Freud and Jung: Conflicts of Interpretation.* London and Boston, Routledge & Kegan Paul.

Stein, M. (1982). Editor's preface to *Jungian Analysis.* La Salle, Open Court.

Winnicott, D.W. (1967). 'Mirror role of mother and family in child development', in *Playing and Reality,* London, Tavistock, 1971.

Paternal psychopathology and the emerging ego

DAVID KAY

I have chosen to put Kay's paper first because of the writer's overt dissatisfaction at the way in which 'the father' is treated in current depth psychology. He writes of the difficulty he had in persuading his colleagues that the father of his patient was an image, a theme, a person worth exploring in relation to early infantile emotional deprivation. A further factor in the positioning of the paper is that, although Kay is in the tradition of analytical writing which sees psychopathology as its source, he also gives an indication of what he believes to be the psychological function of the father in health. Then there is a paradoxical factor: Kay's paper is about an ever-present, enthusiastic, even committed father—and how it was precisely these aspects of the father-child relationship which were problematic. Thus, any attempt to build up the father as an answer to all problems, or to idealize him, is forestalled at the outset. Kay's analytical technique, as revealed in the paper, makes use of transference/countertransference understanding within a Jungian tradition. He is thoroughly involved in the treatment but not in an ostentatious manner. Perhaps it is the balance between his affective investment and his clinical insight that enables him to traverse the sexuality-spirituality spectrum so effectively. *A.S.*

THIS PAPER deals with a subject that I have found to be most conspicuous by its absence, both in my analytic training and in the literature in general. For, if the father does have an important rôle to play in the early months of an infant's life, then my theme merits more than the present cursory acknowledgement and dismissal. Furthermore, in our day-to-day work as analysts it is vital that we possess a good understanding of this subject, because some of our patients may very much need us to have such skills. I am hopeful that my paper will have a twofold effect: namely, to stimulate and to further interest in infant/father psychology and psychopathology, and also to offer some thoughts and ideas on the subject of male bisexuality.

The normal maturational processes which occur during infancy are, to a large extent, dependent upon the provision of a facilitating environment. It may well be that the relationship which the parents have with each other is enhanced by a sharing of the 'mothering' function. However, if pain, depression, or some other factor prevented a mother from carrying out her vital task, most fathers would feel a need and willingness to step in and take over. The extent to which they succeed would, of course, vary from one individual to another. Not every father who, for various reasons, provides the initial 'mothering' can automatically be assumed to be, in Winnicott's terminology, a 'good enough' mother. Fathers can have problems of their own as well as mothers.

In certain circumstances *it may well be the very nature of his psychopathology that is intimately related to why he, rather than mother, provides the initial mothering experience.*

Clinical material will be provided from such a case, and an attempt made to understand some possible effects upon the infant resulting from exposure to such an environment.

Winnicott seems to go as far as acknowledging father's importance as a supportive and an occasional replacement figure, but the quality of that replacement I failed to discover considered in any great depth or detail, e.g., 'to do her job well, the mother needs outside support: usually the husband shields her from external reality and so enables her to protect her child from unpredictable external phenomena to which the child must react.'

Or: 'Often from my notes I have been able to see that the psychiatric state that now exists was already to be discerned in the infant/mother relationship (I leave out infant/father relationships in this context because I am referring to early phenomena, those that concern the infant's relationship to the mother, or to the father as another mother. The father at this very early stage has not become significant as a male person)' (Winnicott, 1963, pp. 71, 142).

A recent paper by John Munder Ross entitled 'Fathering: a review of some psychoanalytic contributions on paternity' makes an excellent and comprehensive survey on the subject to date (Ross, 1979). A little earlier, Ernst L. Abelin's contribution, 'Some further observations and comments on the earliest rôle of the father', describes various sub-phases of development, and its chronological and scientific approach is both helpful and fascinating (Abelin, 1975). Jung himself devoted a whole paper to the subject, 'The significance of the father in the destiny of the individual' (see below). The subject of paternal psychopathology and its importance is underlined. For example:

> The danger is just this unconscious identity with the archetype; not only does it exert a dominating influence in the child by suggestion, it also causes the same unconsciousness in the child, so that it succumbs to the influences from outside and at the same time cannot oppose it from within. The more a father identifies with the archetype, the more unconscious and irresponsible, indeed psychotic, both he and his child will be. (para. 729)

In *Children as Individuals* Michael Fordham discusses the concept of an original self in infancy. Out of this state of completeness, by a process of deintegration/intergration, islets of ego nuclei appear which coalesce to form a rudimentary ego (Fordham, 1969).

In order to encourage the growth and strengthening of this process, a marked degree of identification with the infant is required so that the frustrations of reality will only be applied at a rate which the developing ego can safely manage. Any marked and prolonged degree of failure to provide for, and adapt

47

to, these constantly changing infantile requirements could bring about serious trauma to the psyche; for, by definition, it would be the self that experiences the disturbance.

The newborn and very young infant therefore is, at the same time as being in its most complete form, also at its most vulnerable stage, and therefore exposure to a non-facilitating environment, which a parent possessed by an archetypal experience could undoubtedly produce, might well be crucial.

On the subject of such an early environment failure, Winnicott considers that, during the first few weeks of life, a baby has no means of orientation, so that a failure to meet a need could easily become catastrophic: 'Probably during this time, the basis is being made for the infant to form the first self representations and if an environment exists which is not good enough then the self fails to form and in its place there comes into existence a False Self' (Winnicott, *op. cit.*). Such an infant would lack, to a considerable degree, the freedom and ability to be spontaneous and have a personal sense of identity. His life would be one of a reaction to external stimuli with all the inner rage and despair that such a compliant attitude would unavoidably produce.

The general concept of parental (presumably to include maternal and paternal) psychopathology becoming introjected by the children is, of course, well documented (e.g. Fordham, *op. cit.*).

Jung leaves little doubt in the reader's mind about his feelings on the subject: 'Parents should always be conscious of the fact that they themselves are the principal causes of neurosis in their children' (*CW* 17, para. 84); and, 'Here as elsewhere in practical psychology, we are constantly coming up against the experience that in a family of several children only one of them will react to the unconscious of the parents with a marked degree of identity, whilst the others show no such reaction. The specific constitution of the individual plays a part here that is practically decisive' (para. 85).

In the case of the clinical example shortly to be described, the family consisted of both parents, two boys and one girl. In my opinion, it was not only the girl's constitution that helped her to avoid the full force of the environmental influence but also her gender. Both boys (one of whom was my patient) developed profound disturbances of their personality, while their sister seemed considerably less affected.

Jung goes on to describe in greater detail how parents can bring about these effects on their children, e.g., 'What usually has the strongest psychic effect on the child is the life which the parents (and ancestors too, for we are dealing here with the age-old psychological phenomena of original sin) have not lived'.

> Generally speaking, all the life which the parents could have lived but of which they thwarted themselves for artificial motives is passed on to the children in substitute form. That is to say, the children are driven unconsciously in a direction that is intended to compensate for everything that was unfulfilled in the lives of their parents. (*ibid.*, paras 87, 328)

I should like now to consider and discuss a more specific example of this general concept, and in so doing, start by making some preliminary observations on the subject of male bisexuality. I must confess that I have never felt fully convinced as to the completeness of our understanding concerning the aetiology of homosexual feelings. For even in cases where a patient consciously wishes to change and seems well motivated to do so with psychotherapeutic help, progress can be painfully slow and the outcome often only partially successful. I am, therefore, not surprised to find listed in the psychiatric literature, among possible 'causes' of homosexuality, that it might be 'constitutional' or 'inherited'. The degree of resistance encountered when attempting analytically to help such individuals often makes one feel that this indeed might be so.

If, however, one were to consider the possibility that the origin of confusion and uncertainty about sexual identity might in some cases lie in infancy, then its apparent intractability becomes more understandable. For if the basis is pre-Oedipal, pre-genital and associated with the earliest months of life, then to reach back towards such a time would inevitably involve an encounter with very powerful and primitive defence mechanisms. To regress to that sort of level is not a situation that an analyst would necessarily actively encourage a patient to do, for the dangers and difficulties in practical terms alone can be monumental. Nevertheless, once in a while one meets a patient who seems to need such an experience and is driven towards it by compelling and overwhelming forces from within.

Fortunately for both my patient and myself, in the case to be described, he was able to express to a considerable extent his inner experiences through a tremendous and growing ability to paint and create visual images, and at the height of his inner turmoil, was engaged in this symbolic form of expression most of his nights as well as days.

Clinical Description (1)

When Harry (as I shall call him, for the purposes of this paper) first started his analysis, he was in his late twenties—the eldest child of a family of two boys and one girl. His parents had separated a few years earlier following the breakdown of their marriage, but they continued to live near one another in Devon where Harry was still a frequent visitor.

Analysis was sought because of his inability to maintain relationships, his inability to study and achieve academic success, but most of all his inability to feel real. There was for him no true existence—only an endless series of masks and rôles determined by what he felt others wanted him to be. Even something as basic as which sex he was supposed to be caused him pain and uncertainty, because he was attracted to both but satisfied by neither.

Two years ago, he deliberately crashed the vehicle he was driving at high speed. By forcing himself to remain conscious, the reality of his painful injuries gave him a temporary feeling of being alive and real—such was the measure of his desperation. However, this was not the first time he had put his life at serious risk, because four years earlier he was experimenting with drugs, including LSD. That had undoubtedly caused some borderline psychotic experience and had a powerful effect on him in two ways. First, it confirmed for him beyond all doubt that beneath his compliant rôle-playing exterior there was not, as he feared, an emptiness, but a cauldron of real emotions which included not only despair and rage but also creativity. Secondly, it made him painfully aware how fragile and ill-equipped he was to manage and harness usefully this vital but chaotic source of energy.

50

During the first months of the analysis I became acquainted with those surface qualities towards which he had powerful and ambivalent feelings—namely, his physical appearance and the personality he presented to the outside world. He loathed his ability to charm and influence people and he detested the fact that he was, without doubt, exceedingly handsome, to the point of being beautiful. Yet he clung on to these attributes with a fierceness born out of despair that he might never make contact with himself and others at a deeper and more meaningful level. Trying to deal with his powerful intrusiveness by maintaining strict analytic boundaries caused him great pain. It was only when I began to sense that his need to intrude was based on a terror of loss and separation rather than destructiveness that I was able to become more flexible and the atmosphere between us improved.

His anxiety and fear that our relationship would, like all others, soon end became greatly heightened when I began to carry the maternal projection and to be attacked for it. I seemed to him to be just like his mother, whom he experienced as sweet and suffocating, full of adoration for him *provided he remained adorable*. This apparently conditional aspect of his mother's love would obviously have tended to inhibit ego integration of his shadow-like qualities. During all this time he continued to feel 'dead', unreal and false—and also started to accuse me of being so—'You never say what you *really* feel about what is going on.'

This distressing situation was certainly not alleviated when, some while later, his experience of me became influenced and distorted by paternal projections. The quality of the anxiety produced by this situation was undoubtedly paranoid in nature. As a result, I had to abandon any attempt to follow an interpretative approach as this greatly aggravated the situation. Instead, I continued the difficult and delicate task of attempting to 'hold the situation' while being experienced by Harry as homosexual 'just like father'. It seemed to him that I wanted to penetrate his body and his mind in order to overwhelm him and he needed that 'like a hole in the head'. By not acting out this greatest fear/wish of his, we started on the long road towards unravelling the confusion that existed between infantile love and adult genital sexuality.

51

In reality, his father had not been as unhelpful as a 'hole in the head', for he had talked openly to his son about his own personality and sexual difficulties, and his unhappy and illegitimate background. This seemed to have been a genuine attempt to share and make contact with his son. Furthermore, his father had himself been in therapy for some considerable time, and had actively encouraged Harry to consider this for himself when he realized it might be beneficial.

My relief when these paternal projections started to abate in intensity was short-lived, for we were approaching the beginning of an experience which has permanently changed Harry and without doubt made an unforgettable impression on myself. It coincided with a time when my family was temporarily away from the house where I live and work as an analyst. The unavoidable background noises of other people and cars, etc., was replaced by a profound quietness. To Harry this was crucial and he truly felt he had me 'totally to himself'.

In those comparatively few but vital quiet days, Harry began to paint pictures. He painted day and night and brought along to me literally hundreds of paintings filled with archetypal images of violence, love, death, primitive creatures, sexuality and a central and special one depicting birth or rebirth. Along with this outpouring of creative and unrestrained art, he began to feel real and alive for the first time since his childhood. For my part, I felt deeply moved and involved, and very much a part of this exciting and extraordinary liberation.

The Painting

On 6 October 1980 I read this paper to the London Society of Analytical Psychology and it was at this stage in its presentation that I turned my attention to the painting illustrated (Fig.3).

There are two reasons why I have included it. First, it depicts in many ways, artistically and symbolically, the central theme of this paper, and by describing certain aspects of it, some additional and important facts can be brought to light relating both to Harry's history and to transference/countertransference phenomena. Secondly, the painting became the focal point of several comments, and questions put to me by my colleagues

Figure 3

in the discussion after the paper's presentation. Some of the questions, and my replies to them, I have included in this section, and I am grateful for the fact that this has enhanced and added depth to the paper.

Let us first consider the painting that was given to me, complete in a beautiful solid frame. It is bizarre and disturbing, full of brilliant but harsh colours, and its archetypal nature and symbolic qualities speak for themselves. The central image is of a kidney-shaped sac, suspended by a cord and growing at the tip of a huge phallus-shaped container. The colours within the sac bear a striking resemblance to those of my consulting-room carpet. The red fiery-root of the penis/womb depicts the instinctual side of its nature, counterbalanced at the opposite pole by the cold detached observant eye of the fish. Both of those qualities, Harry felt I possessed. My ability, as he perceived it, to be intimately involved, yet at the same time able to retain a detached and intelligent view of the situation, gave him considerable security. It was between those two archetypal polar opposites that Harry depicted himself as contained, alive and growing.

The artist's palette requires little discussion—its presence portrays the vital rôle that art has played in this experience of transformation.

Some of my colleagues felt I had neglected his mother's rôle in the early months of Harry's life simply because my theme was focused on the father. I would certainly agree that in the very act of concentrating on one aspect of a situation in order to clarify it, some distortion of the totality, albeit by omission, must inevitably occur. Nevertheless 'mother' is, in fact, in the painting. She is represented symbolically by the comb-like side of an infant's cot, to the left of the phallus. Within this cot, you will see a small white object, which Harry informed me was a tombstone (the interpretation of all these symbols was provided by my patient several weeks after the completion of the painting).

The tombstone is quite a complex symbol, for it has more than one meaning; without doubt it could be there because his mother had several miscarriages prior to Harry's birth. This experience must inevitably have tended to reinforce or confirm his mother's perception of herself as someone who can only produce dead or bad things out of her body.

However, when she finally did succeed in giving birth to a beautiful live child, she tended to react towards it in a 'dead' way, if by 'dead' we understand 'fixed' or 'unchanging', so the tombstone would stand for her lost dead babies, but also an important aspect of her mothering qualities, as perceived by Harry. This rigid attitude I have already mentioned when referring to his mother's inability to acknowledge her own shadow or to recognize or permit its existence in her offspring. Even now, years later, Harry has complained bitterly to me after visiting his mother, 'Nothing ever changes for her,' he said. 'People, in her eyes, are either "wonderful" or suddenly totally rejected when discovered to have imperfections.'

The trigger mechanism for the whole archetypal experience was my family being away from home, which permitted Harry to feel he had me totally to himself. This may have reactivated elements of the original experience in early infancy when Harry and his father were for a while almost 'fused'—certainly to the exclusion of anyone else. This supposition could be given valuable support of a reconstructive kind by referring to transference/countertransference phenomena.

It was during this time that I experienced powerful feelings of inflation, and considerable effort on my part was required to remember that I had other patients, my family, and my friends. The importance of the fusion and the resultant creativity seemed to overwhelm and override all else. Harry's father, who doubted his potency and manhood, may well have had similar feelings when his son was born—an event that must have seemed to cure him magically of his lifelong insecurity. In fact, Harry's father's therapist, on reading this paper, stated emphatically that my supposition was correct.

Obviously this fusional state cannot be understood and explained *solely* in reconstructive terms. It must, in addition, have been influenced by me and my present personality and psychopathology. An acknowledgement, therefore, should be made that another analyst might well have handled this 'fusion' somewhat differently. It was pointed out to me, and quite rightly, that the fusional state could be understood in terms of the infantile roots and forerunner of the Oedipus complex.

I was asked by a colleague whether or not I felt my behaviour was confusing and contradictory—being willing to enter into an archetypal experience and then (later) having to struggle to extricate myself in order to regain boundaries. I would reply by saying that my behaviour could be understood as an example of what Jung meant by the therapist and the patient entering into the alchemical crucible in which both undergo a transformation. Without entering into the problem in a *real* way, accepting projections and later on disentangling and clarifying them, there can be no real change. One merely ends up with a 'clever' analyst and a 'clever' patient who can understand and intellectualize about the problems.

The theme of several questions put to me centres on anxieties about the advisability of accepting gifts from patients—quite obviously a number of analysts were uncertain and even doubtful about the wisdom of my having accepted the gift of the painting, and then hanging it on the wall of my consulting-room. I certainly expected to be asked to give an account of my behaviour, and I was not disappointed—the subject deserves a fair and considered response.

The giving and receiving of gifts is in itself a vast and complex subject. For example, was this gift given to express and symbolize loving feelings, or was it an attempt to placate a feared object, or a defence against his hostile and envious feelings towards me? Equally important, was I, by accepting and displaying the painting, colluding with his concept of specialness, and inflating an archetypal situation which was already larger than life? If that were so, I would certainly have been acting irresponsibly.

There were, in fact, two reasons why I unhesitatingly accepted it: first, it symbolized an important event that had occurred between us. Therefore, to have refused the gift would undoubtedly have caused great pain and profound feelings of rejection. Secondly, it is vital to remember that my patient suffered from feelings of unreality and doubts concerning his very existence. Therefore, for his analyst to accept and value a gift which symbolized an important creative psychic event is undeniable *external confirmation of his inner existence.* For if he did not exist, I could not have been affected by him, and if his inner life contained nothing of worth, then he would have been incapable of producing anything that I could experience as valuable and worthy of preserving.

I firmly believe that if an analysis helps a patient to feel that he exists, and that what is contained within includes good internal objects (or hopefully more good ones than bad), then a worthwhile step along the road towards health has been achieved. Gifts are usually accepted 'for the time being'. That understanding permits a patient to feel free to ask for its return at a later date. For example, Harry's fear of his own self-destructiveness prompted him to 'give' me a whole series of paintings at one stage in the analysis, and these were returned to him from 'safe keeping' when he experienced himself as being more in charge of these impulses. The withdrawal of projective mechanisms is another well-recognized situation that could make a patient feel the need for his gift to be, in some sense, returned.

However, the painting described in this section is still in my possession. It is difficult at this point in time to know whether or not this will turn out to be the exception that proves the rule or simply that I have not *yet* been asked to return it. The personal and private message on the reverse side adds to its feeling of permanency. I like it, and am pleased to have it hanging on my wall alongside several other interesting paintings and drawings. I find it to be no more a focus of attention and interest by other patients than any of my numerous *objets d'art* scattered around the room. Nevertheless, we are both aware that it is an important painting, for it symbolizes a turning-point and a psychic event of great magnitude. It is as if once the emotional and chaotic experience that could not be dealt with is objectified, then the danger of its overwhelming the ego recedes.

Jung himself noticed that disturbed patients often show a distinct improvement once the crucial archetypal experience has been depicted in a painting or drawing. There has, in fact, been a tendency for Harry's artistic creativity to show intermittent bursts of activity. Each episode has differed from the previous one in a way which suggests that further psychic development has occurred.

The initial outpouring of paintings coincided with the return of feelings of spontaneity and aliveness. It was intense, had archetypal qualities and was experienced by Harry as including myself, i.e., a boundaryless state of fusion.

The second episode, some months later, was characterized by a less intense state, and one which suggested that some separation between us had occurred. That was presumably for the very reason that he now had a separate psychic existence. He was reluctant to show me his paintings and kept them secretly in his flat. He felt that showing them to me might somehow diminish their meaning and value. However, at the same time (as previously mentioned) he gave me several, and asked me to keep them in a safe place. 'Because if I keep them, they might get destroyed like the others.' This behaviour is without doubt indicative that Harry was struggling with anxieties that characterize the paranoid-schizoid position as described by Melanie Klein. The main fear seemed to be that the powerful external object (myself) would intrude and damage his internal world as symbolized by his paintings. Yet there was also considerable confusion about where exactly the threat lay— externally (i.e., projected on to me), or internally (which would herald the arrival of his ability to own some of his destructiveness).

The third period of painting was most secretive, and I was only informed obliquely of its existence. It seemed that Harry felt the right to have secrets from me without being rejected.

Clinical Description (2)

My family's return home had a profound effect on Harry's behaviour in relation to the *original* period of creative art, for it resulted in his destroying most of his paintings. However, he has clung on to his most treasured possession—his feeling of reality and aliveness. Even this, however, vanishes from time to time as the spiral effect of analysis comes into play and he returns to apparently the same problems, but at a different level. That crucial period in the analysis now feels, and indeed is, a long time ago. The archetypal atmosphere, in which he felt so vital and alive and I felt I had liberated or given birth to a trueself, has faded. What is so important to realize is the sense of loss and depletion that must inevitably follow so intense an event.

58

Since that time more mundane, ordinary and day-to-day problems (earning money to survive at a job, interpersonal relationships, etc.) have been occupying the analysis.

It was while I was formulating my ideas for the purposes of writing this paper that, sad to relate, an event occurred which tended to confirm our understanding of the situation.

Harry was having difficulties at work, and his father became involved as he had knowledge of the subject. He and Harry spent a short but intense period of time together in which Harry was fed with an abundance of helpful, relevant ideas as to how to solve problems. Harry returned to work full of confidence and zeal, but found the task enormous. To carry out his father's ideas with effect really required his sustained support and continued presence to work through the difficulties encountered and *they were not provided.*

Harry began to feel totally alone, out of his depth and very insecure. This culminated in his leaving the job, having also been advised to do so by his father, who felt that if he did not give up he would 'have a nervous breakdown'! I am reliably informed that his father showed this tremendous initial enthusiasm and joy when Harry was born. He adored him, played with him constantly, often in a most unrestrained manner—that is, until he had to go away on business when Harry was about six months old. I am confident that the reader will, without much difficulty, be able to link together these things: the quality of Harry's first few months of infancy, the way in which his father recently 'helped' him in his problems at work, and the intense but short-lived period in the analysis characterised by artistic creativity and an inner experience of vitality.

Harry seems to have been 'programmed' by the original archetypal experience into constantly searching to recreate it in order to bring back his spontaneity. He obviously had preconceived ideas and expectations that this event would occur in his analysis (as indeed it did). Only very slowly does it seem that he might break free from the bonds of this concept and move towards a realization that true growth and inner stability rest more on having a continuous, reliable and *non*-dramatic environment.

Harry is fascinated by, and loves to paint, trees and I have therefore been provided with a symbol which could represent this idea—a slow and sustained nourishment by mother earth helping the roots to draw up and incorporate into its own structure the necessary ingredients for development. My hope is that in time, my reliability and capacity to care will become more consciously appreciated by him as factors which facilitate his true needs. Perhaps then he might become less insistent that I embody some intense archetypal experience and may even come to see and value me for simply being myself.

Having considered a painting in some depth, it might be helpful to make a link with one of Harry's more important dreams, for these also played an important rôle in the analysis.

Dream

> Harry was aggressively demanding that his mother should return to him the 'metal contact point', without which his motorbike remained immobilized. To his surprise, his mother knew exactly what was needed and went into a cellar to retrieve it.

The 'contact point', I might add, was shaped like a spoon or guitar. This seemed to relate to something vital that was missing and which was both masculine and feminine (the elongated and round parts of the spoon). Perhaps it stood for his father, through whom contact was originally made and whom his mother, he felt, had taken away. It also probably stood for his inner self—his vitality and creativity which were combined (masculine/feminine) and to a large extent undifferentiated— the hermaphroditic uroboros.

Our work on the dream quickly led Harry to recognize and identify these two aspects of himself—on the one hand was his desire to please and passively to become for the other person whatever he believed they wanted him to be. Counterbalancing that were his more aggressive, penetrating, intrusive and controlling qualities. His need to be loved usually activated his passive side, but eventually this brought about feelings of being suffocated and overwhelmed by the other person. When that occurred, he changed abruptly and behaved in a most violent and aggressive manner. Although it was really a defensive attack, its effect on the recipient was usually one of shock, both at its unexpectedness and intensity. Following this, there was usually a withdrawal and loss of contact, leading to repeated breakdowns in his relationships.

There have been numerous occasions in the transference in which that pattern of abrupt change in behaviour occurred. They usually caused him great anxiety, based on the fear that I might, like most others, reject him. As far as was possible an attempt was always made to analyse the underlying fear of suffocation in those situations.

He always perceived the source of energy and life as residing *in the other person,* whom he then experienced as powerful and terrifying (like the mother in the dream). This quality had to be stolen or seduced from the other person in order that he might possess it. It never occurred to him that somewhere in his psyche he already owned that which he sought so desperately in others. The feeling that something vital had been stolen was quite central to Harry's personality. It caused him to feel insecure, envious, suspicious and resentful—qualities that he tried his best to hide beneath his more acceptable and pleasing persona.

It is possible to make some sense of this feeling of loss of a vital quality by recalling the archetypally and behaviourally 'mad mothering' experience provided by Harry's father soon after the birth. By having to exist to fulfil his father's needs, Harry was robbed of an opportunity to start to be himself. He was, in addition, deprived of the experience of having *permission and approval* to exist, and this was probably quite crucial. Instead he became filled and haunted by feelings of emptiness, worthlessness and lack of direction.

The dream, in contrast, was full of hope and optimism and one in which agression, to his surprise, brought about the result he so desperately needed, and felt he deserved. Harry realized that in the dream he had done something quite vital that had helped to consolidate his right to a separate existence. This can most simply be defined as having the ability to say 'No' (what was implied in the dream was that he said, 'No, mother you cannot keep what belongs to me any longer, and I demand its return').

61

As a result of this work with the dream, there was a shift in the quality of our relationship, and the transference situation grew calmer and less overshadowed by paranoid anxiety.

In many ways, the inner psychic changes as depicted symbolically by this liberating dream are reflected externally and linked to the return of Harry's ability to paint and feel alive. However, the archetypal, larger-than-life quality of this achievement means that a personal existence, more rooted in reality, still remains some distance away along the psychic pathway.

Perhaps, having so far considered the dream and its symbolism mainly in personal terms, it might be helpful to enlarge our understanding by including the collective and mythological attitude. In particular I should like to concentrate on the symbol of the 'contact point' mentioned in the dream. It was understood to represent masculine and feminine in their undifferentiated form—the hermaphroditic uroboros.

Erich Neumann in *The Origins and History of Consciousness* refers far more eloquently than I to this state of existence:

> While in the beginning the ego germ lay in the embrace of the hermaphroditic uroboros, at the end the self proves to be the golden core of a sublimated uroboros, combining in itself masculine and feminine, conscious and unconscious elements, a unity in which the ego does not perish but experiences itself in the self as a uniting symbol. In this process there is a sublimation of the ego as it reaches its connection with the self, a connection which appears more than once in the paradoxical identity of Horus and Osiris. In the self the ego knows itself immortal and is itself immortal; the connection between the two comes out in the Talmudic saying 'Man and god are twins' and also in the symbolism of the father-son and mother-daughter identity. (1954, p. 414)

Neumann, in describing those crucial developments, refers in mythological and archetypal terms to the symbolic 'separation of the world parents' and later 'the fight with the dragon' (aspects of the terrible mother), leading on to 'the birth of the hero'.

It is interesting that Harry does indeed suffer greatly from a terrible sense of guilt about his very existence, and this is specifically mentioned by Neumann: 'Without the slaying of the old parents, their dismemberment and neutralization, there can be no beginning. We shall have to examine at some length this problem of parental murder. Obviously it entails a genuine and necessary guilt. The emancipation of the youthful lover from the uroboros begins with an act which was shown to be a negative act, an act of destruction' (p. 121). As Harry's ego matures and he can slowly deal more clearly with reality, he must come to understand it is the *archetypal* and not the personal parents who die, so that he might be free to exist spontaneously and separated from the powerful hold of the terrible mother and father archetypes.

Theoretical Considerations

This paper deals with the archetypal masculine and feminine as well as the real parents, and their gender.

Birth is a significant event in the life of most family units. But for a man who has serious doubts and confusion about his sexual identity and potency, the arrival of an infant, particularly a first-born beautiful male child, can have a very powerful and crucial effect. The father, in the example quoted, saw and experienced his son as the 'Divine child hero'—living proof that his self doubts were at an end. In his perfect untarnished image he saw healing for his own wounds and hope for the future.

Although both parents were present from the start, the archetypal intensity of the father's adoration seems to have produced, by its very nature, the more significant effect on the child than did the mother's influence.

The child was compelled to exist to fulfil the needs of the father. This failed to acknowledge the need for the child to develop an identity of his own, and an eventual separate existence. Archetypal experiences have a capacity to fascinate, and there can be little doubt that this was firmly imprinted on the experience of the emerging ego. It seems to have interfered with the normal maturational process, and compelled the child repeatedly to search for situations in which he could re-experience aspects of the original one.

The particular example quoted describes how this father physically went away after six months, but a similar effect might have been achieved had he remained but ceased to project powerfully aspects of his own psyche on to his son.

I must confess I became intrigued with the idea (not dealt with in this paper) that certain cases of post-natal maternal depression might have underlying them elements of this pathological situation—the father, for whatever reason, providing the first mothering experience and later being ousted by the mother who then 'spontaneously recovers' from her depression. In Harry's case the situation seems to have caused him to be unconsciously drawn towards men and through them possibly to re-experience the lost fascination. *Those are the infantile roots* of the so-called homosexual aspect of his bisexuality.

The ambivalence concerning this trait is understandable for, although he is compelled to search for such a fusion, it will never fulfil his real needs which are early and pre-sexual. So men are sought after but also loathed, for they use and penetrate yet fail to bring about any true satisfaction or inner growth.

I am greatly indebted to Harry's father's therapist, who has read this paper and felt able and willing to verify that the description of the father's personality is fundamentally correct.

He has confirmed the extremely powerful, delusional quality about the father's love affairs with protégées in which he sees himself as a selfless maternal protector of a divine child. Like myself, the father's therapist feels that he cannot emphasize too strongly how much importance he attaches to the archetypal situation between father and baby in this patient's case.

To have known the strength of the almost psychotic delusional and intensely powerful quality of the father's relationships and the power of his 'love' puts one in a position to feel one can know something of the aetiology of homosexuality. Perhaps it is only those who have been caught up with such powerful affects who can truly understand them.

Without doubt, it was not normal or good mothering that his father provided but *mad mothering,* and this probably helped to produce the peculiar personality, analytical problems and delusional transference encountered in Harry's therapy.

To work with a patient whose fragile ego is greatly influenced by a powerful archetypal force is a long haul—for to loosen such a grip means exposure to the unknown which is even more terrifying, so there is formidable resistance to change of any sort.

One would try to move towards a situation in which the ego becomes more related to the self, for only this can bring about a feeling of reality and a basis for a personal existence. However, this means approaching the source of all psychic energy—the unconscious, and the fear of disintegration or annihilation by it can be overwhelming; so the ego mobilizes its powerful and primitive defence mechanisms.

To be related to one's self is therefore both highly desirable yet at the same time highly dangerous.

The images and dreams of such a patient tend to confirm the fragility of his psychic equilibrium, and to warn against the possibility of progress. That can only be achieved at a pace which acknowledges the true state of ego development—including its limitations.

I have found it most helpful to have an attitude of non-expectation and to be as free as possible from having ambitions for improvement, although such a state of affairs is consciously longed for by the patient. That well-recognized analytic attitude is mentioned at this point in order to highlight a difficulty that I encountered—namely that the non-expectant attitude can easily be misinterpreted by the patient as signifying absence of hope or even (my) despair. In order to avoid that pitfall, I have had to try to remain aware of how patients can take the analyst's words (and behaviour) as concrete and literally meant.

The transference situation has been characterized by great fluctuations. There have been times when formal analytic procedures have seemed both possible and appropriate, and under such circumstances interpretations could be usefully digested. However, there were other times when to hand back a split-off part of the ego which had been projected seemed to cause further disintegration rather than encourage reintegration. It may well be that at such times the actual acknowledgement of that mechanism was too painful to bear, because it underlined in an unmistakable way how little of the shadow could be owned, and accentuated his feeling of failure. When I understood and sensed this, I held on to the projection.

Interestingly enough, there have been more and more occurrences of a half-way stage. In these, an interpretative comment could be accepted as valid but was also experienced as an attack—my patient would say, 'Look, we both know what's going on, but why do you have to hurt me by putting it into words?' And he is quite right—there are times for him when formal analytic procedures are positively harmful.

The analysis will only survive if my patient trusts me to continue to learn to understand and provide what is right, but I might add that the strain and responsibility of continually tuning in at his level is a draining and emotionally exhausting task.

While recently studying some of the writings of Melanie Klein (1975), I came across a reference to Herbert Rosenfeld's paper entitled 'Remarks on the relation of male homosexuality to paranoia, paranoid anxiety and narcissism' (1949). I was most intrigued by his writings and the above paper in particular, with its implication of a connection between homosexuality and an early state of ego development. While I found no clear explanation of how the homosexuality came into existence at this pregenital stage, it was nevertheless understood as being a defence mechanism against paranoid anxieties. This concept is, of course, not a new one and the paper itself makes reference to as far back as 1908, when Freud discussed with Ferenczi and Jung the intimate relation between paranoia and latent homosexuality. And much more recently Edwards has discussed the same theme in the light of disorders of the self (Edwards, 1978).

However, it seemed to have links with what I was trying to express in archetypal terms in the case of my patient. The grip which for him his early archetypal experience had over his ego caused him compulsively to seek to re-experience it, and at the same time to block thereby further development. However, what it *did* achieve was to afford a *defence,* and to protect him against exposure to the power of the unconscious, of which he was terrified and which would, without doubt, have activated anxieties of a paranoid nature. Therefore the tremendous resistance to change becomes very understandable.

It must be stated that my remarks are in no way meant to imply that I would analyse a borderline patient in the way Rosenfeld describes. He seems to adhere in a most consistent way to seeking ego integration by interpreting the primitive defence mechanisms as and when they occur in the transference psychosis. My approach I have already clarified as being more intuitive and flexible. Indeed, in order to function at all working at this level I must strive at all times to remain myself rather than adhere to any strict format of rules. For I truly believe that in the long run, it is the ability to remain a real person that is one of the most powerful therapeutic tools available. In that way there is a chance of success in mediating archetypal experiences and for the patient to move towards more personal and human relationships.

Summary

This paper focuses on a situation in which a male child failed to develop a sense of personal identity in addition to remaining confused about his gender rôle.

An attempt is made to link these problems with his father's bisexual psychopathology, to which the infant was exposed immediately after birth. The archetypal quality of the father's 'mothering' seems to have blocked the normal maturational processes, and its fascinating effect compelled the child, in later years, to search repeatedly to re-experience it, usually with other men.

If certain cases of homosexuality have their true origins at the very early level, then the tremendous difficulties often encountered in therapy become more understandable, and more meaning is given to the view that it might be 'inherited'—for such degrees of resistance could easily masquerade to give this effect.

I am grateful to my patient for his permission to use some relevant clinical material, dream work and a painting in order to describe aspects of an analysis in which there has been some partial resolution of these problems.

References

Abelin, E. (1975). 'Some further observations and comments on the earliest rôle of the father', *Int. J. Psychoanal.,* 56 (3).

Edwards, A. (1978). 'Schreber's delusional transference—a disorder of the self', *J. Analyt. Psychol.,* 23 (3).

Fordham, M. (1969). *Children as Individuals.* London, Hodder & Stoughton.

Klein, M. (1975). *Envy and Gratitude and Other Works (1946-1963).* London, Hogarth Press.

Neumann, E. (1954). *The Origins and History of Consciousness.* London, Routledge & Kegan Paul.

Rosenfeld, H.A. (1949). 'Remarks on the relation of male homosexuality to paranoia, paranoid anxiety and narcissism, in *Psychotic States: A Psycho-analytic Approach.* London, Hogarth Press, 1965.

Ross, J. M. (1979). 'Fathering: a review of some psychoanalytic contributions on paternity', *Int. J. Psychoanal.* 60 (3).

Winnicott, D.W. (1963). *The Maturational Process and the Facilitating Environment.* London, Hogarth Press.

The half-alive ones

EVA SELIGMAN

From the all-too-present father we move to the absent father. Seligman's paper focuses on the manner in which the problem of the missing father feeds into a person's remaining enmeshed in his or her family of origin, unable to enjoy adult contacts. The idea of a symbolic reinstatement of the father image itself rests on the concept of the archetype, functioning here as a storehouse of potential. The flesh and blood analyst is 'used' by the patient's unconscious psyche to build up a live paternal presence within. Then a true personal identity can begin to take shape. The marital perspective which Seligman brings to her analytical work is also helpful because it serves to underline the need for the practitioner to be aware of the inevitability of fluid movement between internal figures and external, 'real' persons. *A.S.*

THE FATHER

THIS PAPER was conceived many years ago while working with my first ever analytic patient, but it did not take shape until 1980 when I was invited to give a lecture on the topic at the University of British Columbia, Vancouver. I chose to focus on the pattern of the parental marriage, with special reference to the rôle of the father in personality formation. Furthermore, I was unexpectedly asked to do two radio call-in programmes on the same subject. A remarkable feature was that the lecture stimulated, in the main, questions from separated and divorced members of the audience concerned for their fatherless children. The radio callers were exclusively fathers at the point of separation from their wives, desperate about the threatened loss of their children, or else men who had taken on children who were not their own and who were deeply troubled about whether these children would ever accept them as their father.

As an analyst, I had been preoccupied with the inner world of the many patients who presented, and described, themselves as 'half-alive', and I continued my search for some common denominators. They appeared to dwell, as it were, in a state of permanent twilight, of non-differentiation, inexorably trapped. I remember an extreme example, a woman recently divorced, suffering from an acute phobic condition, obsessed with a fear that the sun would never rise again, and that she would spend the rest of her life in everlasting darkness. In the course of her analysis it transpired that, on the one hand, she felt herself to be almost irresistibly pulled back into the powerful, but suffocating, dark embrace of her mother, represented also by her husband, and on the other, she longed to come alive as herself, discovering and developing her own atrophied identity. It was an interminable tug-of-war. She came from a broken home and was effectively a fatherless child. Jung has pointed out that 'the sun is a symbol of the source of life and the ultimate wholeness of man' (*CW* 12).

Gradually, my patient was able to relax into some measure of dependency without feeling smothered and suffocated and, with the diminution of her anxiety and of her fear of fragmentation, her own libido was liberated and she became able to construct a productive and creative existence for herself. She emerged from the darkness of a half-life. During a holiday break early in her analysis, she wrote as follows: 'I have allowed myself to become dependent, and my level of dependence will, I am sure, increase before it decreases. Only through developing an ability to acknowledge my dependency needs will I ever grow in the way that I want.'

Before launching on the main subject-matter, namely the view I shall be putting forward that one of the main connecting-threads in the 'half-alive' patients is the 'absence' of one parent—in my own cases, more usually that of the father—a digression seems unavoidable. My North American experiences, together with a prolonged period doing marital work, have driven home the extent to which the realities of the modern world impinge forcibly on the analyst's foremost preoccupation, that of the life of the psyche.

Certain established facts cannot be ignored. For instance, the divorce rate for first marriages in North America exceeds even that in Britain, which is the highest in Europe, where countless fathers had been lost in two world wars. It has been calculated that three-quarters of these divorces involve children under sixteen, many of them only babies or toddlers. The greater the acrimony, the less is the chance for the children of effectively keeping both parents. As yet, joint legal custody is only awarded in two and a half per cent of cases. Usually it is their father that children lose. Only a small number of them have any continuing contact with him during the formative childhood years. It follows that, if the present trend of broken marriages continues, something over one million children over the next six years, in this country alone, will lose their father as if he had died, and perhaps, psychologically, in a more dangerous way than if he had (Thompson, 1981).

These matters, however much they may give rise to concern, belong more appropriately to the province of the social scientist and cannot be dealt with here, but perhaps they are symptomatic of the matriarchal epoch into which we appear to have moved.

I shall be confining myself to the significance, as I and others see it, of the symbolically 'missing' father. The next section will be concerned with the all-too-present mother. There is a strong connection between those two phenomena. I shall be referring

71

to transference implications and intersperse the sections with clinical illustrations and a diagram, which is a pictorial representation of the vital configurations with parents that concern me here. I shall end by trying to show that the reinstatement of the father can be a potent factor in the development of personality. That reinstatement can take place in analysis through the transference.

The Missing Father

I need to make it clear that, when alluding to the missing father, I am referring to fathers *experienced* as unavailable both by the mother and by the child. In my cases he was physically present at least until the child's puberty, or beyond. If, then, the father is present, why is he being, or allowing himself to be, effectively, obliterated? Is he being excluded or is he excluding himself? More likely than not, a combination of both factors is at work. Firstly, I have evidence that there is an unconscious collusion between mother and child to maintain and prolong their mutually interdependent omnipotence and dependency in a dyad to satisfy one another's needs and wishes, thus postponing the more difficult and conflict-ridden subsequent phase of the triad, the phase of sharing and conflict.

Secondly, as Layland points out: 'Unresolved psychological problems in the father interfere with his role as a loving father' (see below). Furthermore, he draws attention to the evidence from the observations of Greenacre (1966), Abelin (1975) and Mahler *et al.* (1975) that the infant has a sense of father from the very early months of life: 'How much he remains a distant figure or what part he plays in his own right depends on his own temperament as well as that of the mother, and on the relationship between them' (*ibid.*). Abelin found that 'a most definite turning towards the father occurs ... at about the age of four months'. Layland emphasizes the importance of the 'father's own emotional response to the infant' and also the significance of 'the father in supporting the mother in her mothering'. These observations substantiate the most common reproach from the 'half-alive' patients that their father did not support *them* either, in their attempts to emancipate themselves from their mother.

72

The All-Too-Present Mother

Fordham (1971) states that 'in essential respects the infant creates his mother in the light of his own needs and she therefore represents a part of the infant self'. Newton and Redfearn (1977) draw our attention to Mahler's research, which demonstrates 'the way in which the mother's feeling values, both conscious and unconscious, stimulate or inhibit her infant's potentialities'.

By the process of reconstruction in the analyses of the 'half-alive' patients, the impression emerges of a large number of ego-damaging mothers, be they withdrawn, self-absorbed, or efficient but affectionless. Others were experienced as anxiously over-solicitous and over-protective, rigidly controlling, domineering and intrusive, or else seductive and castrating, puritanical and guilt-breeding, or as tyrannizing their children by illness, more often feigned than real. There are martyred and dolorous mothers, others that cannot release a child, exploit or scapegoat him. There are also the jealous mothers who vacillate between hostility and remorse.

I can only conclude that the more unconsciously destructive the mother is, the less the child, even when he becomes an adult, can bear to be separated from her.

The Missing Father and the All-Too-Present Mother

As my clinical examples and the diagram (*Figure 4*) will, I hope, show, the patient as a child was expected to conform to a high standard. The mother was usually seen as the stronger and more determined parent, whereas the father was perceived as the weakling. The mother, most particularly of only sons, was felt to be intensely ambitious beneath a show of martyrdom. The mother was presented as the moral authority, the child becoming cold and unloving, but fearful and desirous of approval. The father was thought of as weak, and useless as a shield against the powerful mother and her phantasized revenge. Some fathers were experienced as siding with the mother or as indifferent and helpless. That would arose anger and contempt in both mother and child, culminating in an exclusive mother-child 'pair', which virtually shut out the father as a significant parent.

73

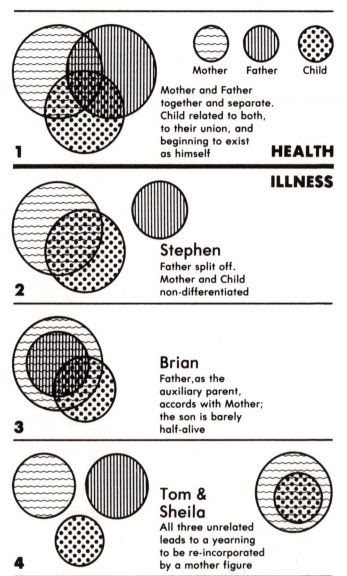

Mother Father Child

Mother and Father together and separate. Child related to both, to their union, and beginning to exist as himself

1 **HEALTH**

ILLNESS

Stephen
Father split off. Mother and Child non-differentiated

2

Brian
Father, as the auxiliary parent, accords with Mother; the son is barely half-alive

3

Tom & Sheila
All three unrelated leads to a yearning to be re-incorporated by a mother figure

4

Figure 4

74

The Rediscovery of the Father

The remainder of this paper will be concerned with my main thesis, namely the significance of the father in the formation of personality, which involves his rediscovery, as it were, within the therapeutic situation. Over and above that, it seems of paramount importance to effect the reconciliation of the parental imagos within the psyche, i.e., the reconciliation of the internalized parents. To support this proposition, I will be presenting clinical material. The names Stephen, Brian, Sheila and Tom are all pseudonyms.

Stephen

Stephen came into analysis because he suffered from a host of debilitating psychosomatic symptoms. As a teacher, his worst afflictions were the acute attacks of anxiety and panic which overcame him in crowded places, such as the daily morning school assembly. These attacks escalated into spells of giddiness, followed by vomiting and fears of fainting. Sometimes they were accompanied by blurred vision and uncontrollable, extended, periods of hiccoughing.

He came with utmost regularity, produced fascinating dreams and paintings, and his distress evaporated. After six months of analysis he concluded that he was 'cured', and well enough to dispense with further treatment.

Such 'transference cures' should make us cautious and watchful, because of the seductive, magical, almost numinous sensations which accompany them, and can infect both therapist and patient. They may lull the protagonists into an artificial sense of achievement and resolution. Stephen's intention to depart hastily was a warning signal that something alarming and painful was about to be uncovered. His defences were threatened, and his newly acquired but precarious equilibrium seemed to him to be at risk. Flight was his only escape. As Fordham states: 'To infer fusion or paradisal bliss as a continuing state is an idealized phantasy' (Fordham, 1980).

Had the sole goal and focus of his therapy been the relief of his symptoms, this might indeed have been the appropriate stage for stopping. But I realized that his attempt to retreat had been engendered by the positive, all too unambiguous, transference relationship to me, which was about to close in on him, as had his mother's suffocating embrace. Newton (1981) refers to related themes: 'An idealized love relationship ... with its counterpart, a sado-masochistic opposite ... a witch mother and a suffering victim child helpless in her clutches ... illustrating a phase of ego immaturity and dependency.' When I made an interpretation to him along those lines, his first dramatic anxiety attack in an analytic session occurred. Eventually, when he became calmer, he began to speak:

> I am really a miserable fool who staggers and blunders about, and does not want to face anything. I am a pathetic, poor little one who cannot attack and who cannot be attacked. I experience phases of nothingness. Life is frozen, sexless, numb. I feel anonymous. Everything I have ever done was for *someone else*, to keep things just as they were. I have never done anything original in my life. My mother told me I was nearly suffocated at birth. I still am. I have travelled half way round the world [he had been in the Armed Forces], but I have never left my mother.

He had already told me that, throughout his school life, he would rather go through agony than use the school lavatories. His excreta were to be entirely preserved for his mother. Sometimes his acute discomfort had become so apparent that he had been sent home, thus also serving to alleviate his separation anxieties. At his demobilization camp, he claims not to have defecated for three weeks, at the end of which he was finally discharged home. When his mother had an eye operation, he had to stay off work because *his own* eyesight was so badly affected—a telling example of projective identification between a son and his mother. During two of her serious illnesses, Stephen developed identical physical symptoms, thus making it impossible for him to feel any concern for *her* at all. It was as if he had become so closely identified with her that the psychic and somatic boundaries between him and her had dissolved.

Newton and Redfearn refer to 'some psychosomatic states in which the patient's real body and the internalized mother's body are identified' (1977). In Stephen's case, an even more primitive process had occurred. He totally identified with his external mother's bodily states. Fordham (1971) speaks of infants in 'states in which there seems to be fusion because the baby has not discovered how to distinguish between himself and the parts of his mother with which he comes into contact.' Newton and Redfearn write on similar lines: 'An inner situation of symbiosis when there are fluid boundaries between the sense of "I" and "other". '

I began to realize that the most important characteristic of the half-alive ones is their reluctance to relinquish the dependency, the close identification and the deceptive sense of safety which are some of their distinctive features. The price they pay is imprisonment—a kind of death within life. Newton's and Redfearn's apposite description is: 'An iron circle tightening around emptiness'. The afflicted participant is prepared to throw away almost everything of value that he has achieved for himself—in Stephen's case, his analysis, too—in order that he might preserve this imaginary state of 'containment' to the bitter end. It had now become clear that this was Stephen's unconscious motive. The ostensible reason, namely that he was 'cured', had deceived him. There can be no doubt that he was beginning to experience in his analysis and in the transference to his analyst, the negative, suffocating aspects of his mother's choking embrace.

The subsequent session confirmed those conjectures. He admitted that his analytic hours had become oppressive, suffocating and inescapable. He now wanted to live his own life.

Stephen further told me that he experienced sensations of suffocating most acutely during sexual intercourse with his wife. Newton and Redfearn refer to 'the shadow aspect of holding. The mother/self is devouring the infant/ego ... it represents a negative partnership.' He had brought with him a painting of a dark tree with overhanging, grasping, branches. When I commented that these branches looked like gripping arms, and that perhaps he felt that they would crush him in a tight embrace, he was thrown into a panic, the second time it had happened in a session with me. Eventually, he muttered almost inaudibly that he could feel the branches suffocating and squeezing the life out of him. He then added that he was seeing me as a witch who could magically give him a good or awful day—a characteristic of the archetypal great mother in her negative guise. I pointed out that this powerful witch was enshrined in his psyche and causing havoc in his inner and outer life; he could temporarily free himself of her by putting her outside himself through projection on to me. I reminded him that he had been referred to me on account of his fears of suffocation, which were in conflict with his yearning to remain united with his mother for all time. I added that his reiterated request to stop seeing me, combined with the fact that he nevertheless continued to come, depicted the crux of his conflict. Much later on, he admitted that he had been intent on parting with me while all was still good between us, that is, while we were still as 'one', and in no way a threat to each other.

Subsequent sessions proved to be crucial, in that they enabled Stephen to resolve his ambivalence and to make a deeper commitment to analysis. Fordham (1971) attributes this development to the 'modification of identifications developed in the course of maturation'. Significantly, an upsurge of Stephen's masculinity occurred. He had the following dream:

> I was visiting my mother and father in different wards of a hospital. I said to them: 'Why can't you be together?' And then I set to moving their beds until they were side by side.

This dream marked the first mention of his father. Moreover, it revealed much concerning his vital childhood relationships. *Both* his internalized parents were in hospital; that is, emotionally sick in terms of Stephen's relationship to each of them, and theirs to each other. He had experienced them apart, and was now taking it upon himself to bring them closer together. This movement towards a reconciliation of the inner parents marked not only the beginning of the dissolution of his state of enmeshment with his mother but ushered in the subsequent reinstatement of his father as a potent figure in his inner life. The stranglehold on his psyche of the pre-Oedipal fixation on his mother was beginning to loosen.

Outwardly, he became more enterprising. He had an engine fitted to his bicycle, and acquired a black imitation leather jacket which made him feel 'more of a man'. It had padded shoulders, big lapels and gilt buttons. Nevertheless, he did not quite feel himself in it. The following dream occurred:

> I decided that my large black riding coat was too clumsy and did not allow me enough freedom of movement. I decided to cut it up, and to remake the coat in a different design. My mum and dad were both watching. I cut up the coat and experienced intense grief. It felt as if I had destroyed something of great value. Then I began laboriously to restitch the pieces, but this time it turned not into a coat but into a close-fitting garment.

This dream confirmed Stephen's statement that he had not felt himself, that is his true self, in the coat he had bought. Rather, he had attempted to acquire a pseudo- or false-self manliness, a camouflage, for the as yet unresolved entanglement with his mother. The cutting up of the coat and its remaking into a close-fitting garment symbolized a resurrection and rebirth of a truer identity. This dream tallied with developments in his analytic sessions and in his life. His personality became more clearly defined, less easily obliterated. Yet, with the growth and unfolding, came the experience of grief and loss, stemming from the relinquishment of the primitive 'fusion-state'; the surrender of idealizations; the 'depressive position'.

A short time later, Stephen began to refer to his father in more positive terms. With the unconscious aim of perpetuating their entwinement, Stephen and his mother had needed to see his father as useless and ineffectual. Together they had conspired to denigrate and dismiss the parental marriage as incompatible, so that Stephen might compensate his mother for the lack of satisfaction from her husband, her failed marriage. Thus, he recompensed her for an 'absent' husband.

In my experience, half-alive patients more often than not have had half-alive mothers, unhappily married, who cling relentlessly to one or other of their children, projecting into this unfortunate child archetypal images of divinity or devilishness which smother the normal unfolding of the child's potential personality. As Newton and Redfearn point out: 'Jung sees the personal mother as the first carrier of the archetype'. These mothers are unable to

79

combine a relationship which simultaneously contains togetherness *and* separateness, and the ego development of the child
becomes atrophied. They tend to relate to the growing child as
if he were still a part of themselves, attached to their own bodies
by the umbilical cord, so that he remains, in part, unborn.

Prior to Stephen's request for help, he had left the parental
home to marry the girl next door. They had set up house near
his mother. The young couple spent all their free time doing
identical things jointly, and Stephen described it as a 'yes, dear,
anything you like, dear' marriage.

After some years, Stephen's wife went into hospital for her
first and only confinement. During her absence of ten days, he
became acutely anxious and feared that he was dying. His
eyesight was blurred, he suffered from nausea, he was afraid that
if he moved he would faint. According to his recollection, it was
as if his legs would fold up under him; he felt utterly forlorn.
I am well aware that I am describing classical hysterical symptoms.
Yet his condition takes on additional meaning, I feel, if perceived
as a kind of developmental block, a defence against his wife's
'otherness', and his being faced with the task of relinquishing
the dyad.

A significant breakthrough occurred when his mother came
to see the baby for the first time. She focused on the new arrival, and completely ignored Stephen. No longer was he number
one for his mother, nor for his wife either. He felt so acutely
cheated and irate that he rushed out of the room, overcome by
murderous impulses towards her, his wife and the child. It was
the first time in his life that he was aware of rage. He was both
elated and terrified, and, at the same time, infused with an upsurge of energy. Change, for him, had ceased to be synonymous
with death.

During his wife's confinement, only two weeks earlier, he had
not gone to work but lay in bed too terrified to move, or at best,
sat huddled in a corner armchair. When his wife and baby girl
subsequently returned home, he completely ignored the baby.
His suffering was acute; her arrival had made him feel cast out.
In his words, 'Someone turning away from me is like experiencing
my own death'.

Stephen had been the youngest child in his family, and the only boy. His mother had restrained herself from becoming angry with him, nor had she ever punished him. When Stephen displeased her, her response had been, 'Can't you see what you are doing to me?', implying that he was damaging her, further intensifying their psychological clinch. This response had effectively left him oblivious of the impact he could have on another person, because any unilateral action on his part was interpreted as destructive or damaging of his mother. Any minor digression left him with a load of guilt for having upset her. The extent and intensity of the attachment between himself and his mother had left no room for a relationship with his father, who had no existence for him.

This situation appears to be typical of the 'half-alive' patients. As already stated, they insist on denying any experience of the father as a positive, effective figure in their own as well as their mothers' lives. The 'non-existent' father is indeed the most noteworthy common denominator in the personal history of these patients. It is the father, nevertheless, who plays a specific and essential rôle as the mediator of the difficult transition from the womb to the world. Without the father's emotional support, it seems to me that it becomes almost insurmountably difficult for a child to be properly born and confirmed in his own identity, and to negotiate the unavoidable separation from the mother, a prerequisite to a satisfactory adult heterosexual commitment. The 'absent father' syndrome encourages a mutually collusive 'embrace' with the mother, nourishing a shared illusion of 'oneness', from which the developing child cannot extricate himself, leaving him neither in, nor out, of the womb, but wedged, so to speak, half-way, half-alive, half-born.

Earlier, I described Stephen as living in a state of twilight. When I looked up the word 'twilight' in the Oxford Dictionary, I was surprised to find, among others, the following definition: 'Twilight is a modern method of making childbirth painless.' How apt! Birth is the first and most fundamental rupture, and of necessity accompanied by pain. To quote Jung: 'Child means something evolving towards independence. This cannot be achieved without the child detaching itself from its origins; abandonment is therefore a necessary condition' (*CW* 12).

The patients and mothers who concern me in this paper have

failed to negotiate even the first unavoidable separation, because neither child nor mother could tolerate the accompanying pain, feared deprivation and sense of abandonment. The results have been pathological. It is my contention that the necessary separation requires the participation of the father. Yet these mothers and their children are unconsciously intent on continuing to perceive the father as weak and useless, or else, as in my later examples, as violent and dangerous. There is an implicit prohibition on the growth of an openly warm and loving bond between father and child, because it does not exist between the parents either. It is noteworthy that Stephen, on his own initiative, opted out of taking an interest in his baby, thus also refuting the father *within*.

In these circumstances, a state of unnatural and ambivalent identification with the mother is prolonged. She is loved and has become indispensable, but surely she is envied for her power and over-competence and possibly she is resented for her suffocating stranglehold and for her stressing of the mutual indispensability between the two of them. I hope to show that their unconscious interdependent needs are mutual, and, therefore, reversible—either one may become the parent to the child within the other. This is by no means always recognized; too often, the problem is tackled only in the partner who presents the symptoms. Both, however, are burdened with acute dependency needs, alternating with sensations of being trapped and crippled, necessitating the erection of increasingly rigid and impenetrable defence systems which serve to camouflage weakness, dependence and helplessness. It is just because of this unconscious imprisonment in an infantile state that these people fear, and consequently avoid, a new and different relationship, one which would present a challenge and demand a commitment. Their only apparent escape is to form the kind of bond that Stephen did in his marriage prior to the birth of their child, as close a replica as possible to the original mother/child bonding.

Transference Implications

I have come to realize that in the initial phases of analysis in such a situation the patient seeks to establish a 'fusion-like' mode of relatedness between himself and the analyst. I am sure that must be resisted. The truth lies in the contradiction, since the individuation process revolves primarily around conflict, the tension and the integration of opposites. Creativity springs from the resolution and the reconciliation of opposing psychic forces within the individual.

The analyst's initial task is to establish a good enough therapeutic alliance with her patient so that basic trust is secured. Hopefully, the analyst's ego-boundaries are better established and more secure than those of the patient, and she is more conscious, more of a whole person, than the patient and his original partner. It is this that eventually facilitates the resolution of the *primary* 'fusion' state. With that goal in mind, transference interpretations which imply separateness between analyst and patient, however violently refuted by the latter, are crucial when the time is ripe. It is perpetually incumbent on the therapist to be aware of, and in touch with, the newly-emerging personality, formerly repressed. It must be remembered that any state of almost infantile dependence of one adult on another may ostensibly be wanted by the patient, but it is simultaneously humiliating and undermining. The patient actually knows, but likes to forget, the painful reality that he can never wholly possess or be possessed by his analyst or by anyone else.

The conflict between the yearning for 'oneness' and the opposite drive to reject it may engender a phase in the analysis when both participants become bogged down. Prolonged periods of passivity and hopelessness may have to be endured. Nothing appears to be happening and the analyst may come to feel that she has nothing to offer. Equally, the patient may feel worthless and inadequate, and he may become trapped in just *preserving* the analyst and the status quo. In Stephen's words, 'It feels like disaster if anything were to change'. People like him have impressed me with their infinite capacity to endure suffering without any awareness of the need which also exists in them to achieve satisfaction and happiness. Unable to relinquish the illusion of safety which imprisons them, they appear to accept calmly a kind of death in life. Nevertheless, their frustration sooner or later catches up with them. Newton (1981) states it succinctly: 'There is a loss of the illusion of "oneness" and the inherent conflict of "twoness" has to be sustained.' Violent out-bursts of rage and exaggerated recriminations ensue. I interpret this as a hopeful development, no matter how unpleasant it may be to find oneself at the receiving end! As a last stand, the patient may threaten to throw out everything, including his analysis, and perhaps even his life. Thus he mistakenly hopes to ensure the preservation of 'oneness' to the very end.

The subject of my paper links with Jung's 'The significance of the father in the destiny of the individual' (see below). To quote from the article in question:

> Freud has pointed out that the emotional relationship of the child to the parents, and particularly to the father, is of decisive significance in regard to the content of any later neurosis. This is indeed the infantile channel along which the libido flows back when it encounters any obstacles in later years, thus reactivating the long forgotten psychic contents of childhood ... If the patient is a neurotic, he reverts back to the childhood relationships he has never quite forsaken, and to which the normal person is fettered by more than one chain—the relationship to father and mother ... The source of the infantile disturbance of adaptation is naturally the emotional relation to the parents ... The neurosis sets in the moment the libido is withdrawn from the infantile relationship, and for the first time comes a bit nearer to an individually determined goal ...

> The power which shapes the life of the psyche has the character of an anonymous personality ... The parental imago is possessed of quite extraordinary power; it influences the psychic life of the child enormously (*CW*4, para 728).

Stephen's material highlights, I believe, the rôle that the reinstatement of his father played in his analysis and, more importantly, in his life. Between us, we needed to enlist the help of his father, previously discarded and dismissed, yet having remained potentially vital and potent, so as to give Stephen sufficient security to relinquish his grip on his mother. With the start of this process, his conscious perception of his father began to alter. 'I wonder if dad was ever *allowed* to be effective' or 'I now think of dad as having been sucked dry by mother like a leech', he would say. His dreams continued to confirm his need of his father. In one of them, he was searching his father's waistcoat and found some valuable gold coins. In another, he went to his father for ammunition for his gun, that is, his father became the classical link with his own sexual potency. In a third dream, he climbed into bed beside his mother *and* father; in this bed, all three of them were together, but, also, each of them was separate. That dream was late in his analysis, and indicates a resolution of the Oedipal conflicts which he had never had to confront in childhood because his father had been successfully obliterated.

Brian

Brian was much more ill than Stephen. Despite his professional success, he was less than half-born, less than half-alive, and drifting towards a state of non-being. Six years of Freudian analysis had freed him of his most distressing symptoms, in particular, a condition of tormenting eczema in his genital area. Though only in his thirties, he had prematurely aged and resembled an emaciated corpse. Every movement of his body appeared as if premeditated. He said of himself that he was like an automaton going through the motions of living. As a baby he had been unable to suck and had very nearly died of starvation. During his analysis, he frequently remarked that he could not take in what I was offering him. In other words, he could not tolerate being fed by me either. Brian had experienced his mother as over-intrusive, and he was never able to look at me, as if he was continuing to simulate the darkness of the womb.

Outside his professional life, Brian was totally passive and unrelated. Clinically, he might have been described as schizoid, although I do not find the labelling of people very helpful. This sketchy picture of Brian contains some typical ingredients of half-alive patients; that is, people whose childhood was too disturbed and distorted for all but minimal ego development to have taken place. They are nowhere within sight of the individuation phase which was close to Jung's heart. In the main, they are sexually frozen, often overtly or potentially homosexual, but above all, asexual. This is equally true of both sexes. They go to infinite pains to preserve the semblance of leading 'normal' lives, that

85

is, socially acceptable lives, but they only succeed up to a point, more generally in their work. Relentlessly, they go through the motions of appearing tough and independent to cover up the extent of their helplessness and overdependent attachment to parents. The inevitable crisis occurs when they embark on their first move towards separating.

Brian and I experienced one session when this dilemma had to be lived through and survived by both of us. It followed his cancellation of an appointment with me in favour of a professional engagement with an influential and older male client.

When he came next day, he was nearly paralysed and had shrivelled up even further than before. He was unable to speak. Although I was acutely aware of his tormented state, I felt that I should resist the temptation to come to his rescue. To do so might forfeit the possibility of taking him beyond this crisis and assisting him to become alive in his own right. When time was up, he hurled his cigarette at me and ran out of my room. He was alight with anger; for the first time I saw in him a nucleus of some life of his own.

This outburst was not unlike Stephen's rage when his mother focused her attention on the new baby. I have worked with many people who presented as affectively dead and who then had a sense of coming to life when they dared to feel emotion.

The following day, Brian returned, still very angry, and accused me of failing to understand how suffocated with guilt he had been, having cancelled an appointment in favour of a male client. He had opted for the father figure, abandoning me, the mother figure. He was terrified that I would avenge myself by abandoning him. The presence of guilt suggests that a two-person interaction was beginning to develop and that notions of attack and retaliation, paranoid fears and defensive aggression had been activated. For Brian, up to then, I had almost been the archetypal great mother who had the absolute power of either nurturing or devouring her young. His subsequent comment was significant: 'The only thing that can save me now is to rediscover a mother who will breathe life into me.' It was then that I understood my reluctance to rescue him. Had I done so, I should have reduced him to a foetus who has little power to communicate and whose needs are met by primitive, instinctual biological processes.

A passage from Genesis came to mind: 'The Lord God formed man of the dust of the ground, and breathed into his nostrils the breath of life; and man became a living soul.' Had I yielded to his pressure, I would have turned into an omnipotent goddess for him. Had I become a numinous archetypal figure, I would have lost for Brian my fallible human qualities, the very attributes which assist in mediating archetypal forces. By renouncing that rôle, I had steered him into some contact with the fragment of the father within him and whatever atrophied masculinity he possessed. As he left, he looked me in the eye for the first time; the point of dissolution of the illusion of 'oneness' had arrived.

Whenever he perceived himself as other than an extension of his parents' personalities and as straying from their rigid image of him, he was overcome by guilt. His father had wanted his only son to be tough, extroverted and successful, a near-impossible target for such a frail, introverted person as Brian, although to some degree he had met his father's expectations in his work situation. In Brian's words:

> To be myself was unacceptable to my father. My mother, on the other hand, wanted me to be her perfect image of a son, so that I should make her feel a perfect mother. She fascinates and repels me simultaneously, and I feel terrible because I don't love her in the way she wants me to. I cannot risk revealing myself to her; I possess no personality in relation to her. I have betrayed my mother and need to protect her from realizing it. I am not what she thinks. If I were to rebel, the world would come to an end—my parents would be destroyed. I would do irreparable harm.

Searles (1961) speaks of patients whose existence as children in their own right received little acknowledgement, i.e., they existed mainly as an extension of their parents' personalities. Searles argues that this may lead to a conviction in the patient that he 'possesses some magical, inhumanly destructive power over people'.

Brian could not allow himself to have any manifest, discernible sexual life of his own which involved *another* person. To do so would have disproved the fact that he was still a part of his mother's body, and established instead that he owned his body in his own right. His marriage of many years remained unconsummated. His sexual life, such as it was, was enacted in the secret dark recesses of his bachelor bedroom, where he masturbated by stimulating himself with sadistic photographs in which women were being beaten and subjugated. In this situation he could feel that he was top dog. It excited him. In addition, he indulged in weekly feasts alone, going to expensive restaurants and indulging himself with large amounts of food and drink. From there, he would take himself to a sleazy pornographic club where women publicly humiliated themselves. Furtively, he went home to masturbate. These pursuits constituted the only pleasure in his life and the only stronghold against complete engulfment by his mother. If they had been interfered with, his frustrated, murderous impulses would have threatened to overwhelm and disintegrate him. He would have become even more paralysed. Open rebellion would have killed his mother. To preserve her, he could at best afford to be less than half-alive.

I should like to say something about the problem of inhibited aggression in the analysis of patients such as Brian. I trust that I have given enough material to demonstrate that even a show of forcefulness strikes them as an uncontrollable explosion, which threatens the shattering of everything and of everyone. Instead, the analyst is commonly confronted by passive withdrawal, or by a withdrawn paranoid response. Rage is turned inwards, producing depression, if not despair, to avoid the obliteration of the indispensable other. The venting of aggression against the seemingly indispensable 'mother' figure is too hazardous, unless the father, the masculine component, can be experienced as protecting and preserving her from the wounds of attack and ultimate separation.

Up to this point, I have been focusing on a father seen as weak, dismissible, and overshadowed by the mother. My last two clinical examples briefly illustrate a father experienced as 'absent' in the sense that he was violent, drunk, unpredictable, unrelated and unloving, eventually removed from the family with the active assistance of the patient when a child. Thus these patients were deprived of nurturing experience from both parents. (Both mothers were emotionally unrelated not only to their husbands but to their child too.)

Sheila

Sheila had a barren childhood; she was a lonely, manipulating, depressed woman, who threatened suicide whenever she felt the illusory 'union' that she imagined she had with me was at risk. I was the first and only person to whom she felt close; I regard her now as the most difficult and alarming patient with whom I have worked. She had never experienced love from either parent, nor did any affection exist between her parents. They were divorced when she was in her early teens. As far as I was concerned, she had a 'delusional transference'—she was besotted with me. The most infinitesimal change would upset her out of all proportion; inwardly, she would scream desperately, like a young baby disrupted at the breast. When I moved house, she was in a severe crisis, as if her small familiar world had totally disintegrated.

After saying that she had lost me, she pronounced that she too was going away. Although I was deeply affected, and feared that she was going away to die, I felt that I must let her go, despite my own, as well as her investment in her analysis. The following day, to my everlasting relief, she screamed over the telephone at me that had she ended her life, she would also have lost me, like throwing out the baby with the bath water. Therefore, she would return for her sessions.

Her background and Tom's were not dissimilar. Both of them described their mothers as withdrawn, depressed and martyred, and their fathers as violent, destructive, with terrifying outbursts of rage. Feeling, as they both did, that they were completely cut off from a human mother, they were in the grip of a more formidable archetypal partner, namely the great mother, in her idealized and in her devouring aspects. The clinical picture of half-aliveness is even more entrenched if there is an 'absent' mother, who cannot at all mediate some experience of humanity, love and holding; the damage far outweighs that inflicted by the suffocating, over-possessive mothers of Stephen or Brian. These people live in an emotional desert, as did their parents, and consequently they manifest schizoid traits, and an overwhelming longing to be reincorporated inside the mother/analyst, which they see as their only secure experience.

89

Whenever Sheila could not avoid the realization that she did not possess me utterly, she attacked me venomously and unmercifully. Gradually, I was able to tolerate her onslaughts better. This occurred when I managed to constellate within myself both my feminine and masculine aspects; that is, I united my own internalized mother and father. In other words, whenever Sheila succeeded in splitting the parents within me, thus separating me from my animus, I became part of her chaos, and I would take evasive action which only heightened her destructiveness and guilt. Her ego boundaries were as fragile as a young infant's might be at 6-9 months, in the grip of both love and hatred, i.e., at the onset of the 'depressive position'. They needed shoring up in the form of a mother/father unity before she was safe enough to express both her positive and her negative feelings. During one crisis she actually said: 'I need the father in you too.' She only came close to achieving an integrated emotional state when she received in her analysis the psychological experience of two united, loving parents. It was at such times that a benevolent regression could take place; she would speak of her longing to be my baby inside me. Only as a foetus, she maintained, had she ever felt safe, wanted and cherished.

Sheila claimed that her parents used to tear each other to pieces. She became their pawn; they tried to win her over to one side or the other. The culmination of these conflicts occurred when she was forced to give evidence in a divorce court. Knowingly, she lied about her father, so that her mother might win the case. From that time on, she disintegrated rapidly, the more so because her worst fear, that she had caused the split between her parents, was confirmed by reality, demolishing any surviving phantasy of a loving pair. At one point, when I had become excessively concerned about her suicidal threats, I arranged for her to see a male psychiatric colleague. She came away with a sense that both he and I cared about her and that she could safely share *both* mother *and* father without depriving either of them. The outcome was a spontaneous alleviation of a near-psychotic depression; she felt wanted and a shared object of concern.

Her parents' failure to come to terms with one another was matched by their incapacity to relate to Sheila as a whole person. That had produced a far-reaching rupture in her personality. She had no experience of wholeness either outside or within herself; she described herself as 'torn to pieces', or 'all in bits'. I had observed that she, like Tom, was quite incapable of retaining the memory of one session to the next, even when her sessions were on consecutive days.

Experiences of fragmentation can occur irrespective of the parental situation; these states are indicative of a fragile ego being overwhelmed by archetypal forces. In another instance, a patient who was becoming better integrated and fulfilled convinced herself that her newly acquired strength had been stolen from her husband. She felt that she had irrevocably wounded him, and a period of guilt and hopelessness ensued.

Tom

Finally, I should like to select a few fragments from my work with Tom, a severely disturbed man in his fifties, exceptionally brilliant; having come from a working-class background with little formal education, he was entirely self-made. His long analysis ended when he retired and had developed his creative side to the full. I hear from him still and know that he now lives a contented and peaceful existence.

Tom began his analysis by rigidly denying his dependency needs. In his sessions, he was so controlling that I was totally blotted out and blocked. He spoke compulsively into empty space, an attempt, as I saw it, to hold me to him inextricably. I felt as isolated and useless as he. Then one day, when, as usual, he was flooding me with words, I said quietly: 'You know you don't *have* to'. The effect was dramatic. For the first time, he relaxed; then added that the only excitement in his life was derived from observing pretty young women at a distance. He had always avoided looking at me because, he said, if he were to become aware of me as a separate entity, his much-needed phantasy of 'oneness' with me would become disturbed. He could not permit me to show him in or out of my consulting-room as was my custom; that would have exposed the fact that there were two of us. It was he who terminated each session. Whenever a holiday break approached, he pleaded for extra sessions so that the ritual number of sessions, which represented his regular feeds and safety to him, should be maintained. In a letter written during the first year of his analysis, he included the following: 'It is almost as if I am a prisoner in a cell. The door is ajar, yet I dare not go out into the bright world. I remain fixed where I am—rigid, terror-stricken, immovable. My present non-existence, in a contrary way, is burning me out ... so much of my energy goes into suppressing and stifling my individuality and spontaneity.'

Conclusion

My work with patients such as Stephen, Brian, Sheila and Tom has shown that an integral, vital stage in the healing process necessitates a reactivation in the patient's unconscious of a steadfast mother/father constellation. Only thus does it become endurable for the patient to relinquish the primary, phantasized state of 'union' with his actual, or with the archetypal mother. The inhibiting effect of divided parents on growth and development can be devastating. Should the analysis go well, however, that area of the patient's personality which has been committed to a real or imaginary 'oneness' with the mother and was thus unavailable for the enrichment of his own life, will gradually be restored to him, making him more alive, more whole. With the re-emergence of the father as an important person, the mother can gradually be safely relinquished to him, and she is no longer perceived as mutilated and impoverished. Briefly, I see the process of reconciling the parents within as a vital ingredient in healing.

Summary

This paper is the outcome of observations made throughout my analytic work as well as the more than twenty years spent doing marital therapy at the Institute of Marital Studies.

Although primarily concerned with the inner world, I acknowledge the frequently tragic and damaging impact which the escalating divorce rates have on children who consequently grow up in 'one-parent' families.

Clinical material and a diagram are presented to illustrate my contention that 'half-aliveness' is often linked with an emotionally 'absent' parent, in my cases more frequently the father. Furthermore, it follows that there is an 'absent' husband also, so that the parental marriage tends to be dilapidated and empty to a degree which lumbers the unfortunate child, most likely the only son, with the rôle of the surrogate 'husband', a psychological trap from which he may be unable to extricate himself well into adult life.

It is suggested that a resolution to this pathological enmeshment may lead to a symbolic, if not actual, reinstatement of the 'absent' parent, enabling a reconciliation of the inner parents to take place, which then frees the previously 'paralysed' individual to discover his own identity, liberating his hitherto atrophied resources.

References

Abelin, E.L. (1975). 'Some further observations and comments on the earliest rôle of the father', *Int. J. Psychoanal.*, 56 (3).

Fordham, M. (1971). 'Primary self, primary narcissism and related concepts', *J. Analyt. Psychol.*, 16 (2).

Fordham, M. (1980). 'The emergence of child analysis', *J. Analyt. Psychol.*, 25 (4).

Greenacre, P. (1966). 'Problems of over-idealization of the analyst and of the analysis', in *Psychoanal. Study of Child*, 21. London, Hogarth Press.

Layland, W.R. (1981). 'In search of a loving father', *Int. J. Psychoanal.*, 62 (2).

Mahler, M.S., Pine, F., Bergman, A. (1975). *The Psychological Birth of the Human Infant.* London, Hutchinson.

Newton, K. (1981). 'Comment on "The emergence of child analysis" by M. Fordham', *J. Analyt. Psychol.*, 26 (1).

Newton, K., Redfearn, J. (1977). 'The real mother, ego-self relations and personal identity', *J. Analyt. Psychol.*, 22 (4).

Searles, H.F. (1961). 'The sources of anxiety in paranoid schizophrenia', *Brit. J. Med. Psychol.*, 34 (2).

Thompson, E. (ed.). (1981). *Social Trends.* Government Statistical Services, No.11. London, HMSO.

The father's anima

JOHN BEEBE

Beebe's paper also explores the internal-external dynamic. But, because he does so by using biblical personages, the paper also serves as an excellent introduction to the use in analytical psychology of *amplification*. By this is meant a method of linking personal imagery with historical and mythological motifs. Amplification is not translation of the enigmatic image into another language, however. Rather, it is an attempt by way of parallels to flesh out (make ample) clinical material which might be rather thin. Though Jung tended to use collective cultural material in his amplifications, an analyst who refers the events of analysis back to a model of infancy may also be seen as carrying out the same task. Another point to watch for in Beebe's paper is his particular demonstration of the reworking of Jung's seminal concepts that is taking place in analytical psychology worldwide. In this instance, we see *anima*, not just a personification, but a perspective or *Weltanschauung*. The paper has been slightly revised. *A.S.*

I WANT TO BEGIN with four clinical examples of the psychodynamic problem I have in mind. Like all clinical examples, they are part fiction, part fact. My first example is of a young man in his late twenties, to whom it would not have occurred to go into analysis. He was a surpassingly beautiful servant in the house of a bisexual captain of the Egyptian Guard. This master had acquired this Jewish youth initially 'for a lewd purpose', but, discovering that his comely servant was serious about his Judaism, managed to sublimate his attraction to the young man. He treated him as a son and gave him a favoured position in his home. The captain's wife could not so easily contain her physical longing. She persistently entreated the servant for sex, which he always refused her, explaining that he could not betray a master who had treated him kindly. Exasperated, the woman finally played a trick: she seized the unsuspecting servant by his shirt as if to draw him near. When, as she expected, he tore himself forcibly from her grasp, she had a bit of his clothing in hand with which to prove to her husband that the young man had made a pass at her. A tribunal was called, and though no one really believed the captain's wife, the young man was sent to prison on the grounds that he had called his mistress's honour into question.

For the biblical Joseph, who was the unfortunate servant, this imprisonment turned out to be decisive. His skill at interpreting other prisoners' dreams became know to the Pharaoh, who had had a 'big' dream which none of his usual consultants could interpret. Joseph's refusal of Potiphar's wife led to his rise under a far more powerful master, the Pharaoh.

My second example, from the analysis of a contemporary man, is an amplification of the Joseph story. This man, also in his late twenties, found himself making rapid advances in his chosen career. He felt supported in his advancement over his fellows at work by the seemingly endless encouragement of his fatherly Jungian analyst. This analyst managed to provide a wonderfully non-intrusive holding environment that contained the patient utterly in a sense that his every step toward self-advancement would meet with the unconditional positive regard of the analyst. Under the spell of this 'anima fathering' the patient had come to regard his entire life as one of continuous advancement. And then he had the following dream:

> I was in a classroom with other students, possibly a nursery
> school. I was absorbed in the positive maternal atmosphere
> of the teacher, humming at her desk. I felt at one with the
> other students, who were all working quietly at their different
> desks. I didn't actually see anyone in the room, nor did I need
> to, so contained was I within the pleasant atmosphere. Sud-
> denly an angry male figure, 'The Father', entered the room,
> harshly interrupting the comfortable atmosphere with angry
> words toward the motherly teacher.

> 'How could you let this happen?' the father demanded. 'Look
> at him!'

> I was suddenly acutely conscious of myself and my surround-
> ings. Now I could see that all the other students were wear-
> ing tunics and I a coat of many colours.

This dream registers the impact of the analyst's stance upon the
patient. For the analyst's anima was in fact the motherly teacher,
so skilled at creating a containing environment that she was not
allowing the patient to become conscious. And the terrrible father
was the split-off envious and hostile side of the analyst's attitude
toward his patient.

This dream was the analysand's first intimation that in and
outside the analytic situation his obvious capacities might arouse
envy and competitive feeling from others, and another anima
response than unconditional positive regard from his analyst.
Yet this experience of his analyst's unconscious hostility toward
him helped to make him aware of the creativity of his own, rather
extraverted, anima. This anima developed into a very useful
political sense that enabled him to survive many difficult situations in the course of the realization of his scholarly gifts.

My third example is also drawn from the analytic situation.
This analysand was a man in his middle thirties who found
himself in the throes of an acute marital crisis. This man became
gripped by a passion for someone younger and more physically
alluring than his faithful and familiar spouse. Discussions with
neither the spouse nor the analyst seemed to transform this all-

consuming passion. In the midst of deciding what to do the man dreamed:

> I'm in the kitchen. I turn on the water, which is badly hooked up to the plumbing in the bathroom in the next room. Water comes out of every pipe in the kitchen. It's good clean water, almost like crystal clear spring water, but the plumbing is in awful shape. My father is there. I say, 'Dad, what do I do about this?' He's absent-minded, absorbed in his thoughts. He doesn't acknowledge that I've said anything.

Shortly afterwards the man terminated both his marriage and his analysis in order to pursue his passion. Despite the aggressive explosivity of his initial decision, the patient was able to find his way back into marriage for another try and into a more focused relationship to his unconscious life than had previously been possible for him. He was ready to fix his own plumbing.

My fourth example involves a similar decision to live out, rather than refuse, the call to eros, and it provides amplification for the third case. This example is taken from the documented life history of the head of a religious state who prayed to God his father to test him in his faith. This wartime political leader's wish was not long in being granted. Shortly after his prayer, the head of state caught sight of the beautiful wife of one of his most loyal military officers. Unable to contain his passion, the leader summoned the wife and slept with her. She conceived that night, and when her pregnancy became known to him the head of state decided that he would get rid of the husband by sending him to the front lines. The loyal officer was killed in action, and Bathsheba married King David of Israel.

God was not slow in expressing his displeasure. For the way in which he took the wife of Uriah the Hittite, David was to suffer greatly. The child conceived of their tryst died in infancy, and continuous warfare was to plague David's forty-year reign. He was not allowed to build the Temple, and for a six-month period suffered from leprosy. And he had to endure a long, troublesome rebellion at the hands of his favourite son, Absalom.

But despite all this, David never regretted his choice of Bathsheba, and apparently neither did God, once the shabby beginning of their intimacy had been punished. David atoned for the enormity of his sin and continued his life with her. Bathsheba and David's second son was Solomon, a personification of the wisdom David had gleaned from his experience.

David was visited at his bedside by Bathsheba for the last time when he was dying, and he followed her good advice to make Solomon the next King of Israel. Solomon turned out to be an excellent King and he was allowed by God to build the Temple.

Those are my four examples. It is obvious, I think, that in each of them a man has an anima experience which requires a choice.

In the first two examples, the men decide to resist the seductions of the anima figure so as to realize the anima potentiality in themselves. The men in the second two examples decide to go with the pull of the anima into a deepened consciousness of eros, even at the cost of betraying loyal partners and traditional values.

What I want to show, however, is that in each case the anima problem that is being presented to the man is not purely his own but rather one posed to him by a father figure. These father figures are: Potiphar, the all-accepting analyst, the affect-isolating personal father, and God. And Potiphar's wife, the warmly maternal nursery school teacher, the outpouring of the pure water of life from the poor plumbing, and Bathsheba in all her glory represent anima problems those father figures have left to the sons to solve.

In each of my examples, the task of the son figure is to relate to his 'father's' anima problem in such a way that its energy becomes his own.

Making the father's anima problem into an inner experience of his own usually requires from the son a refusal to go the way that the father's anima would apparently desire. Joseph realizes his own anima potential by not sleeping with Potiphar's wife. The first analysand stops allowing his analyst to carry the anima function for him, and becomes conscious of his own capabilities. The married second analysand chooses to live out the libidinal problem his father would rather ignore. And David goes against God's will in making someone God has presented as merely temptation into a legitimate wife who will mother his future heir.

These four situations are examples of a transfer of energy I regard as decisive for the individuation of a man, the way in which the anima becomes his own, free of his father's influence. The parallel process by which a woman frees her female energy from her father's sphere of influence is described in Linda Leonard's *The Wounded Woman: Healing the Father-Daughter Relationship* (1982).

The purpose of this paper is to explore the impact of the father's anima on the son's own anima development. In what I want to do, I feel it important to emphasize from earlier Jungian literature two ideas which I think have been insufficiently appreciated as clinically useful. One is Jung's conception of the anima as the archetype of life. I take Jung to mean that the anima is the part of a man that shapes, registers, and experiences his life: to be without anima would be to be depersonalized. The second is Hillman's (1973), that the anima serves the instinct of reflection. I have followed Hillman to think of the anima as the emotional attitude a man takes toward anything (or anyone) he reflects upon. A man's reflections, those musings he so often mistakes for consciousness, are grounded in an unconscious, archetypal base—the anima—and it is in the midst of a man's fondest and most frequent reflections that we can see the anima arranging a pattern of behaviour that will soon affect the target of those reflections. This archetypal ground of a man's reflections is not, I think, necessarily female, any more than it is ever entirely uncontaminated by shadow. Jung speaks in his later writings of anima Mercurius, emphasizing both androgynous and trickster aspects of the anima, and it is these aspects I will emphasize in what follows, since there is often a tendency to think of the anima as the ideal feminine image.

A man's anima is of course multifaceted, but perhaps his most consistent anima is the one towards the rôle he is playing in life. This is certainly the anima that affects his fate. A man with persistent feelings of inferiority, for instance, is the target of a self doubting anima, and this negative anima will arrange an inferior fate for him. The anima is the man's spontaneous working sense of his life, the way he approaches his life and the way he reflects upon it. But when I speak of the father's anima, I am referring to the father's working sense of his son's life, the emotional attitude that the father takes towards his son. This emotional attitude is communicated to the son as his father's felt sense of the younger man's worth.

The father's emotional attitude toward his son is normally ambivalent, and there is usually splitting in any father's experience of that ambivalence. One father feels primarily loving and protecting, while another is painfully aware of an attitude of rejecting resentment towards his son. Often, the surfacing of another pole to what seems to be the dominant attitude comes as a shock to both father and son. Yet, as I have tried to show in my examples, it is the unsuspected side of the father's anima that provides the greatest opportunities for the son's own anima development.

My intent is to highlight the rôle that the anima may play in contributing to the complexities that abound in the father-son relationship, but not to reduce all those complexities to anima. And, of course, this paper's focus is one-sided because it is compensatory—compensatory both to the Freudian tradition (in formulations like 'identification with the aggressor') of confining discussions of father-son dynamics to super-ego and ego consequences only and to the Jungian tradition (in formulations like 'the battle for deliverance from the mother') of seeing the mother's animus as the only, or at least the main, obstacle to the development of the son's anima.

The stories of Joseph and David define two extremes, two opposite patterns of the effect of a father's anima on the later individuation of his son. In the Joseph story, or pattern, the father's anima, in her most approving aspect as idealizing love, is directly projected on to the son. In the David story, or pattern, the father's anima is withheld from the son in an attitude of devaluing, distancing and paranoid envy. Under conditions of love, Joseph becomes ingratiating; under conditions of abandonment, David becomes resourceful. Yet, in later development, Joseph has to learn to protect himself from the tricksterish, envious hostility that is concealed within his father's apparently endless love for him. And David is driven forcibly to seize hold of the affective response that has been withheld, rather than simply to endure his emotional isolation with compensatory efforts at poetic and heroic self-validations. Both men have to deal with the parts of the anima their fathers have not revealed to them, and these split-off parts emerge synchronistically in the sons' encounters with actual women. Joseph is forced to experience the withheld trickster pole of his father's anima through Potiphar's wife. He must learn to withdraw from this kind of woman and survive her treachery if his development is to proceed. David's need for the withheld loving pole of his father's anima drives him to a series of passionate encounters with women—Bathsheba was his hundredth wife—until his own identification with the heroic trickster gives way.

If we look more deeply into the stories of Joseph and of David, as found not only in the Bible but in the legends surrounding these figures collected by Louis Ginzberg, the process of anima differentiation within each pattern becomes more clear (Ginzberg, 1975). What you should be listening for as I retell these stories is how the father's anima is gradually transferred into the son.

I will start again with Joseph. Joseph's father was Jacob, a grandson of Abraham, and though Jacob had four wives, Rachel was by far his favourite. But Rachel watched the other wives bear Jacob ten sons. At last God let her bear Joseph. When a second son, Benjamin, was born to her, Rachel died in childbirth. Ginzberg tells us that

> Joseph's beauty of person was equal to that of his mother Rachel, and Jacob had but to look at him to be consoled for the death of his beloved wife. Reason enough for distinguishing him among his children. As a token of his great love for him, Jacob gave Joseph a coat of many colours, so light and delicate that it could be crushed and concealed in the closed palm of one hand.

Thomas Mann, in his own retelling of the story, makes the coat of many colours into Rachel's wedding garment. We can see that the anima rôle in his father's life had been placed on to Joseph, and the young Joseph behaved accordingly. He 'painted his eyes, dressed his hair carefully, and walked with a mincing step'. And young Joseph also felt called upon to carry his father's relation to the unconscious. He bore tales about his brothers home to Jacob and reported mediumistic dreams which had portent for the future of their tribe. In effect, he began to pre-empt the function of Jacob's anima in looking out for the family unconscious.

In telling one such dream, Joseph said:

'Behold, I have dreamed a dream more; and behold, the sun and the moon and the eleven stars made obeisance to me.' And he told it to his father, and to his brethren: and his father rebuked him, and said unto him, What is this dream that thou has dreamed? Shall I and thy mother and thy brethren indeed come to bow down ourselves to thee and to the earth? And his brethren envied him; but his father observed the saying.

I would like the reader to notice the splitting in the father's response, as reported here. On the one hand Jacob is leading the brothers on in their envy of Joseph. On the other hand, he 'observes the saying', that is profits from the mediumistic anima function that his son is performing for him. Joseph is trapped by Jacob's idealizing transference to him into a grandiose exhibitionism which arouses Jacob's envy, which Jacob then transfers on to the brothers so that his conscious idealization of Joseph can be maintained.

Yet the envy they carry for Jacob, the shadow side of Jacob's idealization, is actually the force that serves to free Joseph from this dangerously inflating situation and pulls him on the road towards his own individuation. Jacob sets Joseph up by sending him out to inquire after his absent brothers; they strip off the coat of many colours and throw Joseph into a pit while they decide whether to kill him or sell him into slavery.

In the father's tricksterish deviousness in sending Joseph to his collapse, we can see that Jacob really wanted to reclaim the anima with which he had invested his son. The coat of many colours is brought back to him stained with the blood of a slaughtered animal, and he is told that Joseph has been torn to pieces by a wild beast, though in fact Joseph has been sold into slavery. Jacob's trick enables him, with the aid of his other sons, to win back his authority over the unconscious destiny of the tribe.

In Egypt, the two sides of the father's anima are expressed by a single figure, Potiphar's wife, whose behaviour fits the pattern of seduce-then-destroy. After initial idealization, she too divests Joseph of part of a fine garment Potiphar gave him, and she deprives Joseph of influence and authority by having him sent to prison.

Prison is a chance for Joseph to reflect, as was the pit, and through these depressing experiences one feels him beginning to grasp that there is a side of any father figure which is bound to resent the anima investment he has made in a son. Indeed, unless a young man realizes this, he is in for some rude shocks, particularly in the area of his career. When a previously encouraging father-figure snatches back his anima, it can feel like a major betrayal.

Yet with Joseph, each divestiture of the father's anima leads not to irreparable narcissistic injury but rather to the further development of interiority. When finally Joseph emerges from prison to take his destined rôle beside the Pharaoh as the steward who will see Egypt and the world through the famine, he is a very different person from the youth who naïvely paraded his dreams before his father and his brothers.

Having demonstrated that Pharaoh's disturbing dream predicts a famine, Joseph advises Pharaoh to 'look out a man discreet and wise and set him over the land of Egypt' to oversee the storing up of food against the lean years.

'Pharaoh said unto his servants, can we find such a one as this is, a man in whom the Spirit of God is?' and then to Joseph, 'Forasmuch as God hath shewed thee all this, there is none so discreet and wise as thou art'. And he then makes Joseph second in command, giving him his ring, a gold chain and 'vestures of fine linen', and 'made him to ride in the second chariot which he had'. As Pharaoh puts it to Joseph, 'only in the throne will I be greater than thou'.

This investiture is a very different process from the one which prevailed in Jacob's house. The Pharaoh manages his ambivalence about sharing power by retaining his own anima connection to his Royal Self as supreme authority.

Joseph, for his part, never tries to pre-empt that authority, even when called to the intimate task of interpreting the Pharaoh's dreams.

It is at this point that Joseph is allowed to marry. The Bible tells us that his bride is a daughter of Potiphera, who is described as a priest. This name is virtually the same as Potiphar, but the change in vocation from military captain to religious priest suggests that the attitude of the father figure has changed towards

104

Joseph from one of defence to one of religious sacrifice in response to Joseph's maturing consciousness. The father figure at this stage is no longer a tribal patriarch using the pattern of seduce-then-destroy in order to maintain his power; he is an initiatory father who yields the anima to the son as his sacred duty to help the son become a father figure in his own right.

The rest of Joseph's story reveals that he can now deal with the tricksterish side of his original father's anima. When his brothers come to Egypt during the famine to buy grain, he plays meaningful tricks upon them, demonstrating not only that he can handle them but also that he is willing to share the guilt of betrayal with them. He really sets them free from having to carry the envious side of Jacob's anima, and makes them glad to yield to him his rightfully superior position over them.

Once Joseph has learned to deal with both the idealizing and the tricksterish pole of his father's anima Jacob is satisfied and ready to die. Joseph has his own anima, his own interior relation to ideals and to tricks, and his father complex is at an end. He has gracefully solved the problem of achieving anima fertility without acquiring it at his father's expense.

When we turn to the David story, we find ourselves in a very different pattern, where anima fertility (represented now by the continuation of the kingship) can *only* be achieved at the father's expense. In this pattern, the son does not suffer from the trickster but is the trickster, and ruthlessness, not grace, is what the son must display to survive. David is the type of son who starts his journey through life feeling that his father is somehow ashamed of him. The trickster side of the father's anima has been pro-jected on to him, and so he is always somewhat doubtful in his father's eyes, however remarkable his attributes and achievements.

Of David's personal father, Ginzberg tells us:

> In spite of his piety, Jesse was not always proof against temp-tation. One of his slaves caught his fancy, and he would have entered into illicit relations with her had his wife, Nazbat, ... not frustrated the plan. She disguised herself as the slave, and Jesse, deceived by the ruse, met his own wife. The child borne by Nazbat was given out as the son of the freed slave, so

that the father might not discover the deception practiced upon him. The child was David.

In our words, the father's anima has projected her trickster pole on to David. David grew up a living reminder of Jesse's 'regrettable lapse of piety', tragically cut off from the idealizing side of Jesse's anima. Therefore his early life is a continuous effort to prove his worth to himself and to father figures, and the tragedies of his mature years can be understood as his ultimate attempts to connect with the love and forgiveness that his father had withheld.

It is clear that the discovery of David's true stature comes as a shock to Jesse. This discovery is made by Samuel the anointer, who is told by God, displeased with the rule of Saul, Israel's first King, that a new King is needed, and that this King will be the son of Jesse. Jesse presents seven sons to Samuel , but the sacred oil will not flow from Samuel's horn on to any of their heads. Finally Jesse brings forth David from the fields, the oil flows, and David's mother 'Nazbat' reveals the deception she had practised. Only then does Jesse recognize David as his legitimate son.

Almost immediately afterwards, David is summoned to Saul's court, to comfort Saul with the musical ability he had learned in his lonely years as a shepherd on his father's estate. Once again, David is in a compromised position, a trickster who knows, as he plays to soothe the paranoid Saul, that he will one day be the usurper of Saul's throne. Nevertheless, though his efforts to win over Saul's moody anima are only temporarily successful, David is able during these years to win a bit of the love from the father that he needs. He gets even more from Saul's son Jonathan. For just as Joseph's brothers carried the envious side of Jacob's idealizing transference to Joseph, so Jonathan carries the homoerotic loving side of Saul's paranoid transference to David. Upon Jonathan's death, David notes, 'very pleasant hast thou been unto me: thy love to me was wonderful, passing the love of women.'

But where Joseph took favouritism for granted, David is much more cautious upon finding appreciation at Saul's court. He asks, for instance, to be Saul's armour-bearer, but he avoids wearing

Saul's armour when he goes to slay Goliath—the counterposition on to Joseph's naïve acceptance of the coat of many colours.

Even so, the slaying of Goliath—David's attempt to win Saul's approval with a grand, heroic gesture—backfires. Saul's ambivalence toward David is resolved in favour of envy, and David is eventually driven from Saul's court to live as a renegade, who hides in caves and gradually gathers supporters for his own cause.

Pathetically, he continues to try to prove his loyalty to Saul whenever the two come into contact, and there is one episode when David cuts off just a snippet of Saul's royal garment with his knife as Saul walks into the cave where David is hiding in darkness. This motif is the reverse of the trick Potiphar's wife played in taking a piece of Joseph's shirt, for David's trick is his way of showing his loyalty to the father figure and his right to his love, demonstrating that he means no bodily harm to Saul. But once again, Saul is only temporarily won over and soon reverts to his murderous pursuit of his hated rival.

During this period David begs bread for his men from a wealthy landowner. Suspicious of this band of renegades, the landowner refuses, but his wife Abigail, meeting David on the road, decides that she wants to help him. When she tells her husband her positive opinion of David and her desire to feed him and his men, her husband has a heart attack and dies. Abigail becomes one of David's wives. Unlike Joseph, David must claim the anima literally over the dead bodies of father figures.

He cannot officially become King of Israel until Saul dies in battle, along with Jonathan. It is in the light of this pattern that we can better understand why the analysand who dreamed that his kitchen was overflowing with poorly-contained libido was forced to seek the solution to his problem outside his marriage and his analysis. The failure of his analysis to contain him (in contrast to the Joseph-like analysand, who was too contained by his analysis) was directly related in his dream to the failure of his original father to lend support or even acknowledgement to his libidinal dilemmas. Where the original father's anima has been this withholding, it is not unusual for the analysand in crisis to find his male analyst's efforts to contain him within the analytic situation relatively unhelpful. Nor may the spouse's empathy be enough to contain him in his marriage when, as sooner or later they must, the possibilities of life emerge that the father has withheld. Often, the father's faulty container must be broken before genuine containment can occur.

I think this is the real reason why David broke God's commandment in sending Uriah to his death; he had to have the connection to Bathsheba on his own terms. For with Bathsheba finally his own, love and not treachery gain the upper hand in David's character. When Absalom, his son, dies during his later political rebellion, David weeps so loudly and so long that he compromises his power over those who have fought so long and hard against Absalom on his behalf (this is the counterpole to Joseph's weeping apart from his brothers in order to maintain his political authority over them in Egypt).

Psalm 51 is said to have been written by David as a prayer for absolution for his guilt over Uriah. In the psalm, one senses that David has begun to reflect upon the pattern of his life. He refers specifically to the tricksterish circumstances of his birth as the genesis of his own longstanding tricksterism:

> Behold, I was shapen in iniquity; and in sin did my mother conceive me.

This self-reflection seems to be based on a genuine interest in the meaning of his own life. His next words to God are:

> Behold, thou desirest truth in the inward parts; and in the hidden part thou shalt make me to know wisdom.

We can therefore understand the sacrifice of the loyal Uriah as a symbolic solution to the problem presented to David by his father's anima. The sacrifice of Uriah represents the end of David's bondage to his original pattern. This pattern had locked him into the rôle of an eternal soldier of God, forever seeking new heroic tests with which to prove himself worthy of God's admiration. His unforgivable sin freed David from such heroic over-compensation and allowed him to become initiated into the experience of God's mercy. In response to David's new attitude of humble supplication, God makes a reciprocal sacrifice of his wrath and allows David to keep Bathsheba. The change in God which accompanies the change in David parallels the way

Potiphar the captain gives way to Potiphera the priest within Joseph's story.

At this point in both stories, heroic devotion to a father who makes use of the anima for his own unfathomable purposes ends, and a truly religious co-operation between son and father begins.

The son experiences the anima for the first time as a more truly caring emotional attitude toward himself. At this stage, the two patterns are really one, the point of both being to effect the father's transfer of the anima to a son conscious enough to make wise use of her protection.

References

Ginzberg, L. (1975). *The Legends of the Bible,* Philadelphia, The Jewish Publication Society of America.

Hillman, J. (1973). 'Anima', *Spring.*

Leonard, L. (1982). *The Wounded Woman: Healing the Father-Daughter Relationship.* Ohio, Swallow Press.

The image of the parents in bed

ANDREW SAMUELS

In this paper I also was trying to rework some of Jung's ideas by placing them in a developmental context. Specifically, this involved seeing the primal scene as an example of the bringing together of opposites. The way in which analytical psychology uses the concept of projection is brought out. Here, we see the way in which the infant first encounters his psychic variety and rich pluralism in images of his parents. I was trying to move fluidly between a personal-historical perspective and a collective-mythological one. A real baby, and then the Hermes mythologem. The thrust of the paper is anti-chronological (at least as far as understanding psychological phenomena is concerned). Hence, there is also an attempt to make a novel use of the forward-looking, synthetic aspect of analytical psychology. The rôle of psychology in the making of morality is also hinted at. The word 'uroboric' may require an explanation. The uroboros is the mythological motif of a serpent, coiled into a circle, eating its own tail. It is used by some analytical psychologists as an organizing metaphor for their understanding of the earliest stages of psychological development. Love and aggression are not delineated, gender identity is unformed, and there is a fantasy of self-sufficiency. The uroboros also suggests fertility and creativity; it is analogous to healthy narcissism in psychoanalytic terminology—with similar possibilities of pathology. *A.S.*

MY THEME is psychological; that is, it is characterized by doubt, uncertainty and possibility. Images and experiences of parental intercourse and the parental marriage hover between and connect inner and outer, personal and archetypal, destructive and creative. Images are the operant element in phantasy; it is they who permit talk of subjective reality. Because the primal scene has to do with origins and the mystery of a beginning it exerts a fascination; because it has to do with outcome and a tangible result it has a compulsive attraction. We know this from our own analyses, from our work with patients and from the history of the early days of the psychoanalytic movement.

Why 'in bed'? Concepts (such as the primal scene) need and create contexts, thereby becoming images. Jung points out 'the term "image" is intended to express not only the form of the activity taking place, but the typical situation in which the activity is released' (*CW* 9i, para. 152). The image of the parents in bed is, quite literally, a matter of chicken and egg. The individual is created out of primal scene activity but the scene, *qua* scene, does not itself exist except as part of a combining of endowment with experience. As a colleague has said, it is hard to get the image of the parents in bed together. It is a creation and a symbol for life as it develops. Bringing things together is a précis of creativity.

The question of the rôle of parental images in the development of personality is still an interesting one. Issues such as the balance between reality and phantasy in the formation of internal imagery, the degree of importance of sexuality and the purposive uses to which inner conceptions and preconceptions may be put are as relevant now as they ever were. In this paper I am concerned with imagery developing over a period of time, changing or not changing as the case may be. Imagery is seen as deriving from the synthesis of phantasy and fact, subjective with objective elements.

In the paper I argue that imagery around the parents in bed can be seen as a conjunction of the divine and the grotesque. Not only are these linked, but what is divine is sometimes primitive and what is grotesque is sometimes sublime. In any event, there is a connection which, it is argued, is central to

112

developing self-image, psychosexual identity and personal relationships.

The conjunction of the grotesque and the divine suggests the presence of a god, and the god who fits the bill, who most aptly could be described as a grotesque divine, is Hermes. Hermes' positive, transforming, connecting aspect is considered together with his tricksterism, his dishonesty, and his sexual perversity and obscenity. Two strands of argument emerge from this. First, that the function of apparently criminal or immoral impulses and behaviour needs reviewing as a developmental factor. The second strand is that Hermes' encapsulation of adaptability and flexibility signifies something central for the resolution of neurotic conflicts generated by the primal scene. Jung says, 'Mercurius consists of all conceivable opposites ... is a unity in spite of the fact that his innumerable inner contradictions can dramatically fly apart into an equal number of disparate and apparently independent figures' (*CW* 13, para. 284). Hermes is 'many-sided' (*ibid.*, para. 267) and has 'a limitless number of names' (*ibid.*, p. 284). My interest in adaptability began first in relation to its opposite—uroboric omnipotence in which, for example, precise inner preconceptions as to the ideal partner controlled heterosexual activity (Samuels, 1980).

The adaptation that is focused on is that which must occur between the world of two-person relationships and that of three-person relationships. As Jung puts it, Mercurius is 'called husband and wife, bridegroom and bride, or lover and beloved' (*CW* 13, para. 268). His hermaphroditism suggests not only early sexualized confusion, but also the possibility of psychic resolution. Jung connects Mercurius with the Trinity in particular and 'triune divinity in general' (*ibid.*, para. 271), and, while the paper does not explore this, it can be said that three-ness and triangles are of the essence of the Oedipus complex and, of course, the image of the parents in bed. Hermes is three-headed, but he is also a unity and therefore contains seeds of acceptance of the fact of family, the family situation and the emergence and integration of differentiated parental images.

The move from two-ness to three-ness takes place, on the one hand, in the outer world as the baby 'discovers' his father in reality and experiences differences from the mother. On the other hand, however, in the inner world of imagery, a move is also taking place in which images of two-ness evolve into images of three-ness as the father separates from the internal family matrix. There are two primary images of two-ness—mother and baby and then the baby's image of his parents—and the paper attempts to describe the interactive processes between these images of two-ness as the individual moves towards three-person operating. Similarities and differences in the style and tone of mother-infant imagery and parents in bed imagery are examined and it is hypothesized that a specific psychic activity is taking place in which these images of two-ness create a climate in which images of three-ness can exist and the paternal image emerge.

One last introductory note: I am considering consequences of infant and child development with regard to levels of adult functioning and am interested in the way an image, postulated as innate, but mediated by the early environment, takes on a wide range of positive and negative patterns of interaction and conjunction. These patterns are projected, introjected and internalized and then reprojected over a lifetime. The clinical material in the paper reflects, I hope, this interplay.

The Antiquities of Human Development

Jung and Freud allowed their argument over how literally to take analytical material concerning parental intercourse to revolve around the question of whether an adult could produce what might look like actual memories but what were in fact subsequent phantasies. Jung's *ex post facto* explanations stimulated Freud to ask where the later phantasies came from. Freud's insistence that the phantasies must come from somewhere led him into man's prehistory. For example, in the *Introductory Lectures on Psychoanalysis* he writes:

> There can be no doubt that the sources [of primal scene phantasies] lie in the instincts; but it still has to be explained why the same phantasies with the same content are created on every occasion. I am prepared with an answer that I know will seem daring to you. I believe that these primal phantasies, and no doubt a few others as well, are a phylogenetic

endowment. In them the individual reaches beyond his own experience into primeval experience at points where his own experience has been too rudimentary ... I have repeatedly been led to suggest that the psychology of the neuroses may have more stored up in it of the antiquities of human development than any other source (Freud, 1916-17, pp. 370-1).

Freud suggests the existence of pre-subjective schemata which might even be strong enough to predominate over the experience of the individual: 'Wherever experiences fail to fit in with the hereditary schema they become remodelled in the imagination' (Freud, 1918, p.119).

We may not agree with Freud's Lamarckian overtones—the suggestion that primal phantasies are a residue of specific memories of prehistoric experiences—but there is less problem with the position that, in general terms, mental structures have a phylogenetic base. In *The Language of Psychoanalysis* Laplanche and Pontalis point out that all the so-called primal phantasies relate to the origins and that 'like collective myths they claim to provide a representation of and a "solution" to whatever constitutes an enigma for the child' (Laplanche/Pontalis, 1980, p. 332). In many respects these views correspond to Jung's 'collective unconscious'.

In 'From the history of an infantile neurosis' (1918) Freud observed that, for the Wolf Man, the main determinants of the primal scene were that it constituted paternal aggression, that therefore the parental marriage was sado-masochistic, that by identifying with either partner in turn the child derived sado-masochistic sexual pleasure causing guilt and anxiety, and that the child phantasized what happened in intercourse as involving anal penetration with attendant imagery of dirt, mess and power struggle. A key problem for the Wolf Man was caused by his feminine side. He conceived of the sexual opposites in terms of active and passive rather than male and female (*ibid.*, p.46). In Jungian terms, the Wolf Man's archetypal images remain unmediated by experiences in the outer world. Summarizing Freud's findings, we can say that the child both projects inner contents and misunderstands on a cognitive level what is happening—his experience is too 'rudimentary'. Possibly he projects *because* he cannot understand; ignorance and phantasy go together.

The 'Parents' are not the Parents At All

Jung disputed the solely sexual significance of innate images of parents. Among many similar statements we find: '[The parents] are, or they represent, vital forces which accompany the child on the winding path of destiny in the form of favourable or dangerous factors from whose influence even the adult can escape only in limited degree' (*CW* 17, para.158). I want to select from Jung's contribution two main features—the idea of the parents as image containers and mediators, and then the theory that the archetypal image of parental union symbolizes the union of opposites and thus the individual's potential for psychic integration. Jung is using his concepts animus, anima and syzygy (a pair of linked opposites). It is these pre-existent psychic entities that the individual is stimulated to project on to his parents. One sees a three-way mix in the parental union—contrasexual imagery, contrasexual reality and integration (represented by the syzygy as a linking of masculine and feminine in the psyche). The copulating parents represent a *coniunctio oppositorum*, perhaps the earliest to be achieved, of masculinity and femininity. I am not sure that the syzygy *is* the primal scene, but the two notions contain components of each other. Jung writes: 'In reality the whole drama takes place in the individual's own psyche, where the "parents" are not the parents at all but only their images; they are representations which have arisen from the conjunction of parental peculiarities with the individual disposition of the child' (*CW* 5, para. 507).

Jung says elsewhere, 'the whole essence of consciousness is *discrimination*...the separation into pairs of opposites is entirely due to conscious differentiation' (*CW* 6, para. 179). So the image of the parents may be a *coniunctio* or it may not, depending on the individual's ego position and his degree of differentiation of his parental images. This point cannot be overstressed. For Jung the syzygy only becomes fertile when the elements are distinguishable. In plain language, it's not a *stuck* image of togetherness he is describing, but something divided and unstuck, hence vital, and also linked, hence imaginable. Image holds the linked division in momentary balance.

EXAMPLE A. A patient referred to her parents' marriage as a 'great big circular jigsaw fuck-up'. She was referring to her incomprehension, her envy and her feeling of exclusion. The word 'jigsaw' contains the seed of a puzzling experience of differentiation—for the moment, only an intellectual solution.

For Jung, differentiation of the parents in bed facilitates looking beyond or through the real parents to membership of the human race and to issues of ontology, purpose and meaning. '...mankind has always instinctively added the pre-existent divine pair to the personal parents—the "god" father and "god" mother of the newborn child—so that from sheer unconsciousness or short-sighted rationalism, he should never forget himself so far as to invest his own parents with divinity' (CW 9i, para. 172). Jung is saying that differentiation within the image of the parents in bed connects directly with the numinous and with ideas regarding the purpose of life. This seems appropriate, for the primal scene is about genesis and you cannot split alpha from omega. Differentiation implies conflict; granted sufficient ego-strength this can lead to conjunction.

Jung is connecting pairs of linked opposites with the individuation process: 'We enter the realm of the syzygies, the paired opposites, where the One is never separated from the Other, its antithesis. It is a field of personal experience which leads directly to the experience of individuation, the attainment of the self' (CW 9i, para. 194).

A further way in which the subjective nature of the primal scene may be understood is by considering the part played by sight and by the eyes in it. Recent developments in neurophysiology have led to the proposal that what we call reality is built up on holographic principles and that we can therefore speak of holographic or holonomic reality. Solid objects are registered by the brain as patterns composed of layer upon layer of waves. Objects vibrate or resonate in tune with the various receptors in the brain. Reality is a harmonic arising out of this interaction. What is true in the physical world may also be true in relation to a patient's experience of his or her emotions, for

117

instance during a primal scene fantasy or experience. What is the rôle of the eyes in this? Traditionally, in science and myth, the eyes are an input channel for the brain or the psyche. But the implication of the theory of archetypes is that the eyes are, in many ways, an output channel, the very means by which projections are conducted to, and placed in, the external world. When we speak of the investment of the world with archetypal expectations, or of the *Umwelt*, the subjectively perceived environment, or of the discernment of pattern in perceptual raw material, or even of deintegration, we should not overlook the eyes as an output channel which facilitates all of these.

It is important to understand the way in which the psyche is using the image of the parents to express itself, discover itself, and, ultimately, get back what has been projected. The bodies involved in the primal scene, and the attributes they seem to have, are symbolic of the various facets and elements of the infant's (or adult's) own psyche.

Merger and Differentiation

Neumann takes up the point about discrimination and works on the differentiation of an early, merged parental imago. My idea is that a process of separating an image of each parent out of an image in which they are merged goes on at the same time as attachment and separation processes with regard to the mother. There is a distinction between separation *of* the parents and separation *from* mother.

It can be argued that the image of merged parents arises from a relatively undifferentiated state of mother-infant relations. As Newton points out, there is a problem here of point of view, both with regard to mother-infant and parents-in-bed imagery, because the lack of two-ness in both images is what is experienced psychically even if we, the observers, can see that two-ness is 'objectively' the case (Newton, 1981, p.73). If the merged parental image persists beyond an age-appropriate point then it becomes psychopathological and hence an example of the 'stuckness' that is not, and cannot be, a true *coniunctio*. The transition on which we are focusing is from images of mergedness and 'stuckness' towards images of true union of separate entities

118

with attendant conflict.

For the 'unsticking' to take place, Neumann ascribed to the infant affect and behaviour of a vigorous, instinctual and hence guilt-inducing kind:

> This destruction (of the merged parents) is closely associated with the act of eating and assimilation ... The formation of consciousness goes hand in hand with a fragmentation of the world continuum into separate objects, parts, figures, which can only then be assimilated, taken in, integrated, made conscious ... in a word, eaten ... Aggression, destruction, dismemberment and killing are intimately associated with the corresponding bodily functions of eating, chewing, biting and particularly with the symbolism of the teeth as instruments of these activities, all of which are essential for the formation of an independent ego. (1954, p.124)

Neumann is arguing that the act of biting and its accompanying phantasies constitute an attempt to differentiate the 'stuck' parental image, to comprehend imaginatively a primal scene in which two distinct parents may have intercourse. 'Not only do ... male and female grow out of this development of opposites ... but opposites like "sacred" and "profane", "good" and "evil" are now assigned their place in the world' (*ibid.*, p. 109).

Neumann goes on to make an interesting point. He refers to the image of the merged parents as a 'primal deity' in the inner life of the child. It follows that the differentiation of the merged parents into the opposites of mother and father clears the way for the emergence of a type of polytheism—'God is now experienced and revealed under as many aspects as there are Gods. This means that the ego's powers of expression and understanding have increased enormously' (*ibid.*, p. 325). I would add that one facet of this increase in range is the capacity to tolerate the emergence of the father. Polytheism is a way of describing the move from paranoid-schizoid mechanisms of control towards variegated two-person exchange and the depressive position. It also stands for the positive aspects of polymorphousness, namely fertility and creative potency. Polytheism idealized phantasies of unitary fusion states (monotheism, if you like).

119

Projection, Introjection
and the Image of the Parents in Bed

Melanie Klein approaches the problem from a different direction. She states that the infant conceives of his parents in an almost continuous state of intercourse and is thus able to project any bodily impulse whatsoever on to the image of the parental couple (or, to be more precise, the image of the parents coupling). As Hanna Segal says, 'The infant will phantasy his parents as exchanging gratifications, oral, urethral, anal or genital, according to the prevalence of his own impulses ... This gives rise to feelings of the most acute deprivation, jealousy and envy, since the parents are perceived as giving each other precisely those gratifications which the infant wishes for himself' (1973, p. 103). The infant then internalizes this heavily coloured image of parental intercourse and the image is then ready for reprojecting, for example when the individual contemplates a marriage of his own.

One interesting overlap between Klein and Jung and involving the figure of Hermes might be mentioned. Jung shows that Mercurius represents 'continuous cohabitation' and comments on the numerous obscene representations of the *coniunctio*. He adds to this 'pictures in old manuscripts of excretory acts including vomiting' (*CW* 13, para. 278).

It is noticeable that Klein's source of positive connotation within the infant concerning his parents in bed is confined to projections of the infant's own real or phantasized gratifications or wishes leading to envy of the parents in coitus (Klein, 1929, p. 111). Jung's stress on the image of the parents in bed symbolizing an innate potential for integration and individuation is foreign to Klein's theory. She argues that

> the Oedipus conflict begins under the complete dominance of sadism...the attack launched [upon the objects] with all the weapons of sadism rouses the subject's dread of an analogous attack upon himself from the external and the internalized objects...a special intensity is imparted by the fact that a union of the two parents is in question...these united parents are extremely cruel and much dreaded assailants. (*ibid.*, pp. 212-13).

Earlier in the same volume she notes with regard to case material that 'aggressive motor discharges' are provoked by the primal scene (*ibid.*, p.122). Riviere demonstrates the extremity of the position in her remark that a patient's unconscious feeling that he has good parents inside him means that the parents are 'idealized...and he is filled with a sense of omnipotence, perfection, grandeur and so on' (1952, p. 21). In essence, Klein is taking what is happening at the breast or anus and, as it were, 'applying' it to the primal scene. There is therefore some interplay between feeding phantasies and primal scene phantasies. One might speculate about the extent to which the interplay *in the adult psyche* is two-way. For instance, do primal scene phantasies have influence on feeding phantasies?

EXAMPLE B. A patient is deeply involved in the animal welfare movement. While making love, she phantasizes that she is a cow being experimented on by scientists, being cut open and so on. She also phantasizes that within her vagina are teeth-like syringes which emit fluids which 'neutralize' her husband's sperm. Her oral aggression is projected into her primal scene imagery, but she also reports her father as supercilious and sadistic towards a less well educated mother. The two sets of imagery influence each other and follow a similar pattern in their movement from states of identity and subjective merging to the formation of positive and negative attachments involving some differentiation and finally to full differentiation and creative or destructive intercourse.

In fact, there is a sense in which it is only after the recognition of the primal scene as involving two people, and the emergence of the father, that a full two-person relationship between mother and infant may be said to be constellated. When the infant becomes aware of the existence of a third person, he is forced to give up any identification with the mother, or fantasies of being fused with her. We find that chronology is not always the most satisfactory perspective from which to view psychic events; three-ness may precede two-ness, psychologically speaking.

121

Emergence of the Father Image

At this point it might be useful to consider what has so far been a missing link—namely the emergence and development of the infant's image of his father and his relationship to him. There would seem to be three strands in this. First, the infant experiences his real father as different from his mother—for example, by discovering a different sort of chest or smell or voice. Second, the image of the father has always been there for the infant as an archetypal potentiality requiring fleshing out through experience. Finally, there is a sense in which the image of the father can be looked at as constructed or synthesized out of the interaction of images of mother and infant with images of the parents in bed. The image of the father and the infant's relation to him is predicated in part on their common relation to the mother.

What we can see is image creating image. The separation of the infant out of an intense feeding dyad and his differentiation of his parents are interactive processes. In the case of the mother-infant relationship the sequence is togetherness-separation-rapprochement. The infant experiences and develops an image of a relationship *he is in*. In the case of the image of the parents, the sequence for the infant is stuckness-differentiation-conjunction; the infant is confronted by a relationship and an image of a relationship *he is not in*. The notion of images interacting in this way to produce a further image or images is strengthened by Stein's idea that archetypes can be arranged in a framework of planes so that '...archetypes as the constituents of the self are interrelated and...this interrelatedness is teleological, i.e., serves the well being of the individual as a whole' (1967, p. 103). From this we can add that the image of mother and infant and the image of the parents are a pair of linked opposites within the self. Their interaction, mutual mediation and conjunction lead to the image of the father—they are transformed.

Parthenogenetic Delusion

Money-Kyrle's remarks concerning parental intercourse in his paper 'The aim of psychoanalysis'are helpful in bringing out the subtle interweave between the developing relationship of mother and infant and the infant's perception and experience of the parental marriage. He says, 'All you can do is to allow your internal parents to come together and they will beget and conceive the child' and 'remember that, in the inner world, parthenogenetic creativity is a megalomanic delusion' (1971, p. 103). This links with Neumann and Klein so that affect surrounding the image of the parents in bed can be looked at as a base for the individual's subsequent creativeness. Money-Kyrle's bringing in of parthenogenesis is significant for two reasons. First, because accepting that one has been created is the foundation of a religious attitude and second, because a teleological factor is implied in parental intercourse from the point of view of the child. Differentiating the parents gives the individual a chance to create something. But, as the following example shows, this does not always happen.

EXAMPLE C. A successful entrepreneur felt his parents always closed ranks against him in family arguments. He could not see their togetherness as anything other than a ploy used against him, a fake trick. His image was of the parents arm-in-arm like an overposed early photograph—static and unreal. A feeling of togetherness with a woman was beyond him because it felt like the nothingness he phantasized in his parents' marriage. Mutuality had to be eliminated and was replaced by hyper-criticism of his partner and competitiveness.

The Grotesque and the Divine

To conclude this section of the paper I want to note Redfearn's comment that experiences of the primal scene antedate the emergence of the human self-image. Thus, one gets 'bizarre and monstrous forms on the one hand or god-like forms on the other' (1978, p. 235). I think that the bizarre and the monstrous, and the divine and the sublime, may be involved in another important *coniunctio oppositorum*. The linking of grotesque and divine would then take its place alongside the linked human and divine parents of Jung's theory. As we shall see, grotesque, divine and human

123

dance a figure round the image of the parents in bed.

Recapitulation

I should like to recapitulate the themes which I shall develop further. From Freud, the need to look at man's prehistory and also to learn how grotesque phantasy about sexuality fills the gaps in rudimentary knowledge. From Jung, valuing of the image of parental intercourse as containing seeds of psychic integration for the individual and also the paramount need for conscious discrimination. Neumann, taking the problem of differentiation further, allocating to the baby's bite the function of separating the merged parental image and also pointing out the increase in experiential variety and flexibility that follows the emergence of masculine and feminine—polytheism. Klein, showing how mother-infant phantasy and primal scene phantasy interact. Money-Kyrle, stating how vital it is to allow the parents their creativity and warning against parthenogenetic inflation. Finally, Redfearn, underlining the enormous range of imagery involved in the primal scene from the most sublime to the most horrendous.

In good-enough development we would see a move from an undifferentiated image of the parents to an image of a conjunction, a true union of opposites involving conflict as well as harmony. Psychopathologically there are two main possibilities: either a failure for the image of merged parents to differentiate or the creation of extreme images representing only one of the opposites.

It might be useful to list some of the conjunctions:

conjunction of human and divine;
conjunction of masculine and feminine;
conjunction of grotesque and divine;
and some of the undifferentiated images:
image of the parents in bed 'stuck' together;
image of the parents in bed fused with mother-infant imagery;
and some of the extremities:
grotesque sexual phantasy (cf. Wolf Man);
idealization—confusion with divine parents.

124

In the next section of the paper I shall go more deeply into some of the connecting factors between these ideas.

Hermes and His Family

As I have been trying to demonstrate, thoughts about, and reactions to the image of the parents in bed as experienced in infancy and then carried through life tend to polarize in particular around the divine and the grotesque ends of a spectrum. Freud, Klein, Neumann and others, while not regarding the process as unhealthy or even avoidable, tend to see and to stress images of a violent, perverted, animal kind. Jung and Money-Kyrle, for instance, tend to see harmony and conjunction first and then the darker side. It occurs to me that this swinging, which is apparent in the theoreticians when perceived as a group, may tell us something about the way in which a child (and later the child in the adult) develops and experiences primal scene imagery.

If this is so, then the need is for some sort of thematic organizer around the polarities of grotesque and divine—which is where Hermes comes in. The god is used as a way of describing the relatively weaker early ego's attempts to come to terms with all that is involved in the primal scene. In one way, I am saying that it is all very well for Money-Kyrle to identify a 'direct line' connecting 'favourable development', 'the first good object', the recognition of parental coitus as a 'supremely creative act', and a good subsequent sexual and marital relationship (1971, p. 105). This is a healthy sounding description of a healthy process and of course Money-Kyrle in no way avoids issues of psychopathology; but his unfolding seems more redolent of (ideal) goals than of journey or process. Although what I detect in the figure of Hermes may ultimately move towards such goals, there is much twisting and turning through which the individual must live. Hermes' multi-faceted nature permits him to link what sometimes seems unlinkable to the observer—and how much more difficult to bring together for the infant. My contention is that, although the hermetic strand in the working through of primal scene emotions may appear to leave us stranded on the darker side of things, in reality this is not the case.

125

Meltzer, speaking of metapsychology, states that 'every person has to have what you might describe as a religion in which his internal objects perform the functions of gods' (1981, p. 179). He argues that this religion derives its power, not from belief, but because these gods do actually perform functions in the mind. Meltzer stresses the god-like functions of internal objects such as parental figures, but does not rule out the idea that part-selves ('the child parts of the personality') with archetypal potentials have a similar divine rôle. Hermes would then stand as a representation of a part-self or archetypal theme.

In the literature, Hermes is seen as an agent and as a principle of transformation and connection; he is also a psychopomp or soul guide. As such he is much involved with change and development. Called Mercurius (quicksilver) he is elusive, always on the move, which is why he has to be contained in the alchemical vessel or consulting room. In alchemy Mercurius acts as a catalytic or linking element. As well as linking masculine and feminine, he also links highest and lowest. In his masculine aspect, Holy Ghost and Devil; in his feminine aspect, wisdom and matter. Like any god he is two-faced—for Hermes the other side is his trickster nature. He is inventive in both senses of the word.

This two-facedness causes problems for commentators. In informal discussions with colleagues the introduction of the word 'Hermes' produced two radically different responses. Either all the 'good' aspects were listed (transformation, psychopomp, etc.) or all the 'bad' ones (trickster, thief, liar). It is hard to hold both sides together and of course there is overlap between Hermes/Mercury the classical god and the alchemical Mercurius. Hermes is part of what Jung calls 'the psychology...of the Mercurius duplex who on the one hand is Hermes the mystagogue and psychopomp and on the other hand is the poisonous dragon, the evil spirit and "trickster"' (CW 9i, p.377, Jung's quotation marks). Jung says this in connection with an artistically gifted patient who produced a 'typical tetradic mandala' and stuck it on a sheet of thick paper. On the other side there was a matching circle packed with drawings of sexual perversions. Jung connects that with the 'chaos' (again, for some reason, the quotation marks) that hides behind the self.

Elsewhere, Jung insists that the trickster myth is actively sustained and promoted by consciousness as a sort of reference point for human origins and indicates that, in the cycle, the trickster does become more civilized and even 'useful and sensible' (*CW* 9i, para. 474). I hope to expand these points in connection with Hermes and primal scene imagery.

Let us now look at the myth in more detail. In the Hermes story he is the son of Zeus and the nymph Maia, who is the daughter of Atlas. On the day of his birth he sees a tortoise near the cave and is overcome by delight. He kills the tortoise and discovers that he can make a musical instrument from the shell, a lyre. He returns to the cave and sings a song to his mother and father referring to their love affair and telling, in the words of *The Homeric Hymn to Hermes,* 'all the glorious tale of his own begetting'. The next thing Hermes experiences is hunger and he wants very much to eat meat. He steals a herd of cattle from his brother Apollo and drives the cattle backwards to the cave, thus cleverly creating confusing tracks. He makes a sacrifice. He manages to fool Apollo and Zeus for a while about what he has done but eventually Apollo finds out and tries to bind Hermes but cannot. A peace deal is made in which each brother imparts or donates certain of his skills to his brother-god. Hermes teaches Apollo music and Apollo becomes the god of music. Apollo hands the rôle of psychopomp to Hermes. The crowning event of Hermes' first day is his audience with Zeus where he is made one of the Olympiads, the messenger of the gods.

Hermes is portrayed as a highly social god, interested in trade and commerce and exchange, befriending men on numerous occasions—for example, he gives Odysseus a magic plant to help him resist Circe and also accompanies Herakles on his descent into Hades. He befriends the gods too—most notably when he rescues his father Zeus in a war with the giants. Interestingly, in the myth Hera consents to suckle Hermes, though she is usually represented as being extremely jealous of Zeus' affairs and the results of them. Apart from being helpful, Hermes plays numerous practical jokes on mortals and immortals alike. He contributes deceit and lies to the construction of Pandora's box. He is intelligent, flexible and creative; he can make fires for cooking and heating, for example. On the other hand, he can take the form of a sudden silence. His altars seem to have been phallic as were many of his representations. His rôle as the guider of souls to Hades overlaps with his functions as the god of travellers and of the crossroads.

Hermes is often depicted as chasing and/or raping some nymph or other—he is rampant sexually. Two of his offspring express this graphically. Priapus, who is sometimes stated to be Hermes' father as well as his son, is highly promiscuous, doubly phallic, front and rear, grotesque, obscene, pornographic, transsexual, transvestite, horrendous. The other son, Pan, is, *inter alia,* the god of masturbation and of nightmares.

Discussion of the Myth

Let us look more closely at this archetypal metaphor for a developmental phase. Lopez-Pedraza points out that Hermes does not seem to have a complex about the primal scene, though his genogram would make interesting reading (1977, p.28). His father, Zeus, is a well-known tyrant, highly insecure and moody. His mother's father feels he carries the world on his shoulders and so on. In fact Hermes *celebrates* his begetting in a song. One thinks here of Money-Kyrle's word 'allow' in connection with creative parental intercourse. Hermes does not indulge in par- thenogenetic inflated phantasy; he sings of the act that brought him into being, specifically acknowledging the participation of both parents. Music-making connects with the idea that differen- tiating the parents is a creative act. Does Hermes deny primal scene envy here? Apparently not, but there is a humorous or even mocking tone to some of his song. And his later actions concerning the cattle theft need to be considered. He takes the meat he craves from the one who has it—his brother Apollo. That is, he makes an envious onslaught on Apollo's wealth. The *envy* can be twinned with the *celebration* mentioned earlier—is not this what we often feel at someone else's good fortune? Then Hermes is deceitful about his theft... .

What does his thieving or taking mean? Why is a god a thief? Jung, following Schopenhauer and Buddhism, points out that it is individuation which lies behind such evils as stealing. In Christianity, for example, human nature has to be tainted by original sin in order to be redeemed by Christ's self-sacrifice. This is because man in a completely natural state would be like an animal, neither good nor pure. Instinctuality and total unconsciousness would prevail if a distinction between good and evil was not drawn. Jung puts it like this: 'Since without guilt there is no moral consciousness and without awareness of differences no consciousness at all, we must concede that the strange intervention [that is, of God introducing the distinction between good and evil to the world—A.S] was absolutely necessary for the development of any kind of consciousness and in this sense was for the good' (*CW* 13, para. 244). Hermes' many good acts and his 'good' development (for example the way in which he and Apollo sort things out) come out of and after the evil act of stealing.

Perhaps the words stealing and thieving have connotations which make them invariably negative. Do they rule out the possibility of the freely offered gift, for instance the mother's devoted offer of her breast? Hermes does get this from Hera, who is able to control any impulse to transfer her hostility towards Zeus on to the baby. So that *is* present in the story; the thieving is something else. I think that taking or stealing are words for what we call today introjection and internalization. Following Laplanche and Pontalis (1980, p. 229) introjection means that 'in phantasy the subject transposes objects and their inherent qualities from the "outside" to the "inside" of himself'. Internalization can be said to mean much the same but with one important difference. In the case of internalization what is transposed is the image of a *relationship* or interpersonal process (*ibid.*, p. 226). Hermes' thieving has much in common with this transposition, which is central to our ideas of internalization and introjection.

Hermes stands at the boundary between two-person and three-person relationships. He connects the part-self that contains masculinity and that which contains femininity; he is part of the cosmic dance of the opposites and hence an early self-representation. In particular, Hermes could be seen as an activation on the archetypal level of the personal 'grandiose self', a term introduced by Kohut. If met and responded to by the parents, the grandiose self forms the basis for ambition and self-esteem later on. Interestingly for my theme, Kohut (1971) differentiates maternal and paternal functions in this regard. The mother provides acceptance of the child's presence and self-assertions and the father some sort of goal-orientation not keyed to performance as much as to direction.

This would throw a different light on Hermes' mendacity and stealing. These features would then be part of a developmental process which would make considerations of morality and approval or disapproval irrelevant. If an infant enters the moral world too soon then the opposites will tend to remain polarized and, in Newton's words, 'zonal bite will be reversed into moral beat...In terms of laying the foundation for ego integration serious damage has occurred' (1975, p. 190).

Pre-morality (and even immorality) is fundamental to being human. The anthropologist Edmund Leach was reported in *The Times* of 3 September 1981 as saying, 'Nature cannot tell lies, but human beings can and do...Human beings engage in wilful deception on a massive scale. The ability to tell lies is perhaps our most striking human characteristic.'

Hermes and Sexuality

Hermes is not a heroic figure; he is basic, down to earth, vital. Nowhere does this vitality show more than in his sexuality. Hermes and his sons Priapus and Pan bring together (at least) rape, sado-masochism, posterior intercourse and all manner of obscenities. These are not completely divorced from genital sexuality—Hermes does have intercourse with his nymphs. But, remembering our search for the god of the primal scene, consider the following. Freud saw paternal aggression, sado-masochism and posterior intercourse as the main grotesque phantasies occasioned by the primal scene. He wondered where they 'came from'. This archetypal metaphor is a partial answer to Freud's archetypal question.

Pan is the god of masturbation and masturbation phantasies and hence closely connected with the signs and symbols of infantile sexuality. He is also the god of nightmares from which we awake or are awoken sweating and frightened. If the primal scene, as a real event, has impact on a child then it will be mainly

130

in the middle of the night. Parents report how often the baby cries or the child intrudes during love-making. The other son Priapus is both homo- and heteroerotic, truly polymorphous in both Freud's and Meltzer's sense (1973).

Hermes is more than pervert or trickster; like any god he is something less than individuated. In his lack of a settled relationship with a female partner his is not an image of maturity either. His naughtiness is baby-like and appealing, it is part of his eternal youth. Part, too, of youth and of growing up is, as Lopez-Pedraza says, 'to be initiated into sexual fantasies...Hermes is the god of sexuality, including cheap sexuality and love by chance' (1977, p. 99). My feeling about Hermes' trickster side is that it is enacted in mocking the parents, denying and envying their separateness and creativeness and in grandiose, parthenogenetic phantasy—sometimes he is described as his own parents and sometimes as parent-less.

Case Illustration

EXAMPLE D. A forty-year-old man who works as a lecturer. We have been meeting weekly for three years. He is a large, bulky, hunched man with a gruff, abrupt manner, superficially masculine. In his inner world he sees himself as a teenage girl. His background involves a home dominated by women, a classic description of a weak father and a phantasy of parental intercourse in which mother initiated, was on top and brought about father's early death by sexual voraciousness. A major theme of the therapy has been a work conflict with his dynamic, quick-thinking and tricky boss who belittles him and interferes with his areas of responsibility. In his dreams the boss, far from being an enemy, is seen as a helpful figure—for instance giving him a rifle in a war, saving him because of knowing a foreign language. The boss appears as a tour guide and as an emissary from the Pope. The hermetic overtones of all this are clear. To complete the picture, on the shady side, my patient and his boss have to hide some stolen goods and when the boss gives my patient some money there is some missing.

It has become clear to me that I, too, adopted a hermetic

131

stance. I became my patient's discussant and shared in devising plans or even tricks with which to fight back. Gradually the work situation improved as my patient won the respect of his boss and in dreams his masculinity slowly appeared. Two dreams (nearly three years apart) concerning the death of his father show this. In the first there is to be a lawsuit against him, concerning a society lady, which he must be educated to contest. In the second, the dream emphasizes that he is not to blame. A final dream on this theme involves him berating an uncle for backing out of a border crossing somewhere in Europe. The uncle *always* backs out. My patient advances into no man's land (!) alone and crosses into the new country (in his association, Poland—this was dreamt at the time of the Soviet-Polish crisis).

The emergent masculinity produced changes in primal scene imagery. These two dreams, given in full, are also separated by approximately three years:

> I am in the river floating downstream. There are sleeping people in all the houses. I don't have keys so I smash a hole in the window to get in. I am afraid. I come across a rat and a space monster copulating. They are lying on a ramp like a crucifix. Small monkey-like creatures dance around and in a box there is a sort of insect that reproduces by splitting itself. I know it has no sex life.

The second, later, dream:

> I am watching a man diving under the water. I tell my wife's brother that *this* is how to dive. On the sea-bed the diver meets his wife who is an animal of some sort but also human. She gives the man an oxygen tube and they have beautiful intercourse buoyed up by the water. As they continue their love-making a glass dome fills with beads of many colours in regular and soothing patterns. Then the couple sit in armchairs like we had at home.

Recently his wife dreamt that they were getting married again. This example naturally leaves out much analytic interaction, interpretation of homosexual transference and aggression towards me. The adoption of a hermetic criminality did lead to the psychic developments outlined above. I cannot say that I remained uninvolved or in control of what was happening.

This patient produced a blending of images of his relation to mother with images of his parents in bed. By tolerating considerable acting-out on his part in the form of flirtations with other types of therapy and growth activity, I fostered a mother-son differentiation and that, in turn, permitted the emergence of differentiated parental imagery. Our hermetic activity also contributed to producing a masculine impetus which put the primal scene into motion as an act between two entities.

Concluding Remarks and Summary

The paper examines the image of the parents in bed and its impact on psychological development over a lifetime. This includes a review of various kinds of primal scene phantasy— conjunctions, undifferentiated mergers and extremities.

I teased out of the works of various theorists a progression of images and ideas concerning the parents in bed which presented themselves as a spectrum divine and grotesque and involving conjunction. The conjunction from divine to grotesque themselves led me to Hermes. Certain aspects of the Hermes story bring together the divine and the grotesque, the bizarre and the sublime, the criminal and the individuated. Hermes is a representation of human adaptability and sexuality as they relate to the paradox of differentiating parental images so as to allow them union.

Interaction between the image of the mother and infant and that of the parents fosters not only the differentiation of the parents, but also the emergence of a father-infant relationship. If this happens then the individual can celebrate 'the glorious tale of his own begetting' and go on to take part in a similar tale in his own right.

References

Freud, S. (1916-17). *Introductory lectures on Psychoanalysis. Std. Edn.*, 15 & 16. London, Hogarth Press.

Freud, S. (1918). 'From the history of an infantile neurosis', *Std. Edn.*, 17. London, Hogarth Press.

Klein, M. (1929). 'Infantile anxiety situations reflected in a work of art and in the creative impulse', in *The Writings of Melanie Klein*. Vol. I. London, Hogarth Press, 1975.

Kohut, H. (1971). *The Analysis of the Self*. New York, Int. Univ. Press.

Laplanche, J., Pontalis, J.-B. (1980). *The Language of Psychoanalysis*. London, Hogarth Press.

Lopez-Pedraza, R. (1977). *Hermes and his Children*. Dallas, Spring Publications.

Meltzer, D. (1973). *Sexual States of Mind*. Strath Tay. Perthshire, Clunie Press.

Meltzer, D. (1981). 'The Kleinian expansion of Freud's meta-psychology', *Int. J. Psychoanal.*, 62 (2).

Money-Kyrle, R. (1971). 'The aim of psychoanalysis', *Int. J. Psychoanal.*, 52 (1).

Neumann, E. (1954). *The Origins and History of Consciousness*. London, Routledge & Kegan Paul.

Newton, K. (1975). 'Separation and pre-oedipal guilt', *J. Analyt. Psychol.*, 20 (2).

Newton, K (1981). 'Comment on "The emergence of child analysis"', *J. Analyt. Psychol.*, 26 (1).

Redfearn, J. (1978). 'The energy of warring and combining opposites', *J. Analyt. Psychol.*, 23 (3).

Riviere, J. (1952). General introduction to *Developments in Psycho-Analysis*. London, Hogarth Press.

Samuels, A. (1980). 'Incest and omnipotence in the internal family', *J. Analyt. Psychol.*, 25 (1).

Segal, H. (1973). *Introduction to the Work of Melanie Klein*. London, Hogarth Press.

Stein, L. (1967). 'Introducing not-self', *J. Analyt. Psychol.*, 12 (2).

The father archetype
in feminine psychology

AMY ALLENBY

It is worth noting that this paper was published in 1955, before contemporary feminism had taken root. It is therefore prescient and also, inevitably, apparently dated. Nevertheless, it is an example of the way in which psychopathology is envisioned in analytical psychology: as a form of psychic expression to be understood and gently transformed, rather than corrected or cured. The author's use of her clinical material, especially the dreams, repays reflection on the part of the reader. We are presented with a gripping account of a negative father-daughter relationship, showing how father fixation despoils a feminine identity (understood as a sense of being a woman). This can be compared with Seligman's remarks on 'enmeshment' (see above). Also significant is Allenby's refusal to idealize her patient, or impose a value system upon her. The patient's scope for growth is accepted as, perhaps, somewhat limited. *A.S.*

IT IS COMMON knowledge that the bond between mother and son, if intense, may decisively influence the son's psychological development. A less-discussed topic, and far less extensively studied, is the attachment between father and daughter. The mother is for the son a symbol of containment. Therefore her influence may either interfere with his masculine role, or may promote it by making him receptive to the irrational, which adds to his masculine nature richness and scope. For the mother also personifies for him the unconscious which holds both the passivity of inertia and the spring of creative life. In many a great personality a deep personal attachment to the mother is the basis of outstanding artistic or other creative achievements.

But what effect has a strong tie to the father on the development of the daughter?

An answer to this question can only be attempted as part of a study of woman's psychology in general. It is a comparatively recent development of analytical psychology to study the feminine psyche as such rather than treat it as a variation of the human average which is typical of both sexes. A pioneer work in this field is Esther Harding's *The Way of All Women,* in which the author investigates what woman is like apart from her relation to man, and apart from the role she plays in man's psychology (1933). In her second book, *Woman's Mysteries,* Esther Harding has drawn attention to the typical problem of modern woman, who, owing to the increasing development of her masculine side, is in danger of losing touch with the instinctive roots of her being (1935, pp. 12 ff.). The inevitable conflict, she says, which characterizes the situation of woman in the modern Western world, and of the professional woman in particular, is rarely if ever experienced by her or even admitted into her consciousness. By nature and inclination woman tends to avoid the consciousness and painfulness of conflict, she identifies instead either with one side or the other. This fact has also been noted by other observers, for instance, by Toni Wolff and Erich Neumann. Woman's difficulty in experiencing conflict in itself, as well as the duality of her own nature, is symptomatic of her affinity with the undifferentiated stream of life; in her, as in nature, 'the opposites sleep side by side'. This characteristic of the feminine

136

psyche has, however, its negative aspect; it accounts for woman's tendency to identification, which with her is more marked than with man. It therefore matters greatly what kind of influence governs her early development; if the mother's, she will model herself on a prototype of her own sex, but if the father's, she is in danger of being shifted from her innate psychic pattern (see Neumann, 1953, pp. 8 ff., 24, *et passim*).

The better we begin to understand the typical features of feminine psychology, the more evident does it become that a father complex in the feminine psyche is not simply a replica of a mother complex in the psyche of the son, with the sexes merely reversed. Nor is the identification between mother and daughter psychologically of the same order as the identification between father and daughter. A mother fixation, in the daughter's case, may have undesirable effects in leaving her arrested in an immature condition of feminine unconsciousness, but at least it does not estrange her from her feminine background. In the case of a father fixation, however, the little girl becomes prematurely immersed in a psychic world for which she is not yet prepared, and which at best she should enter in the course of developing self-conciousness, but not by way of unconscious identification. So her personality development begins on foreign ground. In his archetypal relevance the father embodies for the daughter not only the first heterosexual love object; he also represents the larger world ruled by instinct and spirit; he represents authority and law, the realm of ideas, the domain of religious and spiritual values. In brief, the father represents the sum total of those aspects of life which lie beyond the sphere of immediate, personal feminine concerns.

In the literature on the subject reference is often made to two particular trends of development which are called out in the woman if the attachment to her father has been intense. One such trend is described as a marked orientation towards the realm of the spiritual. I must add, however, that the English 'spiritual' is a very inadequate rendering of the German word '*geistig*'. What is meant by '*geistig*' is rather a blend between intellectual and spiritual, a cast of mind receptive to general cultural issues, whether intellectual, aesthetic, political, or spiritual properly so called. I would like to add—though I am anticipating what this paper is intended to demonstrate—that I personally hesitate to give too much weight to this assumption and would prefer to qualify it. When a woman's early development proceeds under the sign of the father rather than the mother, we may expect to find a considerable animus problem in her psychology; for the father is the first symbolic counter-image of her unconscious, and the first manifestation of her masculine energy later crystallized in the figure of the animus (cf. *CW* 9ii). In some cases the influence of the father is indeed the source of genuine intellectual or spiritual achievement by the daughter, but I do not think this should be taken as a general criterion.

The second factor frequently mentioned in connection with the father-daughter relationship concerns the development of the woman's sexual instinct. Here, however, the situation of son and daughter is not basically different. Wherever a parent's love life is not satisfactorily fulfilled in the marriage relationship and fastens, by substitution, on a child of the opposite sex, the child is caught by the 'unconscious incest' which originates in the parent (cf. *CW* 17, p.125). He is thus contaminated with an infantile sexuality that belongs to the parents, and this can become a serious hindrance in his own development towards sexual maturity.

A fair amount of case material on the problem of the feminine father complex has been published, most of it gleaned from experience with children. Frances Wickes has given excellent descriptions of cases where the little girl, on account of a strong father fixation, 'intuited' his problem and reacted to it in her behaviour as well as in her dreams (cf. Wickes, 1927; esp. pp.25-7, 46-9). One of Frances Wickes' cases has also been discussed at length by Jung (*CW* 17).

Further valuable observations on the problem in question have been added by Fordham. The boy's early attraction to the mother and the girl's early attachment to the father are normally overcome by subsequent identification with the parent of his or her own sex. A little girl of ten and a half, after being released from a negative father fixation, entered naturally into a phase where she was absorbed in 'a long series of mother games', thus establishing that measure of identification with the mother 'which is so necessary if the child is to develop normally' (1969, pp.47,128).

In records of adult development we have a well-known case of Jung's. A young woman who had had rather too 'good' a relation with her father was incapable of entering into full relationship with a man of her own age (*CW* 7). As a matter of fact, in this case Jung does mention that the young woman developed her intellectual abilities as a counterbalance to her feeling side which had been caught up with her father. Here the liberation from the father complex proceeded in two major stages. The first stage was that of the transference, in which an apparent solution of the conflict, which the patient herself could not solve, was projected upon the analyst, who assumed for her the image of father and lover thrown together. In the next stage the idealized image of the analyst changed, so as to reveal what was behind it. This was the archaic image of a father-god who, in one of the patient's dreams, held her in his arms like a child, rocking her gently above fields of swaying corn. From this 'transpersonal control-point', as Jung has called it, the patient's libido was redirected and found eventually its proper channel in an actual heterosexual relationship.

The case which I am proposing to outline in the following pages, in the briefest possible way, is the case of a woman who also suffered from a severe father fixation. But, unlike the cases so far published, it is not a problem of childhood nor of youth, but of the second half of life. The situation is different, and demands a different solution. For a woman in the second half of life it is no longer possible, as it is for the child, to return to an unconscious identification with the mother, in order that in this way she may catch up with her neglected feminine side. Nor is the situation favourable to the redirection of released energy into a heterosexual relationship, as in the case of Jung's patient. In the second half of life, liberation from the past is not enough.

My patient was a little over forty when she began analysis, and unmarried. An acute breakdown, which led to the loss of her job and to temporary incapacity for earning her living, had made her realize the need for reorientation. It may well be said that the first half of her life had been entirely governed by the consequences of the identification with her father, which dated from her early childhood. She had thus started with an acute deficiency in ego development. The ensuing stresses and strains of life had led to a further weakening of the ego position until her ego was in danger of being completely overwhelmed by the unconscious. She was a prolific dreamer and has faithfully recorded several hundred dreams in the course of three and a half years of analysis. What I find striking about this series of dreams is the fact that in a variety of ways the unconscious seems to insist on reorientating the personality first under the sign of the mother, and then to relate her anew to the father image from a fresh vantage-point.

The patient was the younger daughter in a family of several children and had two brothers younger than herself. From early childhood onwards she felt—and her brothers and sister corroborated this impression from their own memories—that she was singled out as her father's favourite. At the onset of puberty she began to realize the erotic element in her father's attachment to her; in fact, this realization amounted to a veritable sexual trauma. After the mother's death the father remarried, and the bond between father and daughter never became normally adjusted. Consciously the daughter turned with contempt against the father. Unconsciously, however, she remained imprisoned in the memory of their early mutual attachment, which had turned into the image of a mythical marriage in which she was both child and wife, partnered by an encompassing figure who was father and mother, deity and lover, all in one.

The patient trained for social work, and was successful in her career. She was unaware of the extent to which she was ruled by the father principle, or let us say by the drive of the animus. Only later, in retrospect, did she realize how deficient her life had been in human warmth. Even the relation to her brothers and sister, to whom she felt genuinely attached, was strained and distorted. For a number of years the symptoms of unconscious disturbance consisted in physical illness.

During several years prior to her breakdown she had frightening dreams about her father, who turned into a negative figure, persecuting her and trying to destroy her. There was a repetitive dream in which the father tried to get hold of her.

Every time I gained ground, he whistled my black spaniel, who stopped, undecided whether to go with me or turn back.

140

This enabled my father to gain ground. I always woke up with his grinning, diabolical face leering at me as he caught me up.

The dream which immediately preceded the beginning of analysis was the following.

She saw her father standing on the bank of a river in which she was swimming. He seemed enormous, of more than human size, and had the same diabolical expression on his face. In front of her, downstream, was a bridge with three arches through which she intended to escape. With more than human strength the father proceeded to hurl huge boulders into the water to block her way of escape. Two arches of the bridge were already completely blocked, and the third was just about to be closed, but with a last desperate effort the dreamer squeezed herself through the small aperture left, and awoke in terror.

This dream reflects the dangerous condition in which the patient found herself at the time of her breakdown. Almost the whole stream of libido had been dammed up by the father, and only a small trickle was left to escape into freedom. Her concrete situation at the time bore this out. Not only did she feel incapable of concentrating on her work, but the attitude to the job itself and also the relation to her friends was entirely governed by animus compulsions and by animus opinions. Even now, as it were, she saw herself in the image of the father's favourite child, who in this rôle set out to dominate her environment instead of relating to it.

Another symptom of the disappearance of her ego into the unconscious was the fact that, at the time, nearly all her psychic life manifested itself in dreams. She dreamed at great length every night. As a rule she woke up in the small hours and lay awake for a long time: when she fell asleep again she would repeat the same dream which she had had earlier in the night or else continue with the dream story exactly where she had left off on awaking. Moreover, thoughts, reactions, and emotions which she should have thought or felt during waking hours, presented themselves in dreams since her ego had failed to register them. It was a laborious task to reconstitute an ego capable of func-

141

tioning from the material scattered about in the dreams.

Her attitude to her mother, who had died several years previously, had a curiously patronizing flavour. She admired her mother's steadfastness of character, but her admiration was aloof, lacking in warmth. Nor could I detect any sense of guilt for having outwitted the mother in monopolizing the father's affection.

As the analysis progressed, the figure of the mother began to appear in several significant dreams. In the first of these, the patient dreamt that she woke up and tried to switch on the light near the bedside. As this did not work she got out of bed and tried the switch at the door which did not function either. Alarmed, she stumbled out of the room and groped her way in the dark, down an interminable flight of stairs, trying on each successive landing, and with increasing urgency, to switch on the light without success, until in a state of frenzy she reached the bottom of the well and fell down in a heap. At this moment her mother appeared in a doorway lit by candles, picked her up, and promised to look after her on condition that she would consent to be treated as a child. The compensatory tendency of the dream is evident. This was the true condition of her ego, left in a terror-stricken state of helplessness through her father's excessive influence, and in need of a mother's care to develop.

Other dreams followed in which the condition of the dreamer's neglected womanhood, personified by the mother, became progressively defined. Sometimes the mother was ill or dying; on one occasion she was insane. In another dream the mother, apparently dead, returned to life, and the father went in to her and slept with her as if at last to consummate a marriage which would release the daughter. In yet another dream burglars raided the house, and the dreamer's greatest distress was that they also took away her mother's silver tea service and silver spoons. 'It seemed like sacrilege,' she said.

At about the same time (I am quoting the dreams mostly in their chronological order) a dream occurred which upset the patient considerably. She dreamt that she was attending a church service at which her father officiated. Near the church entrance stood the crib, consisting only of the three figures of the Holy Family, which struck her as singularly ugly and incongruous against the beautiful background of the architecture. The figure of Our Lady attracted her attention in particular, 'for it seemed so large and crude and was painted in bright unnatural colours'. Moreover, it was lying face down. The three figures were made of iron and crudely covered with paint, a veritable eyesore. Eventually the father consented to having them removed and replaced by another set, smaller, more lifelike, and of better workmanship. I understand the dream as an indication that under the sign of the father the dreamer's feminine attitude was still no better than a fake. It still required the father's permission to have it improved, but at least the father's consent was not withheld.

About two months later another dream occurred in which, as I see it, a preliminary phase of readjustment came to its close.

> My father and I decided to go to X for a holiday, and started off to swim there, as a means of economy. Both naked, we swam along quite happily, my father always behind me. I got tired rather easily, and in consequence we had to stop fairly frequently. We waded on to the beach to find a sheltered cranny in the cliffs where we could light a fire and cook something to eat. Each time we came out of the water, my father disappeared and my mother was there to help me, and she wrapped me in clothes.

I should perhaps mention that X is a holiday resort on the south coast of England, and that the intended journey proceeded along some hundred miles of coast, rounding Land's End. X is also the place in the neighbourhood of which the father, after his second marriage, had settled down and where at the time of the dream he was still living. The great distance which this journey covers may hint at a correspondingly extended time span in which this symbolical pilgrimage is to be accomplished. Further, the dream presents a new situation in which father and mother images balance each other, each being associated with its own native element, the mother with the maternal earth, the father with the sea, the unconscious. Also, the dreamer is shown as potentially capable of relating to both.

The patient's further development revolved around the elaboration of this double theme, father and mother. In the measure in which her capacity increased consciously to define her attitude to these two major spheres of reality the unconscious proceeded to differentiate the psychic contents symbolized by each figure.

However, there is a striking difference between the way in which the contents of the father archetype and those of the mother archetype were developed in subsequent dreams. The father image, as it were, split. While one group of dream figures took over the collective and archetypal function of the masculine principle, the image of the personal father appeared from now on only rarely, and in connection with the dreamer's conscious change of attitude to him. The mother principle, on the other hand, gave rise to an entirely new development, for it released a new aptitude which, the patient felt, had to be integrated in her personal life and given concrete expression. This newly emerging aptitude became a vehicle for relating the patient to the inherently feminine world of matter in a personal and creative way, hitherto unknown and unsuspected by her.

As regards the father image, a threefold differentiation gradually took place into what I would call the image of the personal father, the positive animus, and the father archetype proper.

The positive animus made his distinctive appearance in a dream in which he was introduced to the dreamer as 'the landowner of a neighbouring estate, recently returned from abroad'. In the following dreams she saw him swimming in the sea and then climbing out on to a floating raft, coming towards her. Then again she saw him ploughing a field of rich brown furrows and throwing to her, pencilled on paper, a message of love.

One of the key dreams in which the collective nature of the animus came to dramatic expression occurred a few months later. The patient recorded it as follows:

> I was in a large hall with about an equal number of Chinese people and English people. They were well mixed but one could feel how suspicious they were of each other, and the atmosphere was very tense. Suddenly a Chinaman flourished a knife, and I knew it would be a riot unless something was done. [The dreamer then suggests that a chosen member of each side should search the other party for weapons, and a number of them are found and taken away.] Every scrap of

tension disappeared; I wanted everyone to express their happiness, and I started to dance. I became completely lost in what I was doing, and saw that everyone was watching me, enthralled. As I circled round I noticed a tall, stately, fine Chinese figure; he was obviously the leader of all the Chinese people who were present. I held out my hand to him and he joined me. Together we circled round the room, and as we passed people we invited them to join us. Soon everyone was dancing and all were completely happy.

After this the dream repeated itself with slight variations, the most noteworthy of which was that this time the leader of the Chinese people revealed himself as the Chinese Emperor, 'wearing a wonderful silver kimono which radiated a silver light', while from his forehead shone 'a brilliant light'. This time the dance developed into a kind of orgiastic Dionysian frenzy.

This dream is rich in symbolical material. It should perhaps be noted that the dreamer herself still plays the rôle of the favoured child, even exhibiting an unashamed feminine vanity. The little sentence 'I became completely lost in what I was doing, and saw that everyone was watching me, enthralled' tells its own tale. But the important thing is that the dreamer here enters voluntarily and with abandon into an experience in which the memory image of the relation to her father in childhood is repeated on a collective, symbolical level. One is inclined to say that the incest motif, originally concealed in the relationship with the actual father, is here transmuted into a ritual *hieros gamos* with the animus in his positive aspect. In entering into the ritual, the dreamer takes an active role in reconciling the opposites which in the dream are represented by the Chinese and the English respectively—the masters of the inner life, and the masters of social adjustment and of disciplined activity. The theme as such was already given in earlier dreams, one of which stressed the association of the father with the sea, while in another the young animus figure emerged from the sea. The present dream introduces a new note inasmuch as the animus figure is here represented as the ruler of a collectively valid way of life, and of a way of life which exalts the inner world into a cosmic principle.

145

The theme of the animus presiding over and reconciling two hitherto warring factions, occurred in another dream almost two years later.

> With several other people I was inspecting a building, the property of Winston Churchill, which he was bequeathing to the nation when he retired, for the use of Parliament. It was old, in beautiful repair and well cared for, and although large, was about right for this purpose. It was in a beautiful rural setting ... I had the impression that there would be one Parliament, with no distinction between Lords and Commons. There was a sun-dial in the main hall. One part of it consisted in a rectangular stone slab, placed horizontally on a bench, the style erect in its centre. The dial itself was on a separate stone, placed vertically in an alcove above, and covered with a circle of figures carved in relief in the Roman manner. The light came through a large window at such an angle that the shadow was drawn correctly on the dial, moving across the sculptured relief with the hours.

A considerable process of integration had taken place in the period between the last-mentioned two dreams. In the latter the dreamer is no longer the admired heroine but one spectator among others. The simplicity of the whole setting compares favourably with the excited emotionality of the earlier dream; the patient's ego has become detached from the realm of the impersonal. At the same time yet another stage in the differentiation of the father image has been reached. The Chinese Emperor is the deified Son of Heaven in whom temporal and spiritual powers are jointly invested. Winston Churchill, more humbly, personifies the presiding genius of a specific social unit in its allotted time and space, while the spiritual principle is relegated to the sun, producing the rotation of the sun-dial's shadow across the ancient stone.

In the intervening period between these two dreams the patient had begun to come to terms with the human and fallible personality of her own father. In one of her dreams she met him as she was descending a dark lane with a baby in her arms, and she knew that he could no longer harm her so long as she held on to her child. Then, a little later, she saw in a dream the father

146

sitting in his study, attentively listening to music on the wireless. She had in fact often seen him thus engaged in her youth. Like her, the father had been receptive to the stirrings of the irrational; like her, he had tended to lose his human boundaries in the welter of the unconscious. She no longer had any ground for fear or hate, and compassion was ripe.

Side by side with the progressive differentiation of the father image, as delineated in the dreams, proceeded the separate development of feminine symbols. These revolved around the theme of the human hands.

This theme occurred for the first time shortly after the dream of the swimming excursion to the holiday resort X—that key dream to which I have referred before as indicating a temporary balance between the parental images.

It began with a waking phantasy in which the patient saw two kneeling figures at the foot of the cross, extending their open hands as if to receive the food of communion. The two kneeling figures seemed to be angels, and yet they were herself seen in duplicate, but in the next instant the two pairs of hands merged into one.

At that time the patient began to model in clay. She intended to model the two kneeling figures of her vision, but could make no headway. Then she dreamt:

> In my sleep I was thinking about the hands of the model I was making, knowing that they were full of meaning and of tremendous importance. I knew that if only I could see it, they held the secret to all my searching.

From that time onwards the patient began to find more and more pleasure in using her hands. Free imaginative expression in either painting or clay did not come easily to her, and her attempts were few. But she took up sewing, knitting, embroidery, and even began in a small way to earn a little money with these activities. She felt unaccountably happy and at ease in these pursuits, and became convinced that they should form part of whatever she was going to do in the future. Every time when she became immersed in different activities, a dream would warn her not to neglect her hands, a dream about hands ink-stained or bleeding from wounds, or about tender hands gently enfolding

147

her when she went astray. About the same time when, in a
dream, she met her father, secure in the possession of the child
in her arms, she dreamt the following.

> I was standing before a life-size figure of a Madonna, a figure
> that I was creating. Around her feet and the knees and part
> of her robes was coiled a snake, but there was nothing
> repulsive about it. Indeed it seemed perfectly natural for it
> to be there. The whole thing was changing constantly—
> expression, position, movement. Several times I went away
> and, finding a quiet place where I could be quite alone, I sank
> to my knees, shut my eyes, and meditated about the figure.
> Each time I returned after having 'seen' the next step in her
> creation, I proceded to work on her accordingly. After one
> of these 'meditations' I returned and started to paint her robes,
> applying at first a very deep purple. Then I added a con-
> siderable amount of white until the robe became the softest
> of mauve, iridescent in its loveliness. Looking up into her face,
> tender, sensitive and expressive, I saw how very Eastern her
> features were, and yet at the same time, nothing could have
> been more typically English. Still holding the paint brush,
> I realized that here was something that would keep me
> occupied for a very long time, probably even for years. Then,
> without the slightest dismay, I knew that I was committed
> to her for a lifetime.

Here, at last, the ugly Madonna of the earlier dream was
redeemed.

This dream was by no means the end of the series, nor did
it mark the end of the patient's search for integration. But the
direction was set. The ascendancy of the feminine principle over
the masculine which had almost destroyed the patient can hardly
be expressed more beautifully than as a commitment for life,
to give form and expression to the image of the Divine Mother
in whose presence the destructive power of the snake is rendered
harmless. The tools with which to give actuality to such expression are the patient's own hands—a physical organ, creatively
in touch with the feminine realm of matter. I am inclined to think
that the hands, translated into psychological terms, also stand
for the function of sensation. In my opinion the patient was an

introverted feeling type. It required the development of the function of sensation in order to make available, for extraverted application, the psychic energy accumulated in introverted feeling. This was the condition on which depended the harmonious co-operation of the inner and the outer world, the Chinese and the English, the two Houses of Parliament. When in the previous vision of the two angels their dual pair of hands merged into one, it indicated the way in which the patient's dissociation was to be healed. Sensation should replace what had previously been compulsive extraverted mechanisms, dominated by the animus.

After this delineation of the feminine position the unconscious process turned once more towards the elaboration of the father image.

The last-mentioned dream in the series in which the unconscious appeared to aim at a progressive differentiation of the father principle was about Churchill. As pointed out before, the dream introduced a distinction between the masculine principle that governs the external, collective scene—personified by Winston Churchill—and the spiritual principle, symbolized by the sun. From now onwards the spiritual aspect of the masculine principle, which originally had been hidden in the image of the personal father, became expressed in symbols of increasingly impersonal and abstract character. The following dream occurred a few months later.

I stood by the side of a large and very beautiful old tree. The branches bent over and grew down so that they touched the earth. They were in leaf, and underneath the grass was a glorious green. It was like being in a leafy cave for it formed a complete circle round me and, although this was so, it was wonderfully light within. Yet I knew I could not stay and, stepping out, I stood with my back against the trunk. It gave me strength and I did not grieve for the peace and the quiet I had left behind me in the green haven. Then looking up I saw a golden ball drifting towards me and I stretched out my hands to catch it.

When the patient began to paint this dream, she unconsciously chose for the background the same golden tint with which she had painted the ball, and when she suddenly realized it, she stopped short, surprised, exclaiming, 'The golden ball!' She felt on the verge of a tremendous paradox in which the opposites mysteriously came together, yet in which each created the other—the inward withdrawal and the stepping out of it, the static rootedness of the tree and the dynamic movement of the ball, inviting her to receive it in her hands. And yet it was all contained within a greater golden globe, which would never have been perceived but for what went before.

Again, a few months later, she had another significant dream which, brief though it was, impressed her deeply. She felt rather than saw that she was suspended in the centre of a ball of fire. The fire neither burnt nor hurt, it merely held and contained her, itself an unchanging inexhaustible manifestation of power, and she felt awestruck as if in the very presence of the divine. A lifelong religious search seemed to be answered in this dream, though its nature defied rational explanation.

We know from study of symbolism that the sun, the golden ball, the ball of fire are archaic father images as well as symbols of divinity. 'The well-known fact that worship of the sun is worship of the immense procreative power of nature, shows plainly to anyone to whom as yet it may not be clear, that in the deity man reveres the energy of the archetype' (*CW* 5, p.149). But it was, we may note, only after having found the security of her feminine place that the patient had come face to face with the primordial image of God, in one of the most potent symbols of the father archetype.

One final word about the patient herself. The richness and profundity of the unconscious material should not mislead one into inferring a correspondingly richly equipped personality. She, like every other patient who produces a wealth of unconscious imagery, remained in some sense the person that she had always been. The relative instability of her ego, and her difficulties of relationship had not disappeared. But her attitudes had changed, and so life also had changed for her. She had become aware of a personal centre from which to go out and participate in the stresses of living experience without losing herself, a centre guarded by the parental images in their beneficent aspect. The father archetype had revealed itself as the cosmic source of creative power which no longer destroyed but contained, while the mother archetype presided over the concrete world, which the patient now felt commited to serve in a way expressive of her womanhood. And yet in a sense she still was, and may always remain, conditioned by her early involvement with her father. In her case even the hands are not so much a symbol of personal relationship as instruments for relating her to the impersonal sphere of matter. Their function here is to relate the personality in a feminine way to the impersonal.

This, at least, is my impression, and if I am not mistaken, it has significance. I doubt that it should be assumed as a generally valid principle that a woman's tie to her father is necessarily productive of an intellectual cast of mind, nor should it be taken for granted that her orientation is towards cultural or spiritual interests. While a father fixation remains unresolved it destroys the ground in which womanhood is rooted, but when resolved through the emergence of an appropriate feminine pattern it nevertheless still conditions a woman's basic attitude. In my opinion an excessive attachment to the father commits a woman, perhaps for life, to the impersonal—though the specific nature of this commitment depends on her personal psychology. Furthermore, it prepares her to realize her own duality as well as the cosmic polarity of life, and may even force her to do so. This realization is as such contrary to woman's nature, and contrary to her innate bias towards an undifferentiated unconsciousness in which 'the opposites sleep side by side'. It is presumably only in the second half of life that this realization becomes a challenge which she cannot ignore. But, if this challenge is met, then the problem of the opposites, symbolized by the archetypal figures of father and mother, may reveal itself as the creative point at which the undifferentiated inclusiveness of woman's nature is released into consciousness.

References

Fordham, M. (1969). *Children as Individuals*. London, Hodder & Stoughton.

Harding, M. E. (1933). *The Way of All Women*. London, Longmans, Green & Co.

Harding, M.E. (1935). *Woman's Mysteries*. London, Longmans, Green & Co.

Neumann, E. (1953). 'Zur Psychologie des Weiblichen'. *Umkreisung der Mitte,* 2. *Zürich,* Rascher.

Wickes, F.G. (1927). *The Inner World of Childhood.* London, D. Appleton-Century Co.

Wolff, T. (1941). 'A Few Thoughts on the Process of Individuation in Women', *Spring.*

In search of
a loving father

W. RALPH LAYLAND

This paper by a member of the British Psycho-Analytical Society counterpoints Allenby's. Although Layland in no sense
makes use of analytical psychology, the tenor and content of
his essay shows up the rapprochement that is taking place. In
particular, it is his demonstration of the way an image cultures
feeling and behaviour, and his use of the ideogram of a
'search', that gives his paper a flavour which appealed to
Jungians the moment it was published. The paper is particularly
useful for the light shed on psychosexual development prior
to the Oedipus complex. *A.S.*

TO START A PAPER which has pretensions to being scientific with a generalization would appear to be paradoxical, but it would seem to be the fate of most psychoanalytical concepts that no matter how precisely the concept is defined by its author, over a period of time its meaning will become wider. As more and more psychoanalysts become familiar with the concept, use it in examining their clinical observations and material, and then, if it is found to be acceptable, fit it into the framework of their own theoretical orientation, so gradually will the concept begin to take on slightly differing shades of meaning.

Our inability to measure our scientific concepts mathematically and thus give them precise dimensions could be one of the causes of confusion and disagreement between psychoanalysts of different theoretical persuasions and indeed between psychoanalysts of the same theoretical persuasion. Too often it is automatically assumed by the authors of psychoanalytical papers that when they use a psychoanalytical concept or a piece of psychoanalytical jargon, their colleagues will know and share exactly the meaning of what they are saying. This is a dangerous assumption that can produce unnecessary misunderstanding and possibly conflict.

Winnicott, in his (1960) paper 'Ego distortion in terms of true and false self', defined the good-enough mother as 'one who meets the omnipotence of the infant and to some extent makes sense of it'. For economy of words and preciseness it could not be bettered. He then adds 'She does this repeatedly', suggesting that it is not a 'one-off' experience for the infant but that it takes time for the infant to internalize the good-enough mothering experience.

The concept of the 'good-enough mother' is one which is now widely accepted not only by many analysts of different theoretical backgrounds but also by many members of the so-called 'caring professions'. I would suggest that in the intervening two decades since Winnicott wrote his paper this wide acceptance and use of his concept by many different workers has resulted in a diversity of meaning rather than in a refinement. Indeed, in his book *Playing and Reality*, published in 1971, Winnicott writes 'The good-enough "mother" (not necessarily the infant's own mother) is one who makes active adaptation to the infant's needs, an active adaptation that gradually lessens according to the infant's growing ability to account for failure of adaptation and to tolerate the results of frustration.' For me this restatement of what he defines as the good-enough mother has not quite the same meaning as his definition eleven years earlier, suggesting that in the years between he too had been reconsidering and re-working his concept. When I started to think about the theoretical aspects of this paper, I realized that I had to get clear in my own thoughts what the concept of the good-enough mother meant for me and to define it to the best of my ability, accept-ing at the same time that any definition would be unacceptable to some and irritating to others even to the point of arousing feelings of hostility. Nevertheless it seemed important to state my position. For me the good-enough mother is one who possesses a series of qualities or capacities which when blended together in varying quantities provide the infant with an experience which over a period of time the infant accepts as being good-enough.

It will be seen that I regard the good-enough mother as hav-ing a series of qualities or capacities, and that these are present in varying quantities. For the sake of clarity, suppose it is only a question of two qualities—X and Y. I am suggesting that it is quite possible for mother A to have more of X than Y, and mother B to have more of Y than X, and still be experienced by their respective infants as 'good-enough'. What I am trying to say is that I do not think there is such a thing as the stereotype good-enough mother. The second point I wish to emphasize is that what defines whether a mother is good-enough or not is the infant's experience of her over a period of time. In other words it is the infant's subjective experience which defines whether in retrospect the mother was good-enough, and not some expert's objective observation of the mother-baby relationship.

One of the qualities of the good-enough mother is her capacity to accept that it is the baby's right to bring to her all its needs, wishes, fantasies and feelings which the baby may experience as good or bad, pleasurable or unpleasurable, but not to expect her baby to deal with her own mainly unconscious needs, wishes, fan-tasies or feelings that are inappropriate to the mother-baby relation-ship and for which the mother should seek satisfaction elsewhere.

155

For example, it is the baby's right to be able to take to its mother its own depressive feelings and to expect her to help it with them. It is not the baby's task to cope with its depressed mother. It is this quality of the good-enough mother that I shall call 'the loving mother'.

In this paper, with the help of clinical material, I wish to put forward for consideration the concept of 'the loving father', by which I mean the father who can accept that it is the baby's right to bring to him all its needs, wishes, fantasies and feelings, but does not expect the baby to deal with his own mainly unconscious needs, wishes, fantasies or feelings that are inappropriate to that relationship.

It might be asked why I have not chosen to advance the concept of the good-enough father instead of the loving father. I have emphasized that the quality I have described as 'the loving mother' is only one of those possessed by a good-enough mother. I suspect that a good-enough father must have other qualities in addition to the one I have ascribed to a loving father and that they may be very different from the ones possessed by a good-enough mother. For example, the role of the father in supporting the mother in her mothering.

Clinical Material

My interest in the father-child relationship started after I had completed my analytical training. I found myself taking into analysis and psychoanalytically oriented psychotherapy a series of young women who had had fathers whom they had each experienced as being emotionally unavailable to them in their early childhood years. Either the father had been physically absent from the home for reality reasons such as serving in the Forces during the Second World War, or, because of some difficulties in himself, he had been unable to relate to his very young daughter in an appropriate emotional way. In the first situation, the little girl fantasizes about her idealized father who will come home to her one day, only to deeply disappoint her when she has to discover that he returns not to her but to her mother. He is not at all the Prince Charming she had believed him to be. In the second situation, where the father is experienced as emotionally unavailable, the little girl is left with a confusion of not knowing if her father just doesn't love her or if the feelings she experiences towards him frighten him away.

What I very soon realized was how little I knew, and had been taught as a student, about the effect the emotional absence of the father could have on the girl's subsequent development, especially with regard to her sexual identity. As a student there had been many lectures and seminars on the mother and her child, from the early primitive symbiotic unit through the gradual separation to the two-person mother and baby relationship. But what of the father? What role had he had to play? The more I thought about the material the patients were bringing to the sessions the more dissatisfied I became with my lack of understanding and knowledge of the effect of the father on the very early infant before the Oedipal phase. I decided to let my patients teach me in an attempt to formulate some ideas for myself. This way they would be original for me. I accepted that if I searched through the literature I would find that they had already been original ideas for someone else.

The material which I am presenting is from two young male patients whom I have had the privilege of helping. I have chosen them rather than one of the female patients I have already referred to because they arrived at my consulting room within months of each other and both complained of the same anxiety—the fear that they might be homosexual. Although their background and early histories were in marked contrast, it seemed to me as I listened to them—and it will be realized that I was seeing them in parallel—that their underlying need was the same: to find a loving father.

Michael

Michael was 26 years old when I started to see him for analysis. He had already had a lot of psychiatric help, including a period of psychotherapy from an experienced colleague working in the Student Health Service who referred him to me.

Michael was the eldest of three boys born to a self-made dollar millionaire whom he described in the initial interview as being a 'wimp'. I think the nearest English slang equivalent of this would be to describe someone as being 'wet'. The paternal grand-father committed suicide at the time Michael's father was sitting his exams to enter college, which he failed. Following this event the father seems to have been driven by a need to prove himself in the business world and to become the great provider for his family. When Michael was five years old, the family moved from a working-class quarter of an American industrial city to a rich commuter belt, and there was a further move some ten years later into the millionaires' road. Each day father would leave for his city office at 6.30 a.m., returning home in the evening at 8.30 p.m. when his wife would pour him a coke and the three boys would assemble to give him a ritual kiss. This ceremony continued until all the boys were teenagers. His sons hated him.

As already suggested, the mother was devoted to her husband's wellbeing. She was always telling the boys how much their father loved them and how much they should love him in return. She was described as an affectionate person whom all the boys loved. What gradually emerged in the analysis was Michael's idealization of her as a defence against his feelings of rejection by her. When he was six weeks old he had to be admitted to hospital because he was vomiting back his feeds and not gaining weight. At the end of fourteen months his brother Matthew was born, to be followed two years later by brother Mark.

Michael said that his early childhood was uneventful but that at the age of ten he became 'fanatically pure' (his words) and immersed himself in the family religion, Roman Catholicism. It is worth noting that he always regarded his parents as being 'very pure'. They never showed any form of physical affection to each other in front of the children and neither Michael nor his brothers could ever imagine the parents having sexual intercourse.

By the time he entered high school his intellectual development had far outstripped his emotional growth. He was referred to by his teachers as a genius and was the first boy in the history of the school to be moved up two grades at once. He excelled at sports and was always elected form president. He had no difficulty in getting into an Ivy League college and chose one some distance from his home town. He continued to be academically successful, always coming top of his class. Always popular with his fellow students, he was eventually voted by them as being 'the one most likely to succeed and to become President of the United States'. It was during the time that he was at college that he started broadcasting and writing. About the time he reached his twentieth birthday he was making his mark internationally at journalism.

After graduating at college with honours, it was expected of him that he should go to England to continue his studies at one of the older universities, to which he had no difficulty in getting a scholarship. Six months after his arrival in England he became desperately nostalgic for his élite group of male college friends. He now recognized that he had made them into a surrogate family when he had made his attempt to separate from his home. During the Easter vacation he returned to the States to discover that the group had dispersed. Two months later he had a severe psychotic breakdown in England and once more returned home. He was eventually admitted to a state mental hospital and treated with drugs and ECT. After taking his own discharge he had some supportive psychotherapy as well as a further admission to a private psychiatric clinic.

A year later he decided to finish his university course even though he was far from well. He was determined to get better and worked hard in psychotherapy with my colleague in the Student Health Service. He graduated with a 2:1 honours degree and returned to America. Twelve months later he again crossed the Atlantic as it had become obvious to him that his future career would be better achieved in England. This proved to have been a good decision as he is now recognized as a world expert in his highly specialized field of the arts. He also acknowledged that although he was no longer mad—his description of his breakdown—he still had considerable problems. It was this that brought him to me.

Before describing some of the analysis, it is necessary to give a brief outline of his sexual development. As has already been described, around the onset of puberty Michael became deeply involved in religion. Two significant people had an effect on his thinking. His paternal grandmother had developed a delusional illness. She believed she was a chosen messenger of God and

159

spent her days writing to church dignitaries including the Pope. I do not know if this illness preceded or followed her husband's suicide. The second person was the fervent local priest who instilled in him the idea of sin and everlasting hell with such vehemence that Michael believed that it was evil to think of girls physically, and successfully suppressed any fantasies. Gradually he relinquished his religious beliefs and did some casual dating at college. He indulged in mild petting but was unable to contemplate going further with a girl.

When he was about eighteen years old a friend made a homosexual approach which he rejected. In a subsequent discussion he found out that his friend masturbated. This was something Michael had never done although he had had frequent wet dreams. He started to masturbate, with fantasies of hugging men of his own age. The fantasy figures were always clothed below the waist and he never thought of their genitals. He rationalized the hugging as 'pure'—the same word he had used about himself during his religious period, and about his parents' relationship. At the time of his psychotic breakdown, his masturbation had increased in frequency and his fantasy males were his close friends from his college days. During the time he was having psychotherapy with the doctor attached to the Student Health Service, he worked through some of his homosexual preoccupation. Gradually his fear and guilt of having heterosexual relationships lessened so that he was able to have increasingly successful friendships with girls. Eventually he achieved sexual intercourse.

I shall now relate those aspects of his analysis that I think have to do with the subject of this paper. We often refer to patients 'using the couch'. In my experience no one has used my couch quite like Michael. He would arrive in the room, throw himself onto the couch and begin a non-stop outpouring of words. The predominant theme was his anger with his father for insisting that he was the great provider and that if only Michael put all his trust and love into the family he would be all right. 'You will always have the family' was his father's favourite saying. As he was telling me all this he would be constantly moving on and over the couch; sometimes he was on his back; sometimes on his front. He would roll up into a ball, hugging the pillow, or he would thump it with his fists. At other times he would lash out at the adjacent wall with his hands or feet. At no time was he still, except occasionally when he would suddenly freeze in a kneeling position, his forearms resting on the couch, his head on his hands and his buttocks thrust up into the air. He would hold this position for a matter of seconds and then start his movements once more. So active was his moving that at the end of every session we had to search for everything that had emptied out of his pockets onto the couch and onto the floor.

At first I was unable to understand the meaning of all this activity. I experienced it as if I had a hyper-motile child in the room. I wondered if he was acting out something from early childhood but there was no history of excitability. I resisted any desire to interpret it, hoping that in time I would understand it better.

Eventually a memory started to be recalled of his father coming into his bedroom at night and sitting on his bed. He would put his hand under Michael's pyjama coat and gently rub his chest and belly. During a trip to the States, Michael told his brother Matthew about this memory. Matthew confirmed that their father had done the same thing to him and also to the youngest son, Mark.

Slowly we began to understand that his need to keep moving during a session was a result of the anxiety aroused in him by the analytical setting. Lying on the couch with myself near to him revived the memory of his father coming into his bedroom. If he remained on his back he was open to any attempt by me to rub his chest and abdomen; if he turned onto his front he feared that I might attack him anally so he had to change his position constantly. I understood the kneeling posture that I have described as a need to test out if it was safe to be with me. On thinking about it I have wondered if he was behaving like the frightened animal which when cornered presents its most vulnerable area to the aggressor. As he began to know through interpretation that I understood his anxieties he was able to settle on the couch and his movements lessened.

During the next phase of his analysis he began masturbating again, with a return of his hugging fantasies. He also reported frequent dreams in which he was either hugging a friend or sit-

161

ting on the friend's lap. He would get an erection and wake up ejaculating. In the dreams the friend remained sexually unaroused.

In the second year of the analysis he started to have an intense sexual relationship with Millie, a divorcee with a young child. Unknown to him she stopped taking the pill and became pregnant. He was furious. He felt that she had tricked him and although he accepted responsibility he made it quite clear that he would not be trapped into a permanent relationship. The girl had an abortion and disappeared from his life.

Soon after this incident he returned to the States for a holiday. He was introduced to a young actor, Guy, who had just made his Broadway debut. Guy had been at school with brother Matthew and had hero-worshipped Michael from afar. They spent the weekend in each other's company, during which time Guy told Michael of his life as a homosexual. On his return to England he told me in his first session of how much he loved Guy. He knew that Guy had wanted a sexual relationship with him. He was repulsed by this idea although he would have liked to have held Guy and comforted him. I interpreted that having felt rejected by Millie when she was expecting a baby, he had behaved towards Guy in the way in which he had wanted his own father to respond towards him when he had felt rejected by his mother at the time she was expecting his brother Matthew.

Two weeks later he reported the following incident in a Monday session. On the Saturday he had had dinner with an old college friend, Don, to whom he had been very close. They had returned to Michael's flat. Eventually they had started hugging each other and exchanged gentle kisses. Michael had become aroused and ejaculated. Later he had felt able to tell Don this and was greatly relieved when Don said that he had not been sexually excited.

I considered how I should interpret this piece of material. Should I regard it as a piece of acting-out, which at one level it undeniably was, and say so? Instead I told him that I felt that he had found with Don for a short time what he had been searching for all his life in his fantasies—a loving father. A father who was able to hold him and allow him to experience all kinds of feelings—closeness, loving and sexual ones—without responding in a way that would be inappropriate in a loving father-child relationship.

John

The second patient I shall describe more briefly. Although his presenting anxiety was the same as Michael's, his history and behaviour in the sessions was markedly different.

John was 32 when I first saw him and arranged to take him into three times a week psychoanalytically oriented psychotherapy. He was the first child of a heavy-drinking Merchant Navy Petty Officer and a working-class mother. Soon after his birth his mother emigrated to Australia where John spent the first five years of his life. He had very few memories of this period of his life. He has always believed it was a happy one during which he was very close to his mother. Occasionally the father would come home on leave. John's only recollections of these visits is that his father would give him a packet of sweets and a model boat he had made at sea.

When John was five years old his father left the Merchant Navy and the family returned to England. A year later John's sister Sue was born. The next nine years were very unhappy ones for him. He felt that his mother had rejected him in favour of his father and sister. He experienced intense jealousy towards his sister and great anger towards his father, who appeared to take no interest in him. He felt very lonely and unwanted. His father was drinking very heavily and would arrive home very drunk late at night. John recalled lying awake fearing the quarrels and fights that would take place between his parents when his father came home. His mother suffered frequent periods of depression with paranoid delusions. She made numerous suicide attempts which resulted in admissions to mental hospitals. He never knew when he came home after school what mood he would find his mother in, or if he would even find her there. One day when he was fourteen years old he arrived home to find his mother had killed herself. He immediately developed the idea that his father was to blame for his mother's death. The relationship between them steadily deteriorated. Twelve months later he was unable to remain in the same house as his father any longer because he experienced anger he was afraid to express. He moved to a friend's home where he lived with the family until he was able to buy his own house.

Although he had a place at a grammar school and had obtained a number of 'O' levels, he had to leave in order to support himself. Following a series of jobs, when he was twenty years old he started a business with a friend. It gradually expanded and at the time he came to therapy it had become a financially successful undertaking.

As a teenager he had shown very little interest in girls. He felt an outsider when his friends boasted of their sexual conquests. To quote him: 'I listened to them not really understanding what they were talking about.' It was not until he had reached his early twenties that he started taking girls out. His initiation into sexual intercourse was with a much older married woman with whom he had an intense relationship for a few months. Just before starting therapy he had met a girl, Jean, whom he married twelve months later.

His fear that he might be homosexual arose from his preoccupation with looking at younger boys. He would find himself staring at blond-haired effeminate-looking young teenage boys who seemed to be happy and to enjoy being alive. He had never approached or spoken to any of them. That they should be so carefree at an age when he had been so depressed produced feelings of envy in him. It is interesting that John is himself fair-haired but not at all effeminate-looking. Before starting treatment he had realized that his preoccupations ceased during the periods when he had a girl friend and that they returned when he felt he had been rejected by a girl and had become depressed.

When he was 27 years old he consulted a psychiatrist who advised group therapy. He discontinued after four sessions as he did not feel it was helping him. He tried to work through his problems by himself during the next four years before seeking further help. A few months before his referral to me he decided to test out whether he was a homosexual or not. Through an introduction agency, he arranged to meet a young man one evening. They went to a public house frequented by homosexuals and then to a gay disco. Afterwards they returned to John's house and spent the night together. Mutual masturbation and fellatio took place. The next morning John quickly got the young man out of his house. He felt very guilty about what had happened and decided that it was not 'his scene'. It was soon after this that he met his future wife and looked for further professional help.

His behaviour in the sessions was very different from Michael's. On the couch he took up a rigid posture without a flicker of voluntary movement in his body. He spoke in a quiet, hesitant, monotonous voice. We came to understand that he had a fear of attracting my attention. This was in conflict with his wish to be close to me in order to experience my concern and understanding. He had to keep everything bad inside himself. He feared that I might become depressed by his depression and be unable to sort out my own depression from the depression he had projected into me, in just the same way as he had experienced his mother's inability to do so. After a holiday break he felt rejected by that part of me which he experienced as being like his mother. At the same time the rejection was also experienced as being like that of his father, who had not understood his wish to be close in order to obtain the love he felt his depressed mother could not give him.

Gradually two of the meanings of John's preoccupation with the young boys became clear. He felt envious of them because he believed that if he had been a happy carefree pretty boy, his father would have loved him in the same way that he felt his sister Sue was loved. This wish was in conflict with the fear that his father might become too attracted and be seduced by him. The wish to deny his active masculine self and play the passive feminine rôle was acted out in his sex life with his wife. He preferred Jean to take the initiative and to be on top during intercourse. The other meaning that emerged during the therapy was the unconscious wish to provide the young boys with the love and the caring he had wanted from his own father. This had also been one of the unconscious wishes the first patient, Michael, had had in his relationship with his actor friend Guy.

I trust that enough material from John's therapy has been given to explain his fear of drawing attention to himself during his sessions even though his wish was to have my love and understanding as a loving father to help him cope with his internalized depressed mother.

165

Discussion

To have two people in analysis at the same time, each presenting with the same anxiety, provides an excellent opportunity for comparing and contrasting the material they bring to the sessions. I should like to discuss some of the conclusions I have reached from thinking about the two patients from two aspects—theory and technique.

Burlingham (1973, p.24) writes: 'On the whole, whatever is written by most analysts on the early years of children's lives, the important persons described are the mothers—the fathers remain in the background, unimportant, and, apart from the early, primary identification, scarcely mentioned until they come into their own when the children reach the phallic-Oedipal phase of development. I cannot help feeling that this comparative neglect of the pre-oedipal father not only does an injustice to his rôle but actually distorts in some manner the fate of the infant-mother relationship.' It seems to me that there are times in an infant's very early life when it may experience an overwhelming rejection by the mother. The sort of event in the external world which may precipitate this experience in the infant is the hospitalization of either the mother or the infant, a new pregnancy, or an absence of the mother for some other reason which the infant is unable to understand. The degree to which this rejection is experienced is related to the amount of separation that has already been achieved in the early dependent infant-mother relationship. It is also related to how much the infant's omnipotence has been maintained by the mother's dependency on her child to satisfy her own needs and wishes.

If the mother is unable to deal with the feelings of rejection aroused in the infant, which in turn leads to a rejection of the mother by the infant, the infant has to look to another object for care and help. It needs to find an object that can fulfil two tasks: to help the infant with the feelings aroused by the experienced rejection and to allow the infant to bring to it the needs, wishes, feelings and fantasies that it has now withdrawn from the rejecting and rejected mother, particularly its loving, hating and infantile sexual feelings and wishes. I am suggesting that the appropriate object for the infant is its father. I believe

166

that the way in which the father responds during these crisis periods in the infant's life is crucial to the child's future sexual development and identity.

The evidence from the observations of Greenacre (1966), Abelin (1975), and Mahler *et al.* (1975) is that the infant has a sense of father from the very early months of life. Greenacre suggests that at first the father is probably most frequently sensed as a twilight figure. How much he remains a distant figure or what part he plays in his own right depends on his own temperament as well as that of the mother, and on the relationship between them. Greenacre particularly notes the effects of the physically active father on the child. Abelin found from his research at the Master's Children's Center that a most definite turning towards the father occurs at the beginning of the 'practising sub-phase', that is, at about the age of four months. What I wish to stress is the suggestion that an important factor in how the infant experiences that object that gradually becomes a person called 'father' is the father's own emotional response to the infant. This I have called at the beginning of this paper his capacity to be a 'loving father'.

I disagree with Burlingham when she says that the father *substitutes* for the mother when the child turns to him expecting from him what the mother is unable to provide. To think of the father as a substitute mother is denying him a rôle in his own right. It is also denying the child the capacity to experience him as something different from the mother. To the child he will smell, feel and sound different. It may be that it is how much the child experiences the father as being different from the mother, but at the same time having qualities similar to the mother, that is important to the infant at this stage of the development. I would suggest that it is more correct to use the term substitute mother or substitute father when it refers to someone of the same sex as the parent being replaced, for example, a nanny. Or, in the case of one-parent families where the single parent has to be him or herself and also the substitute other. The purpose of this paper is to demonstrate how unresolved psychological problems in the father interfere with his rôle as a loving father. The two clinical examples presented represent the two extreme ends of the spectrum of the inappropriate way in which a father may respond

167

to the child's needs, wishes, feelings and fantasies.

At one end are those fathers like Michael's who act out their unresolved sexual feelings, which are aroused in them by their infant's sexuality. The other extreme is occupied by those fathers who defend against the feelings aroused in them by rejecting the child, as was John's experience. I believe that the midpoint of the spectrum is where we find the loving father who is neither seduced nor frightened by the infant's needs and wishes, and who responds in a way that is appropriate to the infant-father relationship. It is outside the scope of this paper to discuss what the effect of an inappropriate response by the father to the infant has on the future sexual development and identity of the child. The clinical material provided suggests some of the problems that may result.

Very briefly I would like to give three reasons why I think the subject of the pre-Oedipal father is important from the point of view of analytical technique.

1. Unless the early infant-father relationship is examined and analysed, the analyst is denying the patient—and himself—an important area of the patient's early life experience.

2. The analyst's understanding of some of the transference phenomena will be different. This in turn affects the interpretations and reconstructions he gives to the patient.

3. The later difficulties that the patient experiences in mature sexual identity will be better understood.

Summary

With the help of clinical material obtained from two male patients in therapy at the same time, the concept of the loving father is examined. Both patients presented with a fear of being homosexual. It gradually became clear during the therapy that both of them were searching for a loving father. It is suggested that the rôle of the loving father is the capacity to accept that it is the baby's right to bring to him all its needs, wishes, fantasies and feelings but not to expect the baby to deal with his own mainly unconscious needs, wishes, fantasies and feelings that are inappropriate to that relationship. It is further suggested that this is one of the qualities possessed by the good-enough pre-Oedipal father.

References

Abelin, E.L. (1975). 'Some further observations and comments on the earliest rôle of the father', *Int. J. Psychoanal.,* 56 (3).

Burlingham, D. (1973).'The pre-oedipal infant-father relationship', in *Psychoanal. Study Child,* 28. London, Hogarth Press.

Greenacre, P. (1966). 'Problems of over-idealization of the analyst and of analysis', in *Psychoanal. Study Child,* 21. London, Hogarth Press.

Mahler, M.S., Pine F., Bergman A. (1975). *The Psychological Birth of the Human Infant.* London, Hutchinson.

Winnicott, D. W. (1960). 'Ego distortion in terms of true and false self', in *The Maturational Processes and the Facilitating Environment.* London, Hogarth Press, 1965.

Winnicott, D.W. (1971). *Playing and Reality.* London, Tavistock.

The concealed body language of anorexia nervosa

BANI SHORTER

I would ask the reader to bear Layland's paper in mind when reading Shorter's working out of a similar theme in relation to the daughter, though from her quite different point of view. Hers is the first of three papers that make much of a collective angle on observable personal problems. The paper is interesting for the way it explores the psyche/body link, leading to suggestions of an imaginal body and an embodied psyche. Sometimes analytical psychology neglects physical symptomatology but not here. The reader may struggle with the use of myth and it may be worth pointing out that myths are regarded as root metaphors for basic patterns of human emotion and behaviour. The intent is not to use the myth to fix or ground clinical material but rather to open it up, leading to all manner of suggestive possibilities. To the personal perspective of psychoanalysis (Layland) is added a perspective upon the personal. Our understanding of eating disorders is, hopefully, increased. Shorter's paper is also an attempt to see a balance of the maternal and the paternal in the aetiology of anorexia. *A.S.*

ACCORDING TO some stories, after the Medusa had been slain, Athene wore the severed head upon her breast. Over the shoulders of the goddess was slung the goatskin, the aegis, which represented both armour and authority. Either hanging from it like a trophy or emblazoned upon the hide was the hideous head of the Gorgon encircled by writhing snakes. Later statues show the same moonshaped face engraved upon Athene's shield.

Thus defended, she advanced. Earliest Mycenean art, possibly including more archaic representations of Athene, shows an armed goddess nearly obscured by her enormous shield. But in those days there was no suggestion of the Gorgon's head. This was the plunder of a later time when the chthonic, stultifying power of the threatening earth spirit had been overcome. Perhaps the change from dangling trophy to etched symbol suggests a civilizing influence made possible by the perspective of distance from that encounter. Kerenyi (1978, p.67) saw in Athene's use of the emblem not only the moon-face of a winged deity (for such were the Gorgons) but also the motif of the head taken as booty and feminine mask.

I have given this description because we can see the familiar syndrome of anorexia nervosa reflected in the image of Athene and, figuratively speaking, it is as a person holding the Gorgon shield that we meet an anorexic woman first of all. Characteristically, she appears in maiden form, advancing with tremendous authority and power, like a goddess, hidden behind a formidable defence, ready to attack, always on guard. And, as part of her protective armour, she presents a most distorted face, sign of conquest as well as mask of her real features.

A woman suffering from anorexia nervosa resists her natural mother, resists being a mother, and resists mothering. Her defence is expressed outwardly as defiant, wilful denial of the flesh, excessive drive, and almost superhuman striving. On the psychological level, she combines an inflation of omnipotence with a frustrating sense of not being able to live up to expectations. And, in physical terms, her rejection of motherhood manifests itself in amenorrhoea, and in an emaciation of the body that erases any trace of feminine contour; while, at the same time, she engages in ceaseless, wakeful activity.

It was armed with the Gorgon shield that Athene entered the Greek world. Zeus, the greatest of the gods, was her father, and Metis, her mother, was considered 'the most knowing of all beings'. Fearful that a child of Metis might prove to be even wiser than he, Zeus took the precaution of swallowing the mother when the child was still in her womb. Released at last, Athene sprang from the forehead of her father, fully armed. As woman, she was both martial maiden and maternal protector. Although disinclined to love and marriage, she became the resourceful companion of great men and was known as the guardian of heroes. She seems to have emerged at a threshold between two worlds or states of being, a transitional figure between mother and father realms.

In that dark period when the might of the earth goddess was overthrown, Athene appeared, radiant of bearing, a civilizing agent. But, first of all, she came as conqueror and protectress against the archaic, earthbound aspect of woman. She represented a new style of femininity and was able to hold her own against regressive tendencies. It is in this rôle that we hear her speak to the vengeful Furies, the crones whose static law she undoes:

> I will bear with your anger. You are older. The years have taught you more, much more than I can know. But Zeus, I think, gave me some insight, too, that has its merits ...
>
> Here in our homeland never cast the stones that wet our blood lust. Never waste our youth, inflaming them with the burning wine of strife. Never pluck the heart of the battle cock and plant it in our people ...
>
> This is the life I offer, it is yours to take. Do great things, feel greatness, greatly honoured. (Aeschylus, *The Eumenides*, tr. Eagles, R., p. 269)

These are strong, assertive words; yet Athene is more than a divine warrior and even her exercise of authority is persuasive. She curses civil strife and is the declared enemy of Ares, god of war. At home or abroad she deplores the onrush of battle, the savagery of armed conflict. To see her only as one who advances with the shield is to misread her message or to allow a part to speak for the whole.

Instead, as goddess of wisdom, Athene provides leadership

which counsels, tempers and moulds outcomes. When there is tension, she supplies the clarifying insight needed for decision-making. She causes reflection in the moment, reflection that leads to prudent action. With these attributes she won the epithet *Glaukopis*, bright-eyed, and the sign of her presence was the owl, a bird that finds its way in the dark and sees all round.

Psychologically, Athene brings illuminating perception, the product of reflection in terms of long range and meaningful objectives. For her interests are on the side of applied consciousness. Hers is a civilizing influence. She pays attention to the outcome of the deed and in this way she both guides and relates to these favourites.

Perseus was one of these favourites. When he set out to slay the Medusa, Athene gave him a polished shield to use as mirror lest he be transfixed by sight of the Gorgon's features. Thus she destroyed the Medusa, by producing an instrument for reflection at the crucial moment, and, so, she acquired the trophy. The battle wasn't won either by brute force or calculated logic, but by the insight which made possible immediate, inspired, and ennobling action. In classical Jungian terms, we might say that Athene facilitates reflection which attends upon effective realization of the self.

We see a distortion of this image in the syndrome of anorexia nervosa. Here the patient seems to have undertaken a self-conscious *opus contra naturam*, the realization of spirit by the destruction of matter; and the heroism of Athene, with all its possibilities for the discovery and fulfilment of meaning, is subverted to a single purpose, that of conquest over the feminine body. The anorexic woman looks at her emaciated form but sees something different, a different reality; and, without reflection, she cannot make a wise or informed decision. Moreover, all that suggests companionship, warmth, involvement and caring appears disgusting and unclean to her. She applies herself to ritualized abstention and/or purgation and, as a consequence, becomes increasingly isolated. She detaches herself from meaningful relationship, whether that relationship is to herself, to someone else, to study or to work. So in this way she turns aside from the civilizing opportunities that Athene offers. Wisdom no longer counsels; body commands.

Probably no one archetypal image ever creates or cures an illness. Psychopathologies, like gods, act and interact, combine and recombine with infinite variations. But it is from the perspective of Athene that I would like to consider anorexia nervosa. For this illness, too, belongs to a threshold. Its onset most frequently coincides with adolescence. Like the appearance of Athene, it manifests itself at the intersection of two epochs in feminine life, two worlds, one characterized by the influence of woman and the other by the influence of man.

Before she reaches puberty, a girl expresses herself in conformity or nonconformity to an undifferentiated mother-father ideal. But with the coming of adolescence a change takes place. When she begins to menstruate, she who has been daughter becomes mother, ready and capable of receiving, bearing, giving birth and nurturing. At the same time, the destiny of her life, its direction and decision, confront her in a new way for she is also capable of being mistress, lover, and wife. She can attract, select, allow or reject relationships with men. She is a woman and her virginity is exposed. This is a moment that older and less sophisticated societies prepared for with initiation ceremonies and, by way of ritual, provided a tool, a language for expressing the passage of a changed being into a new world.

Now, in modern times, anorexia nervosa is on the increase. Is this because mothers no longer prepare their daughters to *be* women, wives, and mothers? Is it that women are now presented with new opportunities and pressures for expressing their femininity in ways radically different from those of previous generations? Do we stand at a point somehow reminiscent of the transition occasioned by the slaying of the earth goddess and the advent of masculine consciousness? Or have we no fathers capable of giving birth to daughters who can play the rôle of transitional women?

For anorexia nervosa is a disturbance of a woman's being in the world as a woman, although it involves more than her overt sexuality. There are, in fact, comparatively few cases of anorexia nervosa recorded in men, when probably the reverse is true. It is possible that in these cases the primary disturbance is in a man's relationship to the anima and the rôle that Athene plays there. But amongst women the illness begins most frequently, as Hilde Bruch has observed (1978) and my own work suggests, with an unmet challenge, and the nature of that challenge has to do with the loss of psychological virginity. In *The Virgin Archetype* John Layard summarizes: '...the word *virgin* does not mean chastity but the reverse, the pregnancy of nature, free and uncontrolled, corresponding on the human plane to unmarried love, [and] in contrast to controlled nature, corresponding to married love' (1972).

From my experience, if you listen to the fantasies of women who have suffered from anorexia nervosa, read their writings or receive their dreams—even if you do so long after the crisis of adolescence has passed—it is impossible not to be impressed by the strong impact of the threshold of adolescence upon their continuing self-image. For example, when she was in hospital, a young woman of seventeen wrote of herself, describing how it had been a few years earlier: 'Love exchanged its bonds for shackles of obligation and I submitted and suppressed myself to the figures who sweated obscenities and grabbed out for what they wanted, never noticing their dirty hands.' And one of the most telling biographies was shared with me by a person now in her forties, mother of three. It ended with the following: 'Ever since I was a teenager I have felt like I had to win. Winning implies competition. I have been competing against myself. The self that wore the armour has been competing against the other self that is me.'

Traditionally, both in diagnoses and in treatment, the nature of the triggering challenge for anorexia nervosa has been seen as the demand for a girl to become a woman, lover, wife and mother. But there is a somewhat moralistic tone in the way doctors have written about their anorexic patients. In 1903 Janet perceptively described a case of 'mental anorexia' but suggested that the illness showed the patient's *refusal* to play a feminine sexual rôle. Freud defined the disease as 'melancholia of the sexually immature'. What has not been acknowledged, and what the image of Athene suggests, is that in these women an archetypal image has been activated that prompts them to live out a sexual rôle which is a different one from that of the prevailing cultural expectation.

In my own work I was alerted to this possibility by the way

176

anorexic women first spoke of themselves, by their pictures and by their dreams. With hindsight I now see more in the latent symbolism than I recognized initially. *But what struck me forcefully was the strong influence of the father upon the lives of the daughters who came for therapy.*

From the outset, the image of the father occupied a position of exaggerated importance in the psychic life of these women. One described her father as a forbidding judge who beat his child without mercy when she failed to come up to his expectations. I heard another speak of her father as a rapist and paedophile, a man who seduced little girls into mountain huts or dark cellars. Others portrayed their fathers in glowing terms and described a similar saintly figure, a spiritual leader of extraordinary patience and forbearance. He was presented as a potential head of state, an arbitrator and conciliator among nations. Yet others saw the father as a misunderstood genius whose talents were unrecognized either by his family or his colleagues. He could be a ne'er-do-well and a failure in the eyes of society, but the same man would be a father of awesome and dramatic significance for his anorexic daughter. And the father figures who appeared in dreams were especially powerful. They included Alexander the Great, leaders of mountain climbing expeditions, conductors of great symphonies, wardens of concentration camps, mystics, and liege lords.

These women also defined themselves in father terms. Their aspirations and motivations had a masculine character. Some could even admit to wishing that they had been born men rather than women; though there was seldom much of the tomboy or the homosexual about them. But they emulated men and, if married, wanted to walk alongside (rather than sleep with) their husbands. I heard a man describe his anorexic wife as the only woman he knew who had borne three children and remained a virgin; she referred to these same children as her husband's rather than her own.

Such expressions have led me to examine the nature of the incestuous link between anorexic daughters and their fathers. The actual father's attitudes and his behaviour appear to be determinative in the way the daughter considers and conducts her life. Sexually, these women hold themselves aloof and chaste,

177

but psychologically they are bonded to the father image, and the strength of that unacknowledged incestuous bond is of such proportion that it compels them to adopt a sacrificial attitude of spirit, a purity of body, and an abstinence from involvement with intercourse and childbearing. The anorexic woman is relentlessly committed to holding a special and favoured place in relation to man, although her rôle may be closer to that of the priestess than the paramour; and with her allegiance, her devoted ritual ablutions, her striving, and her loyalty, she tries to assure herself of recognition in man's hierarchy of values. Analytically, we see this as a primary disturbance of the animus, both in its activation and expression.

Again and again, anorexia nervosa has been called *wrong thinking*. From the time it was first written about by an English physician in the seventeenth century, it has been described as an illness of the mind that affects the body (Palazzoli, 1978). Doctors, psychiatrists, and religious leaders, no less than family members, have been confounded and distressed by the tenacity of a conviction that compels a wanton wasting away of the flesh. The behaviour of the anorexic woman has been labelled illogical and the patient's attitude interpreted as stubborn. The emphasis on 'wrong thinking' still persists in diagnosis and therapy even if the focus has been shifted from mind to behaviour and from individual to family. And, although elaborate attention has been given to psychoanalytic investigations, almost no one has tried to piece together the coherence of a story that is being told from within the recesses of the patient's own psyche.

The notable exception to this, of course, is the celebrated 'Case of Ellen West' by Ludwig Binswanger. It is a case which corroborates much of my own thesis (although undertaken initially from a very different point of view, that of psychiatry) and it has been presented as an example of existential analysis. Significantly, however, that case begins with the sentence, 'Ellen West, a non-Swiss, is the only daughter of a Jewish father for whom her love and veneration know no bounds.' This was an observation that—unfortunately, I feel—Binswanger did not follow up (1958).

Trying to unravel the story I was being told by my patients from within, I found that at the beginning of treatment both patients and I were struggling with the language in which their innermost selves were striving to communicate. For these women seemed to have little contact with the reality of psyche as such; its place had been usurped by the flesh of their misshapen bodies. The fleshly figure dominated their lives, and what I was trying to do was to hold a mirror to an image they couldn't see. Yet, out of the basic discrepancy between what the analysand was telling herself and what was being enacted before my eyes, a pattern of certain well-marked characteristics emerged.

I found that the image for a woman suffering from anorexia nervosa is one in which, by way of flesh, her soul has been sacrificed to the patriarchal spirit and, at another level, fantasy is held captive by a chaste and celibate marriage of image and symptom. She is incapable of imagining that she can be other than she is and, so, is caught on a psychological threshold which cannot be crossed. As a woman she finds it impossible to step through the adolescent barrier of mystery and fear to a place where experience can become realized as a new world; and, because of her terror, she takes refuge in identification with her aggressor. This means that she is fixed at a point of entry, remains always on a border, somehow suspended and playing out a rôle for which she has no natural talent. It is an arrested image, starved of individual significance.

The summation of what I observed can be expressed in clinical terms as the fixation of delusion. In personal terms it is a failed initiation which results in a paralysing state of ineffectiveness. From another point of view, the anorexic woman is Athene, swallowed and not yet born. Analytically, this manifests itself as a state of possession in which the animus has usurped control of the personality.

Writing about this dark consequence in mythological terms, Kerenyi says:

> It is to the father, then, that the daughter falls victim in this mythic region... he allows her to descend into the darkness. And it is the daughter who offers the sacrifice; *she* descends into a paternal-masculine darkness... the strange image of the devoured wife of Zeus (Metis) also corresponds to a purely human situation; the binding of the daughter to the father

179

out of which the patriarchal order of the family, as opposed to the matriarchal, could most easily arise... That to which one succumbs and falls defencelessly always has a lethal aspect, the more so here where the masculine appears not *graciously* and paternally but aggressively, like the father in [this] father-daughter mythologem [which] lies at the foundation of the Athene religion. (1978, p.43)

The result of such a sacrifice is that a woman lives her life one-sidedly in terms of a masculine principle and the one-sidedness reveals only the active, conscious part of her being. Such a woman becomes a 'man-woman', as one lover of an anorexic girl put it; and therefore, she often appears ambitious and over zealous. If well enough, she may achieve a great deal academically, in the performing arts, in politics, or in literature. But one notices her creativity is employed in service to a goal which is a projection of her own masculine ideal. Somehow that drive is never mediated by the warmth, the surprise, the pain, or the mystery that are associated with the natural process of childbearing.

The contrast with another kind of womanhood is reflected in the contrast of Hera and Athene, wife and daughter of Zeus. Kerenyi (1978, p.58) helps us to see how they represent two different aspects of feminine being. 'Hera's essence in its fullest development was the full moon', he writes. 'From the viewpoint of Athene, the most essential phase is the exact opposite, the darkest night preceding her birth.' It is this darkness of no reflection against which the anorexic woman is so heavily defended. She has been blinded by the sun of too great an emphasis on masculinity and, being in a defensive position, gives the impression of having no depth, living on the surface, being on the alert, ever wakeful.

During the past few years I have met women who have been exposed to a spectrum of treatment ranging from prolonged hospitalization and forced feeding to systems analysis and family encounter, and as I have worked with them I have been persuaded that if this kind of patient chooses and can tolerate a psychotherapeutic relationship, she belongs in analysis. Here I would like to refer again to the longstanding definition of anorexia

180

nervosa as *wrong thinking*. In my experience, anorexia nervosa is not a disturbance of mind and thought, but a disturbance of psyche and reflection. It is a 'soul problem', but a soul problem of a particular kind, which is summarized as loss of reflection; metaphorically this may be expressed as a disturbance of sun and moon. The moon no longer reflects the sun. It is possessed by the sun instead. For a woman, that condition amounts to 'loss of soul'.

We in analytical psychology do not attempt to find answers to the disturbing and recurrent problems of psychiatry so much as to suggest approaches to perplexing borderlines of psychic development, and we do our work by way of reflected images, constantly observing how they are perceived. Therapy with the anorexic patient must be oriented toward the restoration of imagination and the reflective capacity though, as we all know, attempts at psychological forced feeding are almost never successful. It seems that if therapy is to succeed at all, it has to focus attention elsewhere than on symptoms, concerning itself with events in depth rather than with surface appearances.

Here it is important to differentiate between the structure of delusion and the image contained in the structure. Analysis properly concerns itself with images; that is to say, with the content of what is perceived and with its reflection. The observation of a process in which formerly unconscious contents claim attention and enforce awareness is part of the work involved in analysis. And there is implied in this work a position of importance for fantasy and imagination which is the key issue in the activation of reflection and, so, of psychic movement for the person fixed in delusion. Jung writes: 'The richness of the human psyche and its essential character are probably determined by [the] reflective instinct ... through [which] the stimulus is more or less wholly transformed into a psychic content; that is, it becomes an experience' (*CW* 8, paras 242-3).

In this statement Jung refers to the role of reflection in the process of *apperception*, which he further defines as 'a psychic process by which a new content is articulated with similar, existing contents in such a way that it becomes understood, apprehended or clear.' He distinguishes between active and passive apperception, the first being 'a process by which the subject of his own accord and from his own motives, consciously apprehends a new content' and the second 'a process by which a new content forces itself upon consciousness either from without (through the senses) or from within (from the unconscious) and, as it were, compels attention and enforces apprehension' (*CW* 6, para. 683). Analysis attends the latter.

Initially an anorexic woman is arrested in direct encounter with a fixed image, and she lacks an instrument of reflection with which her gaze can be diverted and her perceptions prevented, like those of Perseus, from turning to stone. In this state she is cut off from the civilizing influence of reflection which would enforce apprehension. In analysis, the familiar reflector is the dream, which can mirror psyche to reality and reality to psyche without the intervention of moral judgement. By the indirection of its commentary, its fascination and self-enforcing character, the dream has the possibility of attracting the overconscious attention of the patient. With a person suffering from anorexia nervosa, this means that if the gaze can be deflected from its fixation upon body imagery to the enigmatic imagery of the dream, psychic movement may again become possible. If this happens, psyche will, paradoxically, assume body (as distinct from spirit) and at the same time acquire a meaning distinct from flesh.

'To see', wrote Merleau-Ponty in his last published essay (1974), 'is to have at a distance.' This, too, is an attribute of Athene's wisdom. She intervenes; she stays the hand upon the sword, she restrains the eagerness to engage and keeps at a distance until counsel can be taken, the plan of the gods revealed. In the therapy situation there is always danger that with its orientation towards action, the impulsive animus of the anorexic patient will seize upon insight and apply it for heroic purposes. The work of the therapist is to encourage distance and detached reflection until perception changes by the *self-enforcement* of new psychic content.

This new content usually makes its initial appearance by way of a dream image that not only attracts attention but releases imagination; for it is imagination that breaks the bounds of a given reality. And once the constricting form of existing reality is loosed, there is a possibility that it can be perceived in a new way. Therapy with anorexic women involves the loosening of the hold of delusion by allowing attraction to new images and fantasizing about them. Importantly, this will involve choicemaking.

Psychic images have a way of presenting alternatives, suggesting first one possibility and then another. Where there are alternatives, choices must be made, and questions of significance and meaning inevitably arise. With questions of significance and meaning the cultural and civilizing potential of Athene has a chance to reassert itself.

If there is a play of changing images which involve choicemaking, psychic movement is restored, and some sort of breakthrough or personal initiation is possible. In this connection, when working with anorexic patients more so than when working with others, I have been struck by the way significant rituals have been devised and spontaneously enacted to safeguard the initiatory passage between two states of being, the old and new. These spontaneous ceremonies often have an archaic and mythic resonance, but they arise within an individual context which makes them memorable. In these ceremonies I find evidence that the person has been released from her identification with her delusion and has begun to speak the language of her individual self.

What I have been describing is a process which is familiar to the analyst. 'The most remarkable thing about this method', wrote Jung, '[is] that it [does] not involve a *reductio in primam figuram* but rather a synthesis—supported by an attitude voluntarily adopted, though for the rest wholly natural—of passive conscious material and unconscious influences, hence a kind of spontaneous amplification of the archetypes' (*CW* 8, para. 403). This quotation leads to my final point in support of analysis for cases involving anorexia nervosa. To me, the body language of the anorexic patient conveys an ontological obsession no less bizarre than that of the fakir or mystic, but it can also be spoken of in Eliade's words (1959, p.94) as 'at once [a] thirst for the sacred and [a] nostalgia for being.' To contradict it is to deprive a woman of significance, for contradiction separates her from her living myth, without which there is no chance of psychological survival. If her story is allowed to unfold itself naturally, however, we can see that she will fulfil herself *primarily* (though never entirely) within the context of an Athene image and this carries with it both promise and responsibility.

If anorexic women see this possibility, in its fullest sense, they are able to enter into themselves. However, a purely intellectual understanding is not enough. The long, slow work of analysis may succeed in release from the bond of identification with the aggressor, though that bond will remain a threat from within the confines of the shadow. However, these women can now face other women without shame, recognizing they are different from those who fulfil other images such as those of Hera, Aphrodite, or even the virgin Artemis. They realize that suffering the constraints of certain boundaries nevertheless enables them to explore new borders of individual and feminine expression.

Each of the goddesses has her own style, her own way of being in the world, and you will remember my reference to Athene as having emerged at a threshold, a transitional figure between two states of being, between mother and father realms. 'She is what she is,' Kerenyi (1978) wrote of this goddess, 'fully apart from whether she ever belongs to a man or not.' What this means for anorexic patients in therapy is that they need to come to terms with their animus identification and allow the male spirit to counsel and inspire, rather than to dominate, the proper work of the animus being not the *pursuit* of consciousness but its *realization*. At the same time, with these women, allowance has to be made for independence, since it reflects psychological virginity, and when that allowance is made they can be valuable, supportive companions in relationship. Like Athene, such women have the resources to meet the challenge of new possibilities with inventiveness, though their forthrightness and assertiveness must be tempered by *reflected* wisdom if they are to remain true to their feminine nature. These are women of action, and today especially they are drawn to the forefront of change.

The archetypal image provides a theme upon which an individual plays infinite variations. And yet, the Athene image holds the possibility of combining strongly opposed tendencies. When it can be sustained, analysis provides the experience of becoming acquainted with *both* sides of an opposed nature. This process

184

in anorexia nervosa is illustrated by the dream of a woman who worked with me for two and a half years. Near the end of her analysis she dreamed:

> I came out of the forest and stood on the edge of a lighted clearing. Here I saw two handsome horses. One was dark, high-spirited and unruly. The other was chestnut coloured, lively, well formed and intelligent. This was a training ground and these horses were being trained. But there weren't any fences and there wasn't a trainer. Instead, the horses moved round the circle themselves. What was happening fascinated me. When one of the horses stepped out of line or failed to keep pace, the other reached across and nudged him back into place. In this way they moved round and round the circle, training themselves.

The dream says many things and, like most dreams, speaks both to analyst and analysand. Athene's connection with the horse is well known: at times she was worshipped as mistress of horses (Otto, 1979). Reflecting upon the dream when it was received, however, I was reminded that the bridle, too, was one of her gifts to man.

References

Aeschylus. 'The Eumenides', in *The Oresteia*, trans. Eagles, R. Harmondsworth, Penguin, 1976.

Binswanger, L. (1958). 'The case of Ellen West', trans. Mendel, W., Lyons, J., in *Existence* ed. May, R., Angel, E., Ellenberger, H. New York, Simon & Schuster.

Bruch, H. (1978). *The Golden Cage: The Enigma of Anorexia Nervosa*. London, Open Books.

Eliade, M. (1959). *The Sacred and the Profane*, trans. Trask, W. New York, Harcourt, Brace.

Kerenyi, K. (1978). *Athene: Virgin and Mother*. Zürich, Spring Publications.

Layard, J. (1972). *The Virgin Archetype*. Zürich, Spring Publications.

Merleau-Ponty, M. (1974). 'Eye and mind', trans. Dallery, C. in *Phenomenology, Language and Sociology: Collected Essays*, Ed. O'Neill, J. London, Heinemann.

185

Otto, W. (1979). *The Homeric Gods,* trans. Hadas, M. London, Thames and Hudson.

Palazzoli, M. (1978). *Self-Starvation,* trans. Pomerans, A. New York, Jason Aronson.

The archetypal masculine: its manifestation in myth, and its significance for women

BARBARA GREENFIELD

Though this writer does not incorporate the clinical dimension, the ingenuity of the central idea is of considerable interest. She cuts across the often fruitless debate about what is or is not 'essential' regarding masculinity and femininity by offering an analysis of what is the case. In other words, she takes the position of a psychologically oriented cultural phenomenologist. She dissects what our culture has understood and understands by masculinity, and her subdividing of this enormous theme is extremely useful. Her evocation at depth of what we mean by masculinity is both timely and vital for a book on the father. 'The trickster' may require some explanation (it is a favourite motif of Jungians). Many cultures, but notably American Indians, produce legendary or mythic figures which are characterized by their extreme primitivity and possession of magical powers. Such personages have not achieved a state of consciousness and are rather infantile. At the same time, in the way the trickster disobeys every aspect of reality, he is a symbol for the psyche itself (cf. *CW* 9i). *A.S.*

MOST OF US who were duly socialized in the gender traditions of Western culture grew up learning to characterize certain aspects of reality as 'masculine' and others as 'feminine'. Sometimes the source of this categorization can clearly be traced to biological differences between the sexes, or to the different positions held by women and men in society. At a certain point, however, the categories of 'masculine' and 'feminine' take on a life of their own; in other words, culture elaborates upon simple differences until an entire *mythos* is created. Our current gender stereotypes, of course, come out of a long tradition of Western myth, and are thus invested with a great deal of psychological significance. If we are to be concerned with modifying these stereotypes, then we must begin by attempting to understand as deeply as possible not only the nature of our cultural myths and categories, but also their significance for the psychological development of the individual.

One useful way of psychologically analysing cultural myths, stereotypes and images is to reduce them to their most basic underlying principles in the manner of Jungian psychology. Jung's method of pulling together disparate segments of experience into single, unified metaphorical structures called archetypes will help to define the essential features of cultural stereotypes which continue to structure much of our thought. Much work has already been done in Jungian and post-Jungian psychology discussing the meaning of the archetype of woman and the effect of this archetype on men (e.g., Neumann's *The Great Mother* (1955), or Lederer's *The Fear of Women* (1968)). Very little work, however, has been done to analyse the archetype of man—the animus—and the meaning of this archetype for women. Although Neumann, Campbell and others have written extensively about the figure of the hero, theirs have been incomplete treatments of the manifold forms of the archetypal (traditional) masculine.

In response to the dearth of analysis of the animus, the present paper seeks to construct a characterization of the archetypal masculine by looking at the way in which it is traditionally presented in our heritage of myths and literature.

Whereas the archetypal feminine has usually been associated with the unconscious, one finds that the masculine is associated in myth and cultural tradition with the ego and its functions. Since the ego shows obvious development in individuals as they mature, the expression of the ego as the archetypal masculine takes various forms which correspond to various stages of ego development. These include the boy, Don Juan, the trickster, the hero, the father, and the wise old man. Thus, the archetypal masculine will be discussed in terms of its various levels of development, its major characteristics, and its rôle in the psychological development of women. Emma Jung has also noted that women have a variety of experiences of the animus, although she attributes this to the fact that men assume a wide variety of professional roles (1957).

The Nature of the Archetype

It may be wisest to begin by describing the archetype in its most stripped down and essential form. Neumann (*op. cit.*) has characterized the archetypal feminine as self-contained, material, enclosing, and static. By contrast, then, we may characterize the archetypal masculine as an *intrusive, active* principle that pushes the development of consciousness out of primal undifferentiation and unity with the mother. Unlike the anima, this male principle is *mental* rather than material, pertaining to activated spirit, intellect, and will. In short, those aspects of the psyche that we characterize as ego are traditionally identified with the masculine. Quite possibly the identification of the feminine with earlier, unconscious stages of the mind and the masculine with later, more developed stages arose out of a cultural situation in which women were given the primary responsibility for early child-rearing and men did not play an important rôle until later on: we can only speculate what sorts of identifications might be produced by a society in which child care was shared equally between the sexes.

One way to conceptualize the animus is to see it as being composed of mental elements which are expressed in an *active* mode via *intrusive* and *generative* behaviours. These mental elements consist primarily of intellect and will, which, as Neumann suggests, begin by an act of negation. This negation is the denial of being identified with the primal, maternal feminine, to say, 'I am *not*

189

that.' It involves differentiating between self and other or, more precisely, self and mother. The creation of this split is often characterized in myth as the birth of opposites and the first expression of human will in the form of disobedience (straying from natural order to human order). It is this same primal will and intelligence that is responsible for creating a universe out of chaos by imposing order upon it; the word or order (*Logos*) generates the transformation and differentiation of the world, the first movement out of the self-contained slumber of the feminine.

As with any awakening, literal or figurative, the effect of this is to disturb or stir up the given state of the world and transform it, and to aggress in constructive and sexual functions. The active mode is expressed in myth as the mobility of the hero (e.g., fleet-footed Mercury, or the picaro). The spirit aspect of the animus may appear in myth as the wind or breath that animates inanimate matter. The Creator puts the 'breath of life' into man to mobilize him and give him consciousness; the Creator himself appears first in the Bible as a wind or spirit moving over the waters (which may be taken to symbolize the uroboric feminine). Neumann calls this form of the masculine the 'procreative wind-ruach-pneuma-animus, which animates through inspiration' (Neumann, 1954).

The active mode of functioning of the animus results in behaviours which have an intrusive and generative character. This is, of course, most obvious in sexuality; in its positive form the masculine is that which impregnates and creates, and in its negative form that which rapes and destroys. At the beginning of time in myth, Father Sky does all of these, and this introduction of the male seed initiates not only the birth of an inhabited world, but also the birth of world order. Male generativity is thus identified with the creation of structure and oppositions and is not purely a matter of physical impregnation. Jung suggests this when he writes,

> The animus is the deposit, as it were, of all woman's ancestral experiences of man—and not only that, he is also a creative and procreative being, not in the sense of masculine creativity, but in the sense that he brings forth something we might call

190

the *Logos spermaticos*, the spermatic word. (*CW7*, para. 551)

This generativity through the introduction of structure is also reflected in later transformations of nature which characterize as builder or creator. Again, this generativity is identified with masculine intrusiveness or aggressiveness in the sense that man creates his own world through the conquest of nature. Since nature is often associated with the feminine, it is appropriate that this domination of nature, when taken to extremes, is characterized as rape. In its benevolent form, this aggressiveness is expressed as mastery or competence, and is a reflection of ego strength.

Since the archetypal masculine is identified with the ego, it is given conscious expression in myth as various male figures who represent the ego at different stages of development. All of these figures, however, incorporate to some degree all of the principles named above which distinguish the ego: will, intelligence, activity, intrusiveness, and generativity. In myth, of course, these abstract terms are given meaning through their embodiment in mythological characters. The boy, Don Juan, and the trickster show us the ego in its early stages of development, while the hero, the father and the wise old man represent later stages of development. As a whole, the animus, or male archetype, unifies these disparate figures because it exists as those principles which underlie them all.

The most powerful mythological forms of the archetype, and certainly the most important forms from the standpoint of a psychology of women, are those of the father and trickster (Jung saw these as being two separate archetypes, but the trickster is rather an early incarnation of the father). The boy is not extremely significant for adults because he represents such an early phase of the ego. Don Juan borders on being a trickster, whereas the hero borders on being a father; and the wise old man, being so old and developed that he is ready to return to the uroboros, is beyond the experience of most adults. Thus, the father and the trickster stand out most clearly as representatives of different and sometimes opposing aspects of the masculine. They also correspond roughly to Emma Jung's characterizations of 'upper' and 'lower' animus (*op. cit.*). When

C. G. Jung speaks of the animus bringing forth the spermatic word, we might say that the 'word' component belongs to the father, while the 'spermatic' component belongs to the trickster. The trickster represents the infancy of consciousness, mobility, the penis, and the transformation of nature; the father figure encompasses the rôles of creator, lawgiver, impregnator, and master. Whereas the father is the lawgiver, and stands for order or even for repression, the trickster is the lawbreaker who represents the expression of instinctual desires. The opposition of these two is seen especially clearly in the relationship of the masculine to women. The masculine as a father is a protector, benefactor or owner whose protectiveness may become restrictive and whose power may overwhelm (as in the burning of Semele). The trickster, on the other hand, is a liberator through the force of his expressiveness, but may also be a deceiver, seducer, or thief. He is a son more than a father, and this youthfulness is the basis for much of his appeal. On a political level, the trickster is also the son who overthrows the authority of the father in the name of freedom and transformation; often this is symbolically achieved in the form of castration. Sometimes, however, the power of the father wins out and it is the trickster who must undergo mutilation.

At this point, it will be most useful to examine the development of the archetypal masculine as it appears in myth, paying particular attention to the figures of the father and the trickster. It will become obvious that the same ego traits of will, intelligence, activity, intrusiveness and generativity are present at each level of development of the masculine, but in varying proportions. The tricks which characterize a trickster, for example, are an early manifestation of the *logos* of the father, whereas a wise old man like Merlin may still display much of the trickster's playfulness. The path of development of the archetype is best conceived of as a cycle beginning with the emergence out of the uroboros and continuing in its development into forms such as the boy, the trickster, the father and finally the old man, whose death is identical with a return to the uroboros. It is for this reason that the image of the uroboric snake is so often shown as biting its own tail.

The Development of the Archetype in Myth and Literature

The birth of ego consciousness is simultaneous with the birth of the cosmos just as in the individual the birth of ego consciousness is the beginning of his, or her, world through the creation of individual self-awareness. On all levels the birth of ego consciousness is initiated by the forces of emotion. For Freud, this emotion consists of frustrations suffered by the newborn; in Hesiod's *Theogony,* this emotion is desire, which activates the union of Mother Earth and Father Sky. Jung writes: 'Emotion is the moment when steel meets flint and a spark is struck forth, for emotion is the chief source of consciousness. There is no change from darkness to light or from inertia to movement without emotion' (*CW* 9i).

In many myths about a primordial Golden Age, which corresponds to the infantile state of feeling united with the mother and having all one's needs met by her, the blissful ignorance of paradise is destroyed when emotion disrupts the status quo and forces human consciousness into existence. Usually this emotion is personified as a woman, as in the case of Eve and Pandora, and her presence functions to stir the masculine into action by arousing him in psychological and cognitive as well as sexual ways. In fact, the introduction to sexual knowledge produced by the presence of the woman is identified with the introduction to all other types of knowledge. This knowledge is responsible for destroying the primal unity with Mother Earth and is thus seen as a negative act and the origin of all pain and need. There is also the feeling that the disruption of paradise is a betrayal of Mother Earth and a disobeying of the natural order. In this action, human will asserts itself as an independent force for the first time. The loss of innocence is the basis for knowledge, and the feeling of guilt creates the first moral awareness.

In its early stages of development, ego consciousness is a fragile thing that always runs the risk of losing its autonomy and falling back into a state of union with the mother. In Greek and American Indian mythology, and in biblical accounts, the world is destroyed soon after its creation by a flood; because they did not have enough strength of character, the inhabitants of the world were engulfed and metaphorically drawn back into the womb. The figure of the boy in myth also expresses the danger of failing to develop a sufficiently strong and autonomous ego. Metman (1958) has effectively characterized the psychology of the boy in his discussion of incipient ego—i.e., ego at the point where it is just barely independent of the self-mother-ego complex. If the incipient ego cannot acquire its own centre of gravity and develop autonomously, it runs the risk of becoming dominated by other complexes and losing its ability to function.

The Boy

The boy is often depicted in early Greek and Egyptian sculpture as a small phallic figure that accompanies an impressive figure of a fertility goddess. In later Greek mythology, the boy appears as a young, beautiful man who is also a sort of consort of the mother and does not have the strength to achieve a break with her. These 'flower boys' include Hyacinth, whose friendship with Apollo indicates a desire to achieve full male development, but who dies too soon to accomplish it and is reclaimed by the earth; Adonis, who was the beloved companion of Aphrodite until he decided to go hunting by himself and thus died an untimely death in an attempt at autonomy; and Narcissus, who scorned love in order to dwell on his own beauty and ended up pining away because he could not progress out of his fixation. Ganymede escaped this fate because Zeus lifted him out of the reach of Earth into the kingdom of Father Sky, but Orpheus was torn to pieces by raving women. The figure of Jesus derives some of its appeal from being that of a young, beautiful man who died an early and tragic death. In modern terms, the boy takes the form of the suicidal poet of romantic literature and the self-destructive rock musician who lives too fast and too hard. The appeal of the boy for girls is perhaps that he is not only young and beautiful, but that he is not powerful enough to be threatening; he does not have the sort of strong will and intelligence that make the father potentially overwhelming. For older women, the figure of the boy may arouse the desire to mother him; according to Lederer (1968), there are certain types of women who consistently seek out such 'suicidal poet' types as companions.

194

The Trickster: Don Juan

In many respects, the figure of Don Juan is still a boy. Over and over, his compulsion drives him back into the arms of the mother. He is attractive, narcissistic, and dies at a fairly young age. However, it may be seen that Don Juan is a more developed figure in terms of ego strengths than is the boy, which makes him closer to the trickster. First of all Don Juan has explicitly developed sexuality which demonstrates the intrusiveness of the masculine; in comparison, the boy is asexual and androgynous, appealing to both sexes. Don Juan sweeps women off their feet in the kind of dynamic mode of functioning that is characteristic of the masculine, and part of his skill in doing this lies in his ingenuity in tricking women and their fatherly protectors. Don Juan also shows a strength of will that does not exist in the boy; he is an aggressive, self-serving person with defined ambitions. In fact, the nature of his ambition—to conquer as many women as possible—indicates that he is seeking not only to establish independence from the mother but even to gain control over her in the same exploitative way that man sometimes approaches nature. In Metman's terms, Don Juan represents in this capacity the autonomous ego trying to dissociate itself from the self-mother-ego complex and shift the centre of psychic gravity over to itself. Don Juan needs to disparage and control women in order to separate from them psychologically. However, the myth clearly shows that he is still compulsively attached to the mother, creating the irony whereby Don Juan's desire to conquer women ultimately conquers him.

Despite the fact that Don Juan is looked upon as a rascal and must ultimately be overcome and suppressed by the protective father, he nevertheless succeeds in practically all of his attempts to sweep women off their feet. This is because, as a young version of the trickster, he has the appeal of free and explicit sexuality, much as the figure of the whore has appeal for men (the whore, however, receives greater reprobation for her sexuality as a result of the double standard). Don Juan is denounced as a 'devil' because he represents the same temptation of the instinctual and the forbidden for people who are compelled by social taboos to restrict those drives (it is no coincidence that the Don

Juan figure comes out of the highly repressive society of medieval Spain). For such people, sexuality can only be acknowledged when it is blatant, one-sided, and takes the form of a devil who can 'possess' the otherwise innocent (asexual) subject. In a more positive light, an affair with a trickster may allow a woman who had formerly accepted the sexually passive rôle of child-bride to develop a more active and expressive sexuality. It seems likely that in sexually unrestrictive societies, both Don Juan and the whore become less compelling because their function of freeing up sexuality is not needed.

The Trickster and the Father

Another source of Don Juan's appeal is that, as a picaresque trickster, he has no ties to anyone and guards this freedom carefully. The unlikelihood that he will hang around anywhere for very long gives women the protection of anonymity; they feel that they are free to indulge in a fling without worrying that there will be consequences. On the other hand, Don Juan may also present a challenge to women to try to possess his freedom, both in the sense of experiencing it themselves and of capturing his desire. As in the image of the wind carrying off Orithyia or Psyche, the woman who is 'swept away' participates in freedom for a brief while. Note that the princess who is carried off by Prince Charming has usually been spending her days locked up in a tower; today the image is of a housewife who feels locked into her suburban home and has an affair to escape it. If women are kept unnaturally chaste, passive and immobile through the overprotection of the father, they are allured by the picaro's sexuality, activity and mobility; Don Juan trickster figures are thus more compelling in myths and stories than father figures, for they represent liberation from the repressive laws laid down by the father. From the point of view of the unconscious, expression of desire is always more attractive than repression, even if this entails risking the loss of the father's support as provider and protector (the risk, of course, lends dramatic tension to any story). Furthermore, when a woman leaves or disobeys a father to follow a trickster, she asserts herself as an independent person and opens herself to transformation and growth. Unfortunately, the superior and socially sanctioned strength of the father and his patriarchy usually operates in myth to defeat the woman in this endeavour by portraying the experience as a betrayal or a failure. The woman is either left older, sadder and wiser (Natasha in *War and Peace*; the Princess of Cleves; Guinevere) or is destroyed by the experience (Anna Karenina; Hedda Gabler). The failure of the experience is sometimes a result of social pressures against it, but often the woman who has been sheltered all her life is simply not ready for independence, much less with a volatile trickster.

We are just beginning to see works of art emerge in which the woman who leaves a father figure for a trickster is strengthened by the experience (e.g., Atwood's *Lady Oracle* or the film *Coming Home*). In these works, the association with the trickster, i.e., a male figure who is less strong and thus less overpowering than a father while being sexually alluring, is the crucial factor permitting the woman to break out of her dependency on a protector and establish her own independence. This experience is highly meaningful because it forces the woman to develop ego strengths that had formerly always been projected on to a father/husband. In other words, since the father/husband had always dictated certain values and beliefs to the woman, or at least served as an external reference point for values and opinions, the woman may never have had to think for herself. Particularly if she was discouraged from thinking independently, she may have never developed her own individualized, internalized belief system. The trickster is thus useful in that his sexual appeal lures the woman away from the dominance of the father and puts her in a position where she is forced to be autonomous and rely on her own strengths, or develop strengths if she did not have them. According to Ulanov (1971) the trickster may also help a woman to break away from her mother. In this situation it is important that the trickster be a picaro who clearly shows no promise for a permanent relationship; otherwise, the woman might simply transfer her dependency from one person to another, without ever having to find her own strengths. The trickster thus serves as a transitional figure for the woman rather than the life partner.

The trickster, in relation to the father who gives the Law, is

197

the son who breaks it (and, in Oedipal style, often suffers mutilation for it). The trickster represents undeveloped ego, being a creature of instinct and unrepressed, unsublimated desire; for this reason he often takes the form of an animal, i.e., a creature lacking in conscious awareness and self-control.

A useful example of the way a real-life trickster may function has been described by Plaut (1959). Plaut's subject had difficulty with any situation that required him to exercise control over himself or threatened his fragile sense of autonomy. He would use tricks as a way of avoiding responsibility in relationships, or to express sexuality without fear of commitment. He wanted freedom from his desires because so often they would overwhelm him, and he experienced himself as a disunified collection of body zones.

Because the trickster's self-control is relatively underdeveloped, especially with regard to his sexuality, he is often characterized in terms of his penis; usually it is described as being exceptionally long and uncontrollable. In the Winnebago trickster cycle, Trickster's penis behaves as a trickster to Trickster himself (Radin, 1956). Similarly, in the Garden of Eden, a phallic snake functions as a trickster in persuading Eve to eat the apple. Because a trickster has little control of his desires and therefore never represses them, he has symbolic significance as a liberator. However, when this lack of control is combined with masculine intrusiveness, the trickster may also become a rapist.

Trickster's freedom and his sexuality are sometimes given expression by images of a wind or a wanderer who, like Don Juan, 'sweeps away' women as he travels. The wind is, of course, an uncontrolled force, with the effect of stirring nature (often characterized as female) into activity, while the picaro is unbound to society and goes wherever the mood takes him. Both the wind and the wanderer embody the active aspect of the archetypal masculine by their ceaseless motion, and the wind displays the masculine non-material aspect (it is an incarnation of the spirit-wind associated with the father). In a figurative sense, the wanderer is also insubstantial, for he has no possessions or ties to society.

The constant, picaresque mobility of the trickster reflects his lack of full development; the father is a more stable figure by comparison, often to the point of rigidity. Trickster's ceaseless activity also makes him a builder, complementing the creator-father. One learns that a certain rock has special markings because Trickster sat on it, or that the human anus is wrinkled because once Trickster burned his. In this manner, Trickster expressed the generative, building-transforming functions of the archetypal masculine. This function is noted by Erik Erikson in his discussion of the male's *'erecting, constructing* and *elaborating* tendency'* that he observed in the play of young boys. Erikson believes that sex-typed modes of behaviour 'parallel the morphology of the sex organs: in the male, *external* organs, *erectable* and *intrusive* in character, *conducting* highly *mobile* sperm cells' (Erikson, 1963, p. 106). Furthermore, the ingenuity displayed in Trickster's building activities and in the tricks that he is famous for are an early form of masculine intelligence.

The Trickster and the Monster

One guise in which the trickster regularly appears in myth is that of a monster. This is not to be confused with the monster who represents the terrible mother that the hero must kill in order to achieve individuation (Grendel, Medusa, etc.). Instead, when the monster is male and is presented in relation to a woman, a different dynamic occurs. While men fight and defeat monsters in myth, women instead tend to marry them—and often fall in love with them besides. Examples of this are abundant: Zeus rapes Leda in the form of a swan, and carries off Europa in the form of a bull; Hephaestos, the most ugly and misshapen of the Olympians, is given Aphrodite as a wife. Minos' wife Pasiphae falls in love with a bull and gives birth to the Minotaur. In European tales, one finds Beauty who marries the Beast and the princess who kisses the frog. Often, the woman who is offered to a monster is paying for the sins of her parents, which are usually greed or hubris; for example, Psyche and Andromeda are offered to serpents. The rape/marriage to a monster is a form of scapegoating an innocent daughter and might be interpreted as sado-masochistic phantasy. On the other hand, since women often choose to marry monsters, it might also be interpreted as a woman's phantasy of attracting a male by appearing helpless

199

and in distress. Sometimes the monster is not explicitly connected with women, such as the werewolf, the vampire, and Mr Hyde. Today, the monster persists in such forms as King Kong and the Incredible Hulk.

The monster is generally an expression of instinctual man. Although the instinct in question is often aggression (e.g., the Minotaur demands nine men and nine women from Thebes at regular intervals, and King Kong is a threat to New York), when the myth involves women the instinct expressed by the monster is sexual. Helene Deutsch comments

> Every time I see one of the humorous pictures in popular movies or magazines showing an anthropomorphic ape or a powerful bear-like masculine creature with a completely helpless female in his arms I am reminded of my old favourite speculation: thus it was that man took possession of woman and subjected her to sexual desire. (quoted in Brownmiller, 1975)

Whether or not woman was forcibly 'subjected' to sex in the dawn of civilization is open to debate, but the point is clear that the monster is a projection of masculine intrusive sexuality. Occasionally the monster shows up as the shadow side of a character who is ostensibly a father figure; Dr Jekyll turns into Mr Hyde, and werewolves and vampires appear civilized enough by day but turn into monsters at night. From a woman's point of view, a man who rapes, deflowers or is even an insensitive lover may be seen as someone who becomes a monster at night. Or, a woman who cannot acknowledge her own sexuality may fantasize about sex in the form of being raped by a monster such that she has no responsibility for the deed. She may even use such phantasies as a means of 'trying out' in a safe way, some alternative forms of sexuality. Trickster is not necessarily represented in monster-like forms in these phantasies; he may also take the form of the 'strong, silent type', e.g., a highly aggressive man whose dominance frees the immature woman from taking responsibility in the relationship. Although this dominance is often more characteristic of the father than the trickster, the 'strong, silent type' is identified with the trickster because his dominance is largely confined to the sexual sphere. Furthermore, he remains a sort of 'untamed' person, and it is this existence on a more 'natural' and/or instinctual plane that gives him his sex appeal (examples of this would be Tarzan, Lady Chatterley's lover, the cowboy, etc.). The trickster/son/animal is often shown to be more virile than Father Sky, who is castrated by his sons in myth.

The Hero

Ego consciousness does not remain at the level of the trickster, however; otherwise the frog would never become a prince, and neither would Beauty's Beast. In the Winnebago trickster cycle, Trickster learns more and more self-control during his exploits and becomes more and more of a builder until he finally ceases to be a trickster and is better called a culture hero. The hero is a figure who is midway between the father and the trickster, the lawgiver and the lawbreaker; he has the youth, vitality and audacity of the trickster, but has acquired more of the father's maturity as a result of his travels and exploits (Raglan, 1936). Some obvious examples of this are Oedipus after destroying the Sphinx, Jason after capturing the Fleece, or Theseus after killing the Minotaur. We do not, however, receive a very detailed psychological portrait of the hero at this point. Once he has assumed command of his realm and captured the woman he desired, the myth moves on quickly to the next major conflict. In part, of course, this is because it is nearly impossible to have a good story line without conflict to provide dramatic tension. But it is still worth asking why it is that we have no clear portrait of a hero who is neither a trickster nor a father and thus is neither immature or rigid, and neither a protector nor a seducer. We do not have pictures of men who are simply the peers of women. The reason for this is probably that, traditionally, men and women have never been in peer relationships; the marriage ceremony is a striking example of how women may be passed from one protector to another. The exception to this rule comes when the man and woman in question are brother and sister (e.g., Apollo and Artemis); they can be peers because there are no property relations between them and because their shared parentage gives them a shared history and many traits in common. In most myths, however, men exist as either

201

tricksters or fathers in relation to women, and not as this sort of soul-mate.

The Father

The dearth of representations of the hero as a mature peer sometimes results in representations of the hero as a rather uneasy unity of a trickster and a father. A good example of this is the Greek god Zeus, who is a Father Sky figure that displays trickster-like characteristics in his endless affairs with mortal women and his susceptibility to being tricked by his wife Hera and other gods. The Zeus figure resulted from the unification of many diverse local gods, and this helped to endow him with these conflicting aspects of the archetypal masculine. Both licentiousness and majesty coexist in Zeus. Edith Hamilton writes:

> Zeus became the Supreme Ruler. He was Lord of the Sky, the Rain-god and the Cloud-gatherer, who wielded the awful thunderbolt. His power was greater than that of all the other divinities together ... Nevertheless he was not omnipotent or omniscient, either. He could be opposed and deceived ... The two ideas of him, the high and the low, persisted side by side for a long time. (Hamilton, 1942, p. 27)

A similar unification of the father and the trickster may also be glimpsed in the God of the Old Testament, who is generally a father but behaves as a trickster in his treatment of Job and his destruction of Sodom and Gomorrah.

The father is the most powerful incarnation of the archetypal masculine. He embodies mature will, intelligence, and generativity. Represented by sky imagery in myth, he is the primal seed that fertilizes Mother Earth and causes her unity to differentiate and bring forth the manifold forms of life. In comparison to the materiality of Mother Earth, the father is a mental or spiritual principle, as might be suggested by the imagery of light and sky (space) associated with him. He is in this sense secondary, an afterthought to the material world, much as the father is for the child a secondary love object. The father is also the first person the child loves on a purely mental/spiritual basis, because unlike the mother the father was not bodily united with the child and is not an immediate source of nurturance. The father principle is important for the child at later stages of its development, however, because of his significance as (1) the word, and (2) power or authority.

The Word and the Law

The father often makes his first appearance in myth cycles as the word or Logos, i.e., divine intelligence, as in the biblical creation story: 'In the beginning was the Word.' The symbol of this intelligence is light, which is the first product of the father when he creates the world and the first ingredient in bringing order out of chaos, and is appropriately immaterial rather than physical. We speak of revelation and inspiration (which also suggests the image of divine logos as breath) in terms of light metaphors. The word is not, as Jung points out, merely an abstract phenomenon; its ordering power is the basis of male generativity such that offspring and knowledge come into being simultaneously and inseparably. Without its generative capacity, the intelligence of the masculine would not be divine.

In terms of the development of consciousness, the word is important because the learning of language is the child's first step in starting to think. Words are the first level of abstraction by which objects and events are categorized and ordered in the world. Even much of the most sophisticated scientific thought is, in the last analysis, an attempt to ascribe order to nature by naming the structures and functions within it. By freeing thought from one-to-one concrete associations and allowing it to manipulate and recombine different concepts, the word provides the foundation for creative thought. Furthermore, the ability given by language to evaluate our actions and project ourselves into the future is what pulls us out of the uroboros and into higher development and moral awareness. The word thus imposes order and makes distinctions in the chaos of primal, unconscious thought, and, in the form of law, imposes order on nature and society.

Perhaps 'order' is the best single word by which to characterize the father principle. Not only does the word order the world by its power to differentiate and create structure, but this creation

203

of structure is identical with the introduction of both natural and human law (order). The intrusiveness of the archetypal masculine may be seen here in the sense that the law is imposed from without on the physical and emotional world. Because it is imposed on material reality without being part of it, the principle of law can only be benevolent if it is responsive to the constant changes which characterize material reality. If the law becomes too rigid or outmoded, it must be replaced, and this theme is seen over and over again in myth when old Father Sky is castrated by his sons and forced to turn his rule over to them.

The archetypal masculine has tremendous power in its incarnation as word or law. First of all, it is responsible for the creation of the cosmos. Secondly, as a mental, spiritual principle that is 'above' and 'beyond' the material world, the masculine represents a sort of divine perfection that is, in its pure form, beyond the reach of mortals still tied to the physical world. In fact, it is highly dangerous for mortals even to attempt to approach it. Icarus dies because he flies too close to the sun (the light of the father), and Greek seers like Teiresias were typically blinded (as was Oedipus) from their exposure to divine knowledge. Similarly, Semele burns to death when Zeus reveals himself to her in his full glory. The power of the masculine is also the power of authority that makes the word or law meaningful. Sometimes this power assumes the form of sexual potency and physical strength, as in the case when Father Sky throws thunderbolts down from heaven or when Apollo acts in the capacity of the archer god. In addition to their phallic significance, the arrow and thunderbolt also express the authority of the father, because they are instruments of punishment. Father Sky is the ruler of the pantheon as well as of mortals. The father himself can do no wrong because, as lawgiver, he is the source of right and wrong, and this applies no less to the child's view of a parent than to the adult's view of God.

The Father and Development

The authority of the father principle is very important in the development of a child, both during the anal stage (when he, or she, is dealing with issues of obedience and autonomy) and in the dynamics of the Oedipal conflict and the formation of the super-ego. This father principle may, however, have a different meaning for boys and girls in the development of ego strengths. A boy develops a strong ego by breaking away from the mother and identifying with the father; a girl, on the other hand, may also establish some independence from the mother, but cannot make as clean a break because she still has to identify with her mother. She does not, however, have to identify with the father, and thus the ego strengths that he represents and helps to develop may never be internalized. The girl may become familiar with and accepting of all that the father represents, and yet never incorporate it fully into her own psyche because it is always seen as something that is, like the law, imposed from without. Intelligence and will of the masculine sort may even be feared or rejected as something foreign and inappropriate. The boy, however, must internalize those strengths in order some day to become a father himself. If a woman is to develop herself fully, she must cease to view her own ideas and values as something imposed on her from without by the external authority of the father, and must either affirm them as her own or develop a new set of beliefs. This issue is often raised, as we have seen, by the intervention of a trickster. Unfortunately, the woman is usually punished in myth for her attempt to break away from the dominance of the father.

Although men are punished in myth by the father in such ways as castration or being struck down by arrows and thunderbolts, for women punishment often takes the form of rape. We are accustomed to portraying the criminal who gives expression to the archetypal threat of rape as a trickster, because we characterize rape as an individual crime of lust and inadequate self-control. However, as Susan Brownmiller has pointed out, rape is an implicit (and in some societies, explicit) means of enforcing male dominance (1975). Thus the man who uses rape or the threat of rape to assert male superiority and the social-sexual status quo behaves as a father figure, affirming his power and the law he set down. In a twisted, punitive way, rape may become an act that supports society and therefore draws approval. One example of this is the immensely popular rape scene in *Gone With the Wind,* in which Rhett explicitly says he is going to assert his rights (!) as Scarlett's husband, and in which even Scarlett wakes up the next day with a smile on her face. There is also the theme in this culture that prostitutes (or indeed, any women who show their sexuality) can be raped with impunity because they are 'bad' women who deserve punishment by the father.

The authoritarian father often balances out the lawlessness of the trickster in myth. In the Don Juan stories, for instance, the ghost of Don Carlo (the father of a woman whom Don Juan has seduced) drags Don Juan to hell; in the fairy tale 'Little Red Riding Hood', the hunter kills the wolf; Odysseus slaughters the suitors; God wipes out Sodom and Gomorrah. The restoration of order by the father is not exclusively related to the chastisement, as it were, of the trickster, but may be a response to any type of fallen order, as when God gives the Ten Commandments to the Israelites. This occurs on a historical as well as a mythological level, as when Napoleon gave the Code to France or Hitler created the Third Reich. When this law becomes too repressive, revolution occurs and the cycle begins again. A variant of this tension is seen in the distinction between Apollonian and Dionysian art; the former is ordered, rational and sublimated, while the latter is irrational, expressive and instinctual.

Often in myth the woman is shown as being caught between these poles of the archetypal masculine. Her choice is whether or not to leave a protective father to go with a trickster who promises individual fulfilment in the form of romantic sexuality and freedom. Very often this is the first major life decision that the woman has ever made for herself and so it is a form of growth and a step toward autonomy regardless of the outcome. Anna Karenina is destroyed by the experience, but largely as a result of social disapproval, whereas Lady Chatterley fares better and manages to run off successfully with her trickster lover. An interesting recent version of this conflict is seen in John Barth's *The End of the Road,* in which it is made clear through the use of existentialist language and religious metaphor that Joe is the protective Father/God who creates and maintains structure, whereas Jake is the Trickster/Devil who represents transformation and destroys structure. Rennie, who had always defined herself in accordance with Joe's ideas, is forced after an affair

206

with Jake to do some thinking on her own in choosing between them. A charming phantasy resolution of the father-trickster conflict may be seen in Jorge Amado's novel *Dona Flor and her Two Husbands.* Flor's first husband, whose licentiousness caused him to die a premature death, was a trickster who deceived her, mistreated her, and was generally irresponsible; still, he was a sensual and virile lover. When Flor remarries, it is to a father-type pharmacist who is respectable, respectful, and a good companion although he is unexciting sexually. At the conclusion of the novel, the ghost of Flor's first husband returns to her so that she is able to 'have her cake and eat it too'—i.e., she can still enjoy the trickster's sensuality while remaining under the protection of the father. This father/trickster conflict seems largely to be an issue for women who have been sheltered by men and have not been autonomous in any economic or psychological sense. With social rôles beginning to change, this conflict may be replaced by other conflicts that characterize more independent and mature women. We are beginning to see this in some of the literature that is currently coming out of the women's movement (e.g., Marilyn French's *The Women's Room*).

The Wise Old Man

When the archetypal masculine has passed its prime in terms of developing beyond the father figure, the result is, not surprisingly, the wise old man figure. The wise old man is a person like Teiresias, Merlin, Oedipus and Theseus at an older age, or Aschenbach of Thomas Mann's *Death in Venice,* who has gone beyond the mastery of the father and is more likely to use his skills to assist younger men who are still developing. Thus, the generativity of the old man is effected indirectly, through influencing other men, rather than through direct interaction with the world. This is partly because the Old Man is preparing to leave the world and is loosening his ties to it. His proximity to death and the uroboros enriches his wisdom both by giving him an outsider's detachment and by allowing him to be a more androgynous figure than the other incarnations of the masculine. His intelligence becomes wisdom because he has incorporated feminine forms of knowledge into himself (i.e., insight in the

207

realm of human emotion and relationships, as is shown by Diotima in Plato's *Symposium*).

This coming to terms with the anima allows him to be both more androgynous and more differentiated. Unlike the boy, who seems androgynous because he is not fully developed, the old man's androgyny is a result of having developed the animus to a point where he can go beyond it and incorporate other aspects of his psyche. Metman has noted the deceptive similarity between men with a poorly developed ego, who seem to have the sort of intuitive insight of a Zen master, and men who really are Zen masters. The former are intuitive out of a failure to establish clear self-other boundaries; the latter have established them, but have gone beyond them. The old man's intuitiveness is transcendental rather than uroboric.

Despite his age, the old man may still show hints of retaining the attributes of his earlier days. Besides retaining the father's intelligence and like ways, Aschenbach devises tricks by which to impress Tadzio, and Merlin runs off with Nimue when Arthur needs him. The old man is thus not immune to being tricked into love or tricking others when he wishes. Eventually, however, the old man dies (usually by jumping into an abyss, ocean, or other symbol of the feminine), returns to the uroboros, and the cycle of the masculine begins again. In the sense that it rises out of the uroboros and then collapses back into it at the end, the archetypal masculine may thus be seen to parallel male sexuality as well as the life cycle of consciousness.

Conclusion

In conclusion, then, the masculine has traditionally been characterized in Western myth as those principles which demonstrate the development of ego consciousness, in contrast to the association of the feminine with the unconscious. The archetypal masculine consists of attributes of will and intelligence which are manifested in an active mode via intrusive and generative behaviours. These principles are seen in varying proportions at each level of ego development, and at each level there exist mythological figures which correspond to that stage. Some of the figures discussed were those of the boy, Don Juan, the trickster, the father and the wise old man. The trickster and the father play the most significant rôle in the psyche of most adults because they represent instinctual expression/transformation/freedom and repression/stability/order respectively. For women, the choice of the trickster's freedom in a conflict between the two is often a move towards independence and growth; perhaps this theme will change when women are able to associate themselves with men who are peers rather than protectors or seducers. When the masculine has completed its development, it falls back into the uroboros and begins anew.

Summary

Our conceptions of masculinity and femininity have often been formulated in terms of a 'male' principle and a 'female' principle, and over the years these principles have come to be associated with different areas of psychological experience. Although psychologists have extensively analysed the significance of the 'female' principle, less work has been done on that of the 'male'. Thus, this paper is an attempt to analyse the 'male' principle, following in the tradition of Jungian psychology. It is shown through an examination of myths and literature that the traditional masculine is associated with the functions of the ego, with different stages of ego development being represented by different mythological features. These figures are discussed individually, and special attention is given to their significance in the psychological development of women.

References

Brownmiller, S. (1975). *Against our Will: Men, Women and Rape.* New York, Bantam Books.

Erikson, E. H. (1963). *Childhood and Society.* New York, Norton.

Hamilton, E. (1942). *Mythology.* New York, Mentor Books.

Jung, .E. (1957). *Animus and Anima.* Zürich, Spring Publications.

Lederer, W. (1968), *The Fear of Women.* New York, Grune & Stratton.

Metman, P. (1958). 'The trickster figure in schizophrenia', *J. Analyt. Psychol.,* 3 (1).

Neumann, E. (1954). *The Origins and History of Consciousness.* London, Routledge & Kegan Paul.

Neumann, E.(1955). *The Great Mother*. London, Routledge & Kegan Paul.

Plaut, A. (1959). 'A case of tricksterism illustrating ego defences', *J. Analyt. Psychol.,* 4 (1).

Radin, P. (1956). *The Trickster*. London, Routledge & Kegan Paul.

Raglan, F. (1936). *The Hero: A Study in Tradition, Myth and Drama*. London, Methuen.

Ulanov. A. B. (1971). *The Feminine in Jungian Psychology and Christian Theology*. Evanston, Illinois, Northwestern University Press.

Some aspects of
the development
of authority

HANS DIECKMANN

This paper also has a comprehensive aim: to anatomize
'authority' from a psychological standpoint. The author writes
of positive and negative aspects of authority and, in a neat
twist, speaks of authority as a kind of instinct, and hence subject to all the usual vicissitudes—repression, loss of control,
denial, idealization, etc. Though the 'instinct' may be said to
be fixed, its manifestations are not and the paper is an example of analytical psychology's capacity to blend together the
innate and the environmental or situational. Dieckmann, a very
experienced analyst, is standing back from his work and pick-
ing out clinical illustrations of this one theme. Having
established what is meant by authority, and its relation to the
father, he focuses on our attitude towards it. For a definition
of individuation, see glossary. *A.S.*

I F WE CONSIDER the problem of authority from the viewpoint of analytical psychology, we should begin by first giving a phenomenological account of the structure of authority as we find it in the collective consciousness. After which we can raise the question as to how this structure came into being, how it developed, and what direction it may further take within the framework of our own practice: that is, which characteristic tendencies of such a development could be linked with the individuation process—if individuation is not to degenerate into a mere word in the vocabulary of a *Brave New World*.

Authority comprises three levels: (1) violence and power; (2) reputation and prestige; (3) knowledge and wisdom. All these may be either personal or impersonal. Personal if authority is based on real personal superiority in relation to other people, be it of greater strength, position or wisdom; impersonal if authority is based on an institution, an office or on higher social position. As we all know, the man clothed in impersonal authority may himself be weak, of low personal reputation and even stupid. This is not very important so long as the institution works. There is a famous German proverb which says: '*Wem Gott ein Amt gibt, dem gibt er auch den Verstand, es auszuüben*' (When God gives someone a position, he also gives him the intelligence to administer it). Only if the institution degenerates does the man also collapse.

Of these three levels of personal and impersonal authority, usually only one is accentuated, the other two playing a more or less secondary rôle like two auxiliary functions. An American President, for example, may have great power but can have a very questionable personal reputation and lack wisdom—as we have seen in recent years. The Pope has a solid reputation but less essential power and often less knowledge. An Indian guru has more of the third, and less of the first two qualities. Nevertheless all three, in differing degrees, exist together, along with a strong subjective factor based on the relationship between the authority and the people who acknowledge this authority. For a Catholic the Pope has a far higher reputation, more power and more wisdom than he has for a Marxist. He feels the reverse about Marx and Lenin. Authority, then, is always based on a relationship and never exists as a mere object like a mountain, which is always there even if nobody is around.

In the structure of collective consciousness we can also delimit three different categories:

1. religious authority, based either on the canonized traditions of the cult, or on the numinous evocation of a god in a prophet or a reformer;
2. the authority of the state based on its constitution and laws;
3. the authority of parents and teachers over children based on the differences between the generations and the degree of experience.

Freud, who was a prisoner of his own fascination with the Oedipus complex and his own father problem, developed the theory that our third category, that of parental authority, is the original biological model and the cause of the other two, i.e. religious and state authority. We are all familiar with his concept of the *Urhorde* (primal horde) in his book *Totem and Taboo* (1913). This has a rather problematical objective background since it is based solely on a few observations of gorillas described by Savage in 1845-1847. According to Freud's concept the younger males of the *Urhorde*, the sons, killed their father, who possessed all the women, and ate him. Thereby they acquired, on the one hand, sexual freedom and, on the other, as a negation of this freedom, murderous guilt feelings. These guilt feelings again brought about the creation of an imaginary father who then ruled as god, or totem, over the clan.

Recently Jacoby has shown that this private myth of Freud's is a condensed version of the old Greek cosmogonic myth of Uranos and Kronos (1975). In this myth Uranos also oppresses his children. After his castration by the sickle of Kronos his phallus was thrown into the sea. This led to the birth of Aphrodite (sexuality), and the blood of the castration engendered the birth of the Erinyes (guilt feelings). As so often happens, Freud was unconsciously fascinated by an idea based on an archetypal image and, without realizing it, applied a cosmogonic myth on the personal level in order to explain the origin of religious authority.

We know today, from the early history of human evolution, that we are not the descendants of the gorillas and that the links between the apes and early man, e.g. the Neanderthal, have not

213

survived. Today the relevant problem in zoology is not to discover the 'missing link'; it is rather a problem of 'Gestalt psychology' whether we find the 'link' between ape and man convincing or not. We know also that we are unable to name the specific quality which differentiates man from animal because we are aware, at least since Köhler (1917), that the higher vertebrates are capable of complicated learning processes, including memory, and display other characteristics formerly believed to be specifically human. All we are sure of, so far as we are able to reconstruct human history and prehistory, is that man was always a herd animal, never living alone, but in larger or smaller groups. It is a fact that all herd animals are compelled by a very restricted and powerful instinctual system. The leading animal of the group, and the absolute authority, is not chosen by himself nor by other members of the group, but by the force of instinct itself, and survives only until a stronger and better animal appears. We have, in all probability, a remnant of this process in the cosmogonic myth, when Kronos defeats Uranos and Zeus defeats Kronos, Zeus himself becoming the father of mankind, signifying that here, for the first time, man wins a certain freedom from the compulsion of the instincts.

The main thing, in my opinion, is that, even from the biological point of view, we should not concern ourselves with the personal problem, as Freud did, but do exactly the reverse. That means, first, we have an impersonal or transpersonal force, an instinctual drive which gives the chaotic herd a structure. This determines that a certain animal be chosen as leader and have absolute authority over the group. In other words, the god is the primary datum, the father is secondary. Otherwise nature would be explained in reverse, by anthropomorphic projections.

From instinct to god seems to be a dangerous leap, but analytical psychologists should be used to thinking in such terms. Behind the often very complicated reactions of the instincts stands the formative principle, and this almost always connected with the image of a deity. In all creation myths, from the earliest known Babylonian myth of Marduk and Tiamat up to that of Jahweh, the father god begins the creation of the world by giving structure and form to the maternal chaotic *materia prima*. We know that in very primitive cultures like that of the Bushmen of the Kalahari all gods are animals, and a descendant of the animal-god lives still in our fairy tales (von Franz, 1964).

Morenz (1960) has shown that in the development of Egyptian culture and religion the Pharaoh, as the highest authority of religion and state, was, in the Old Kingdom, at first identified with the god, and the god was identical with the creature. Hence a Pharaoh is often shown as the Horus falcon. In the Egyptian Middle Kingdom this connexion became more flexible. The Pharaoh was still god, but more the son of God, one who will become God himself only after his death. Finally, in the New Kingdom we find inscriptions which come very near to later feudalistic ideas of the king as a human person, but one whose authority belongs to him by the grace of God. Morenz's ideas are not universally acknowledged; Hornung, for example, contradicts them (1967). Nor is the idea of an evolutionary development from polytheism to monotheism accepted by everyone. I simply want to show here, however, that there is also a symbolic connexion between the animal and religious authority, as well as state authority. This may indicate that one of the roots of authority is based on the innate forces of a structuring principle which, on the deeper levels of evolution, is *identical with instinct*.

Man, more than the other higher vertebrates, is characterized by a certain freedom in relation to instinctual powers, by a greater flexibility, by his ability to learn, and by the possibility of adaptation to different natural surroundings. Gehlen (1950) defines man first by this 'hiatus' between drive, or instinct, on the one hand, and satisfaction of needs on the other. His second definition sees man as a being whose needs have the possibility of changing, and of adaptation to those surroundings which he himself has altered. That means man changes nature. Once this has occurred the changed nature and the changed environment create, in turn, new needs which have to be satisfied.

The second classification is derived from the first: man is an instinctual cripple, and this fact is of the utmost importance for the development of human civilization and culture. We see this from the earliest beginnings of the race down to modern times. In the first primitive epochs, for example, man needed only caves in which to live. After he had learned to build huts and houses,

215

however, these became a need for the whole human race and, some regressive tendencies apart, man will always build houses instead of hollowing out caves when he wants to live somewhere for any length of time. To take another example, modern man has developed a need for worldwide information, and this need for information shows the same characteristics as the need for the satisfaction of a drive. This can go to such extremes that on a Sunday the only services available are the emergency medical services and television!

In view of these typically human characteristics we have to understand authority not as a static, unchanging, innate principle, granted to man by the will of God, but as *a principle capable of changing*, of taking different forms of growth and of development towards certain goals which are, in the final analysis, determined by our value systems.

At the same time, it is not possible to do away with authority itself so long as man is related to other men, and to smaller and larger groups. Right now we are just emerging from an anti-authoritarian period, by no means the first in modern history.

In 1872 there existed an anti-authoritarian movement under the early socialists. It was at that time that Engels wrote his article on authority, often discussed today, in which he asserts the basic necessity for authority and illustrates this by the example of a factory, or a ship at sea, neither of which can function without authority (1933).

Such authority is also needed in a revolution, an authority to be enforced by the use of arms if necessary. For Engels authority is a neutral principle. It depends on man whether he uses it for good or evil. Engels simply pleads that the political authority be discarded and be substituted by a purely administrative state authority. God alone knows if this may one day be possible since man is connected not only with fact and matter, but also with his value system and with his ideas. Nevertheless, this basically political idea of Engels' is one of those utopian concepts which are a basic necessity of human life, growth and unfolding, as Ernst Bloch has shown (1967).

Taking all this into consideration we can assert that authority is a principle which is inherent in nature, which is connected

216

with the instinctual force of structure and order, and which can be observed even on the level of animal life. From this point of view also, the personal father is neither the creator nor the first authority, but only the projection screen of an impersonal principle. At the same time, this principle changes during the development of humanity due to social and economic factors. It cannot simply be reduced to biological, personal or individual factors, but has always to be seen in its relationship to man's environment.

At this point we may have to raise the question of what our own utopian view of authority looks like, and how individuation handles this problem. Is our final goal the same as that of the Freudians—to introject or to build up a so-called sane superego, concerning which nobody can ever determine what is really sane and what is not, especially with regard to its contents? One might, perhaps, at least be able to define its function. Or do we have other goals which are the result of our different concept of the human psyche?

In analytical psychology authority is very closely connected with drive limitation and drive repression. The newborn child has to start very early struggling with the basic conflict between his primitive natural being, his social surroundings and his highly differentiated inheritance. The inhibiting principle is experienced mainly as a paternal principle, and its images, as we meet them in dreams, phantasies and in mythology, etc., consist of father figures.

These images, whether they fit or not, are at first projected onto the personal parents, especially onto the father or, in his absence, onto the animus of the mother. It is this that gives rise to the misconception that the father, in personalistic understanding of psychology, is the primary carrier of authority. As early as 1938 Jung wrote in his essay 'On psychic energy' that, 'The mind, as the active principle in the inheritance, consists of the sum of the ancestral minds, the "unseen fathers", whose authority is born anew with the child' (CW 8, para. 54). A very similar view was taken by Erich Fromm in 1936, only from a more extraverted social point of view. Fromm says that the authority the father has in the family has not come about by mere chance, being later filled up by the social authority, but as such rests basically on the authority of the whole social community. The family father is, in his epoch, the first mediator of the social authority and its contents. He is not their prototype but their copy.

Along with Jung's conception mentioned above, the problem of authority is closely linked with the problem of spirit which, in analytical psychology, is a principle *sui generis* and not to be reduced to other drives, the sublimation of which spirit could then be taken to be. It is, on the contrary, the equivalent counterpart of the drives themselves and their needs. In 1945 Jung gave a deeper and more comprehensive explanation of the problem of spirit in his paper, 'On the phenomenology of the spirit in fairly-tales' (*CW* 9). I do not know whether there is a satisfactory English word which can express what is meant by the German word, *Geist*. So I shall use the German word in what follows.

According to Jung, *Geist* is the principle which is in opposition to *materia*. It is also used to refer to very different forms of this principle, for example, for all those phenomena in fairy-tales and myths we call 'ghosts'. For this reason the word lends itself to personification, a fact which is of special significance for our work. In the above-mentioned paper Jung points out, for example, that we carry out education in the '*Geist* of Pestalozzi' or, more impersonally, we speak of the 'spirit (*Geist*) of Weimar'. On the primitive level *Geist* is the *ligamentum animae et corporis* (that which holds body and soul together). The idealistic philosophers made *Geist* into a supernatural cosmic principle of law and order which transcended this world and became a God, or at least an attribute of the one God. The opposition was claimed by the materialistic philosophers, for whom *Geist* originated from the evolution of matter, a product of cerebral cells and metabolism. In his last book, *Mysterium Coniunctionis*, Jung postulated the hypothesis, based on the ideas of the *unus mundus* of Gerard Dorn, that beyond matter and spirit there is a third substance, hitherto unknown, out of which both *Geist* and matter originate (*CW* 14). We are not today in a position to answer this question scientifically, and philosophical argument over the matter seems to me to be a repetition of the old question of what came first, the chicken or the egg.

All these qualities of *Geist* can be applied to the instincts, except that we do not know whether animals experience images (Fischel, 1949). But we have known, since Fabre's observations on wasps, that they act out images or certain structures which are the equivalent of a highly emotional archetypal image. It is especially by virtue of that quality by which *Geist* can manipulate images autonomously that it also obtains the authority to order images and, along with these emotional images, also action and structure.

Thus far it is neutral, neither a good principle nor a bad one. *Geist* will be experienced as 'good' so long as man identifies himself with it. It becomes a 'bad' or dangerous *Geist* (father) if man rebels against it, a necessity, as we all know, in the individuation process. The rebellion is independent of the ideas and conceptions of the social environment. If this rebellion does not take place there is no progress, no dynamism and no self-realization. As mentioned before, man has a certain freedom with regard to his instinctual needs, though this is at times very limited. He is also able to alter these needs, and this enables us, in like manner, to change the inhibiting principle of structure as such and, along with it, the contents of authority. Consequently individuation, especially in the analytical situation, can bring about not only a changing, and a rebirth, of the inner nature of man, but, to the same degree, a change and a rebirth as regards structure and authority.

After these theoretical considerations it may be of interest to look at the problem from a practical point of view. I have examined the initial dreams of eighty-two patients whom I treated during my first ten years as an analyst. I can scarcely claim, during that time, either in terms of age or experience, to represent myself as a highly qualified authority.

The 'initial dream' (which I have also referred to in earlier papers, Dieckmann, 1969; 1972) I define as the first dream which occurs after the first personal contact with the analyst. In the literature of analytical psychology we often find this term given to the first great archetypal dream which may be reported several sessions later or even before the commencement of analytical treatment, as in the case described by Adler (1961). This definition is highly subjective and not satisfactory for the purpose of comparison. I propose, therefore, to refer to that type of dream as an 'initiation dream'. I want to make it clear that in the following pages I am speaking of initial dreams, i.e. the first dream the patient had after seeing me for the first time.

The first result of my review of these dreams was that there was a fairly high number of dreams which contained the problem of authority personified by a male personal figure such as teacher, father, wise old man, etc., or an impersonal authority principle like government, court, etc. I did not include dreams which dealt with mother figures or other female figures, even if these figures had certain aspects of authority. Of the 82 patients, 45—that is, more than half—had dreams containing paternal authority figures. In these 45 dreamers the unconscious of most chose a figure with whom there was no personal relationship at all, or a very loose connexion such as a little-known uncle. Only in seven dreams did the real father appear and only in three the analyst himself.

In dealing with dream interpretation on the subjective level, Jung pointed out that, in his opinion, the tendency of the unconscious is not to hide personal images behind impersonal ones and that, on the contrary, there is a special meaning in the use of the impersonal image (*CW* 15). By the use of impersonal images the dream specifies that it is not a personal struggle between father and son, or father and daughter, but is rather concerned with a basic problem of the inner world of the patient, which is connected with the transpersonal father image. As we mentioned above, authority has a close link with the principle of structure and order. So we may now say that a very high percentage of patients disclose, as early as in their first dreams, that they have a severe problem with this formative principle inside their own psyche. In the transference this problem is mostly projected onto the person of the analyst or onto the analytic situation, but it does not refer to the analyst himself, or to the personal father. Even in the seven cases out of the 82 quoted where the personal father appeared in their initial dreams, this personal father is, in all probability and contrary to Freud's opinion, only the projection screen for this impersonal, intrapsychic problem.

Looking at the dream images in question, we find that for the most part authority is experienced as negative and destructive. Only ten patients had a positive authority image in their initial dreams, and it is interesting that of these ten, three had a psychosis, two were alcoholics, one had a perversion and only four a neurosis. In two cases out of the four the person of the analyst was the positive authority, so that there remained only two neurotic cases with other positive authority figures. All the other patients had a negative or destructive authority which was sharply accentuated in the dreams of 27 patients. In ten cases the authority figure was neutral.

Of these 27 patients with a negative authority figure I found two different types: either an aggressive, compulsive and oppressive image of authority (seventeen patients), or an impotent and weak one (ten patients). I will now give two examples of these different types. The first is that of a nineteen-year-old student with a compulsive schizoid neurotic structure causing severe disturbances in his human relationships as well as in his work. He dreamt:

> I was living in a state with a dictatorship similar to that of the Nazis. The atmosphere was grey and oppressive. I was in a garden and there was a road along a river. It was very dark. In the background there was a garden fête, and a drunk approached me who had taken prohibited alcoholic beverages or hydrocyanic acid. Anyone who did this would immediately be executed. I was very afraid and brought him to a small hotel. He became more and more sick. The proprietress looked after us and saw to it that we were left alone. Suddenly a man with a beard looked into the room. I closed the door quickly. He did not denounce us, however. The sick man died and I went home.

I do not want to interpret this dream in any detail. All I want to demonstrate is that the dream ego is living under a very oppressive, dangerous and dictatorial authority which is impersonal and constantly threatens it with prison and even death. Marie-Louise von Franz (1964) also mentioned this type of dream in the initial phase of analytical treatment, showing themes of prison, concentration camps and oppression. She gives the explanation that these themes are connected with the psycho-

221

logical types in so far as, in our extraverted culture, the analytical process of individuation and introversion is frequently experienced in its first stages as negative and oppressive. But as the patient whose dream I have just described was a very introverted youngster, von Franz's explanation does not seem to apply. Here, therefore, I prefer Jung's concept, i.e. that the dream represents a true image of the present situation of the psyche and shows a picture of the inner world in which this young man was living. So we may say that in spite of his outward way of living, as a rebel with an ideology of total freedom, inside his own soul he was really living in a state of very severe oppression under a corrupt authority principle.

The second dream is that of a 33-year-old patient with gastritis and a rather depressive disposition. He dreamt:

> I was living with my fiancée in a very primitive room. Opposite the house was a bar in front of which a Spanish-looking thief was strutting about. We two wanted to take a walk and did so. Then I came home alone and did not find our room in the house which had become very large and labyrinthine. In an empty yellow room I found an old man. I asked him for my room, but he only shrugged his shoulders and pointed to a window. Evidently he was unable to say anything or to help me.

In this dream, authority is represented by the not so wise and helpless old man who is not able to lead the ego back into the room in which it could find security and the possibility of living. Also the structure of the patient's psychic house has become labyrinthine and poor. Nobody is able to find the right way and the old king in his yellow sun-room is weak and helpless, too. It seems also impossible to control the thief, who is allowed to act in the open.

When we look at the statistical values and the contents of these dreams, the question arises of how to interpret the results and what consequences they might eventually have in the treatment of these patients. If we see authority as linked with the basic principle of structure and order, the patriarchal principle in our culture, then the antithesis would be the matriarchal principle, that of matter, drives, wish-fulfilment and of the unstructured freedom of paradise. However, matter (*materia*) without structure is synonymous with chaos, and this, I believe, is the important basic problem of every patient who has a neurotic illness. The individual's own psychic system is no longer experienced as stabilized or as harmoniously ordered. The patient has, on the contrary, a profound feeling of disorder, insecurity, disharmony, and usually experiences anxiety of being overwhelmed by the chaotic forces inside himself. As a rule there is only one possible way to deal with this situation, and one which everyone tries at first. It is to build up a strong and rather inflexible barrier against these chaotic forces. At the same time the inner cry for a strong man who is able to give back law and order plays an important rôle. This barrier may be constructed against contents threatening either from within or without. If the authority is a so-called strong man, and there is a strong man within one's own psyche, as in the example of the first dream, then rebellion is directed against the outside. However, it is really a rebel who is acting from inside, figuring as a very oppressive and compulsive dictator. At any time the system can swing into its opposite form.

If you give a rebel the possibility of winning and coming to power, he will be a far more ruthless dictator than those against whom he previously rebelled. This is not only an individual problem, but also a collective one, and history has, right up to the present day, given many examples of this situation. Translated into the psychological situation of individual patients, it means that you can often observe that a case of severe self-neglect and chaotic behaviour can change into a compulsive neurosis with a very rigid persona and a tendency towards very narrow ideologies. This situation can also be reversed.

The second possibility is to build up a strong authority outside oneself. That was what the other patient had done. He had a strong persona on the outside, a supporter of law and order in the world about him. The patient who had the second dream was actually a police officer. Quite the opposite situation reigned in his inside world, as the dream images show. There we find self-neglect and poverty along with robbery and a weak authority which is incapable of finding any means of solving the problem. This may also be regarded as a collective problem. A political system which places great emphasis on law and order, or on a strong ruler, is usually accompanied by the greatest thievery and injustice as its shadow.

There is, however, an exception to the above, when the greatest inner chaos prevails and yet, in spite of this, a positive authority figure turns up. Let us have a look at a typical dream of a patient with a positive authority figure. This patient was an alcoholic. He dreamt:

> I was standing in a long queue before the throne of the English queen. I behaved as correctly as I could. When at last I stood before her I was extremely pleased and honoured that she spoke some words to me and shook hands.

As I mentioned before, this is the only dream I have selected with a female figure since, in my view, the significance lies not in the queen as a woman but as representing the system of the English monarchy as a conservative principle. It would seem that the only help for this patient's psychic situation lay in the restoration of an old and traditional authority system as a defence against his own inner disorder. He was in danger of losing his means of support and his family, which had been part of the motivation for analytical treatment. The outcome of the treatment was almost the same as that revealed in this initial dream. It did not exactly entail a regressive restoration of the old persona, because the patient did experience some ego development and took a few steps towards individuation up to the point where he lost his symptoms. A very conservative personality remained, however—one which, like a good citizen, uncritically accepted authority.

The most disturbing finding of my review was the very great number of negative authority figures with sado-masochistic tendencies, as seen in the first example, of the student's dream. As early as 1936, Erich Fromm, in the above-mentioned paper, gave an excellent study of this type of authority as seen from the psychoanalytic point of view. What I want to point out is the serious danger this phenomenon constitutes for our civilization. Nearly one third of my patients presented this problem in their initial dream, and it turned up in most of the others in the course of treatment. I am aware that it is not very scientific to

224

extrapolate from a small number of results relevant to a wider population. However, we all know, not only from history but also from our present-day situation, that this problem is not merely confined to a few neurotic patients. The fact that the structure of a sado-masochistic authority is a part of the inner psychic system not only of the members of the ruling class, but also of those people who rebel against oppression and struggle for more freedom and liberty, as I mentioned previously when describing the student's dream, brings us to the notorious situation of the cat biting its own tail. These rebels for freedom change oppressive and compulsive dictators the very moment they succeed, and are compelled to become rulers because their own psychic structure forces them to do so. It seems, therefore, impossible to solve this problem by merely changing outer circumstances; we have no alternative but to take the longer route of changing the psychic structure as well, a route extending probably over many generations and even centuries. We can only hope that our work with the individual will act like a stone thrown into the water whose ripples spread wider and wider.

It has always been a sound analytical principle to begin, not by trying to convert the world, but with ourselves. I think we have a lot of compulsive and restrictive rules and patterns within our own system, not only with regard to our patients but also in our training programmes. Although not so narrow as orthodox Freudians, we all have a system of regulations which we apply to our patients, often not well thought out and sometimes completely unconscious, as, for example, the decision as to whether our patients shall sit or lie, whether they shall be asked to write down their dreams or not, etc. An analyst may consider himself very individual if he applies such a rule or pattern not by order of his professional organization but as a result of his so-called personal experience; nevertheless, for the patient it appears as a very collective and uniform system as to whether, for instance, he is expected to write down his dreams or not. It happens not infrequently that such an analytical ritual, often considered as a prerequisite for bringing about the 'hermetic situation' (*vas hermeticum*) necessary for analysis, can have quite the opposite effect. The ritual then does not provide the necessary structure, help, safety and security intended. Rather, owing to the negative authority projected onto the analyst, the ritual becomes restrictive, oppressive and a useful means of resistance. Take, for example, the directive that none of the contents of analytical sessions should be discussed with outsiders. If you have a patient suffering from a severe regressive introversion who has never been able to tell anybody anything about his inner life, including his dreams, this directive would be totally wrong, since such a patient has to learn to share his inner world with partners and friends. It is precisely many of the problems raised in the analytical situation which have to be shared outside as well. This example, which is only one of many, shows how standard methods and a fixed system of rules are unsuitable for analytical work. On the contrary, we have to build up an analytical structure which arises out of the conscious, as well as the unconscious, relationship between the analyst and his patient. The old alchemists were aware of this problem. Their hermetic vessel was a *vas mirabile,* a mystical idea and not a real retort, and it had to be rounded since it was an analogy to the spherical cosmos, where the stars had to assist in the operation. The woman alchemist Maria Prophetissa says, 'The whole secret lies in knowing about the Hermetic vessel' (*CW* 12, p. 236). This *vas* had a very curious and secret connexion with the *materia prima* on the one hand, and the *lapis* on the other. *Lapis, materia prima* and *vas hermeticum* were all in the deepest essence connected with the spirit of Mercurius and originated, therefore, from the same substance.

What does this mean for the analytical process? I believe that we have first to abandon all rules given by outside authorities when we start a treatment, and have to find, together with the patient, during the whole process of analysis, an analytical *vas* which may be built and rebuilt again and again and which can fit the needs of the patient as well as the needs of the analyst. This should not mean chaos and an untrammelled living-out of inner drives. It means, rather, that we must often undertake a difficult search for compromises, that we should be willing to accept necessary sacrifices. It is possible that at the end of such a process a structured hermeneutic *vas* has emerged, the authority of which can be introjected and act directively, making life worth living again.

References

Adler, G. (1961). *The Living Symbol.* London, Routledge & Kegan Paul.

Bloch, E. (1967). *Das Prinzip Hoffnung.* Frankfurt/Main, Suhrkamp-Verlag.

Dieckmann, H. (1969). 'Vergleichende Untersuchung über die Initialträume von 90 Patienten', *Z. Analyt. Psych.,* 1 (1).

Dieckmann, H. (1972). *Träume als Sprache der Seele.* Stuttgart, Bonz-Verlag.

Engels, F. (1933). 'Von der Autorität', in *Ges. Werke Marx-Engels,* Bd. 18. Berlin, Dietz-Verlag.

Fischel, W. (1949). *Leben und Erlebnis bei Tieren und Menschen.* München, Johann-Ambrosius Barth-Verlag.

Franz, M.-L. von (1964). 'Religiöse oder magische Einstellung zum Unbewussten', in *Psychotherapeutische Probleme.* (Studien aus dem C.G. Jung-Institut.) Zürich, Rascher.

Franz, M. L. von (1970). 'Die Bremer Stadtmusikanten', *Z. Analyt. Psych.,* 2 (1).

Fromm, E. (1936). *Autorität und Familie.* Junius-Drucke, Librairie Félix Alcan.

Freud, S. (1913). *Totem and Taboo.* Std. Edn. 13. London, Hogarth Press.

Gehlen, A. (1950). *Der Mensch.* Bonn, Atenäum-Verlag.

Hornung, E. (1967). *Einführung in die Ägyptologie.* Darmstadt, Wissenschaftliche Buchgesellschaft.

Jacoby, M. (1975). 'Autorität und Revolte—der Mythos vom Vatermord', *Z. Analyt. Psych.,* 6 (4).

Köhler, W. (1917). *Intelligenzprüfung an Menschenaffen.* Privately printed edition.

Morenz, S. (1960). *Ägyptische Religionen.* Stuttgart, Kohlhammer-Verlag.

The significance of the father in the destiny of the individual

C. G. JUNG

Jung revised an early (1909) psychoanalytic paper on the father in 1949 (*CW* 4). The 1949 version is published here with the omission of some technical data from word-association tests. The word-association test was used by Jung to establish the existence of the unconscious and the findings were valued by Freud as empirical proof of his ideas. The paper is noteworthy for the way in which the archetypal perspective is shown to add something to personal clinical material. The paper is also interesting because in very few other places does Jung assemble quite as much clinical material. In his Foreword to the 1949 version, Jung wrote that it was the discovery of the collective unconscious and the archetypes which raised problems for the theory of complexes: 'Previously the personality appeared to be unique and as if rooted in nothing; but now, associated with the individually acquired causes of the complex, there was found to be a general human precondition, the inherited and inborn biological structure which is the instinctual basis of every human being ... the structure brings with it an inborn tendency to seek out, or to produce, such situations instinctively' (*CW* 4, p. 302). *A.S.*

The Fates lead the willing,
but drag the unwilling.

Cleanthes

FREUD HAS POINTED OUT that the emotional relationship of the child to the parents, and particularly to the father, is of a decisive significance in regard to the content of any later neurosis. This relationship is indeed the infantile channel along which the libido flows back when it encounters any obstacles in later years, thus reactivating the long-forgotten psychic contents of childhood. It is ever so in life when we draw back before too great an obstacle, say the threat of some severe disappointment or the risk of some too far-reaching decision. The energy stored up for the solution of the task flows back and the old river-beds, the obsolete systems of the past, are filled up again. A man disillusioned in love falls back, as a substitute, upon some sentimental friendship or false religiosity; if he is a neurotic he regresses still further back to the childhood relationships he has never quite forsaken, and to which even the normal person is fettered by more than one chain—the relationship to father and mother.

Every analysis carried out at all thoroughly shows this regression more or less plainly. One peculiarity which stands out in the works of Freud is that the relationship to the father seems to possess a special significance. This is not to say that the father always has a greater influence on the moulding of the child's fate than the mother. His influence is of a specific nature and differs typically from hers.[1]

The significance of the father in moulding the child's psyche may be discovered in quite another field—the study of the family.[2] The latest investigations show the predominating influence of the father's character in a family, often lasting for centuries. The mother seems to play a less important role. If this is true of heredity, we may expect it to be true also of the psychological influences emanating from the father. The scope of the problem has been widened by the researches of my pupil, Dr. Emma Fürst, on the similarity of reaction-type within families.[3] ...

The similarity of reaction-type in children and parents pro-

230

vides matter for thought. For the association experiment is nothing other than a small segment of the psychological life of a man, and everyday life is at bottom an extensive and greatly varied association experiment; in principle we react in one as we do in the other. Obvious as this truth is, it still requires some reflection—and limitation. Take the case of a 45-year-old mother and her sixteen-year-old daughter ... The daughter had not really lived at all; she was not yet married, and yet she reacted as if she were her mother and had endless disillusions behind her. She had her mother's attitude, and to that extent was identified with her mother. The mother's attitude was explained by her relationship to the father. But the daughter was not married to the father and therefore did not need this attitude. She simply took it over from the environmental influences and later on will try to adapt herself to the world under the influence of this family problem. To the extent that an ill-assorted marriage is unsuitable, the attitude resulting from it will be unsuitable too. In order to adapt, the girl in later life will have to overcome the obstacles of her family milieu; if she does not, she will succumb to the fate to which her attitude predisposes her.

Clearly such a fate has many possibilities. The glossing over of the family problem and the development of the negative of the parental character may take place deep within, unnoticed by anyone, in the form of inhibitions and conflicts which she herself does not understand. Or, as she grows up, she will come into conflict with the world of actualities, fitting in nowhere, until one stroke of fate after another gradually opens her eyes to her own infantile, unadapted qualities. The source of the infantile disturbance of adaptation is naturally the emotional relation to the parents. It is a kind of psychic contagion, caused, as we know, not by logical truths but by affects and their physical manifestations.[4] In the most formative period between the first and fifth year all the essential characteristics, which fit exactly into the parental mould, are already developed, for experience teaches us that the first signs of the later conflict between the parental constellation and the individual's longing for independence occur as a rule before the fifth year.

I would like to show, with the help of a few case-histories, how the parental constellation hinders the child's adaptation.

Case 1

A well-preserved woman of 55, dressed poorly but carefully, with a certain elegance, in black; hair carefully arranged; a polite rather affected manner, fastidious in speech, devout. The patient might be the wife of a minor official or shopkeeper. She informed me, blushing and dropping her eyes, that she was the divorced wife of a common peasant. She had come to the clinic on account of depression, night terrors, palpitations, and nervous twitches in the arms—typical features of a mild climacteric neurosis. To complete the picture, the patient added that she suffered from severe anxiety-dreams; some man was pursuing her, wild animals attacked her, and so on.

Her anamnesis began with the family history. (So far as possible I give her own words.) Her father was a fine, stately, rather corpulent man of imposing appearance. He was very happily married, for her mother worshipped him. He was a clever man, a master craftsman, and held a dignified position. There were only two children, the patient and an elder sister. The sister was the mother's and the patient the father's favourite. When she was five years old her father suddenly died of a stroke at the age of 42. She felt very lonely, and also from then on she was treated by her mother and sister as the Cinderella. She noticed clearly enough that her mother preferred her sister to herself. The mother remained a widow, her respect for her husband being too great to allow her to marry a second time. She preserved his memory 'like a religious cult' and taught her children to do likewise.

The sister married relatively young; the patient did not marry till she was 24. She had never cared for young men, they all seemed insipid; her mind turned always to more mature men. When about twenty she became acquainted with a 'stately' gentleman of over 40, to whom she was much drawn, but for various reasons the relationship was broken off. At 24 she got to know a widower who had two children. He was a fine, stately, rather corpulent man, with an imposing presence, like her father; he was 44. She married him and respected him enormously. The marriage was childless; his children by the first marriage died of an infectious disease. After four years of married life her

232

husband died of a stroke. For eighteen years she remained his faithful widow. But at 46 (just before the menopause) she felt a great need of love. As she had no acquaintances she went to a matrimonial agency and married the first comer, a peasant of about 60 who had already been twice divorced on account of brutality and perverseness; the patient knew this before marriage. She remained five unbearable years with him, then she also obtained a divorce. The neurosis set in a little later.

For the reader with psychological experience no further elucidation is needed; the case is too obvious. I would only emphasize that up to her forty-sixth year the patient did nothing but live a faithful copy of the milieu of her early youth. The exacerbation of sexuality at the climacteric led to an even worse edition of the father-substitute, thanks to which she was cheated out of the late blossoming of her sexuality. The neurosis reveals, flickering under the repression, the eroticism of the aging woman who still wants to please.

Case 2

A man of 34, of small build, with a clever, kindly expression. He was easily embarrassed, blushed often. He had come for treatment on account of 'nervousness'. He said he was very irritable, readily fatigued, had nervous stomach-trouble, was often so deeply depressed that he sometimes thought of suicide.

Before coming to me for treatment he had sent me a circumstantial autobiography, or rather a history of his illness, in order to prepare me for his visit. His story began: 'My father was a very big and strong man.' This sentence awakened my curiosity; I turned over a page and there read: 'When I was fifteen a big lad of nineteen took me into a wood and indecently assaulted me.'

The numerous gaps in the patient's story induced me to obtain a more exact anamnesis from him, which led to the following disclosures: The patient was the youngest of three brothers. His father, a big, red-haired man, was formerly a soldier in the Swiss Guard at the Vatican; later he became a policeman. He was a stern, gruff old soldier, who brought up his sons with military discipline; he issued commands, did not call them by name, but whistled for them. He had spent his youth in Rome, and during his gay life there had contracted syphilis, from the consequences of which he still suffered in old age. He was fond of talking about his adventures in early life. His eldest son (considerably older than the patient) was exactly like him, a big, strong man with red hair. The mother was an ailing woman, prematurely aged. Exhausted and tired of life, she died at 40 when the patient was eight years old. He preserved a tender and beautiful memory of his mother.

At school he was always the whipping boy and always the object of his schoolfellows' mockery. He thought his peculiar dialect might be to blame. Later he was apprenticed to a strict and unkind master, with whom he stuck it out for over two years, under conditions so trying that all the other apprentices ran away. At fifteen the assault already mentioned took place, together with several other, milder homosexual experiences. Then fate packed him off to France. There he made the acquaintance of a man from the south, a great boaster and Don Juan. He dragged the patient to a brothel; he went unwillingly and out of fear, and found he was impotent. Later he went to Paris, where his eldest brother, a master-mason and the replica of his father, was leading a dissolute life. The patient stayed there a long time, badly paid and helping his sister-in-law out of pity. The brother often took him along to a brothel, but he was always impotent.

One day his brother asked him to make over to him his inheritance, 6,000 francs. The patient consulted his second brother, who was also in Paris, and who urgently tried to dissuade him from handing over the money, because it would only be squandered. Nevertheless the patient went and gave his inheritance to his brother, who naturally ran through it in the shortest possible time. And the second brother, who would have dissuaded him, was also let in for 500 francs. To my astonished question why he had so light-heartedly given the money to his brother without any guarantee he replied: well, he asked for it. He was not a bit sorry about the money, he would give him another 6,000 francs if he had it. The eldest brother afterwards went to the bad altogether and his wife divorced him.

The patient returned to Switzerland and remained for a year without regular employment, often suffering from hunger. During this time he made the acquaintance of a family and became a frequent visitor. The husband belonged to some peculiar sect, was a hypocrite, and neglected his family. The wife was elderly, ill, and weak, and moreover pregnant. There were six children, all living in great poverty. For this woman the patient developed a warm affection and shared with her the little he possessed. She told him her troubles, saying she felt sure she would die in childbirth. He promised her (although he possessed nothing) that he would take charge of the children and bring them up. The woman did die in childbed, but the orphanage interfered and allowed him only one child. So now he had a child but no family, and naturally could not bring it up by himself. He thus came to think of marrying. But as he had never yet fallen in love with a girl he was in great perplexity.

It then occurred to him that his elder brother was divorced from his wife, and he resolved to marry her. He wrote to her in Paris, saying what he intended. She was seventeen years older than he, but not averse to his plan. She invited him to come to Paris to talk matters over. But on the eve of the journey fate willed that he should run an iron nail into his foot, so that he could not travel. After a while, when the wound was healed, he went to Paris and found that he had imagined his sister-in-law, now his fiancée, to be younger and prettier than she really was. The wedding took place, however, and three months later the first coitus, on his wife's initiative. He himself had no desire for it. They brought up the child together, he in Swiss and she in the Parisian fashion, as she was a French woman. At the age of nine the child was run over and killed by a cyclist. The patient then felt very lonely and dismal at home. He proposed to his wife that they should adopt a young girl, whereupon she broke out into a fury of jealousy. Then, for the first time in his life, he fell in love with a young girl, and simultaneously the neurosis started with deep depression and nervous exhaustion, for meanwhile his life at home had become a hell.

My suggestion that he should separate from his wife was dismissed out of hand, on the ground that he could not take it upon himself to make the old woman unhappy on his account. He obviously preferred to go on being tormented, for the memories of his youth seemed to him more precious than any present joys.

This patient, too, moved all through his life in the magic circle of the family constellation. The strongest and most fateful factor was the relationship to the father; its masochistic-homosexual colouring is clearly apparent in everything he did. Even the unfortunate marriage was determined by the father, for the patient married the divorced wife of his elder brother, which amounted to marrying his mother. At the same time, his wife was the mother-substitute for the woman who died in childbed. The neurosis set in the moment the libido was withdrawn from the infantile relationship and for the first time came a bit nearer to an individually determined goal. In this as in the previous case, the family constellation proved to be by far the stronger, so that the narrow field of neurosis was all that was left over for the struggling individuality.

Case 3

A 36-year-old peasant woman, of average intelligence, healthy appearance, and robust build, mother of three healthy children. Comfortable economic circumstances. She came to the clinic for the following reasons: for some weeks she had been terribly wretched and anxious, slept badly, had terrifying dreams, and also suffered by day from anxiety and depression. She stated that all these things were without foundation, she herself was surprised at them, and had to admit that her husband was quite right when he insisted that it was 'stuff and nonsense'. Nevertheless, she simply could not get over them. Often strange thoughts came into her head; she was going to die and would go to hell. She got on very well with her husband.

Examination of the case yielded the following results. Some weeks before, she happened to take up some religious tracts which had long lain about the house unread. There she was informed that people who swore would go to hell. She took this very much to heart, and ever since had been thinking that she must stop people swearing or she would go to hell too. About a fortnight before she read these tracts her father, who lived with her, had suddenly died of a stroke. She was not actually present at his death, but arrived only when he was already dead. Her terror and grief were very great.

236

In the days following his death she thought much about it all, wondering why her father had to die so suddenly. During these meditations, she suddenly remembered that the last words she had heard her father say were: 'I am one of those who have got into the devil's clutches.' This memory filled her with trepidation, and she recalled how often her father had sworn savagely. She also began to wonder whether there was really a life after death, and whether her father was in heaven or hell. It was during these musings that she came across the tracts and began to read them, until she came to the place where it said that people who swore would go to hell. Then great fear and terror fell upon her; she covered herself with reproaches, she ought to have stopped her father's swearing and deserved to be punished for her negligence. She would die and would be condemned to hell. From that hour she was filled with sorrow, grew moody, tormented her husband with her obsessive ideas, and shunned all joy and conviviality.

The patient's life-history was as follows: she was the youngest of five brothers and sisters and had always been her father's favourite. Her father gave her everything she wanted if he possibly could. If she wanted a new dress and her mother refused it, she could be sure her father would bring her one next time he went to town. Her mother died rather early. At 24 she married the man of her choice, against her father's wishes. The father flatly disapproved of her choice although he had nothing particular against the man. After the wedding she made her father come and live with them. That seemed the obvious thing, she said, since the others had never suggested having him with them. He was, as a matter or fact, a quarrelsome, foulmouthed old drunkard. Husband and father-in-law, as may easily be imagined, did not get on at all. There were endless squabbles and altercations, in spite of which the patient would always dutifully fetch drink for her father from the inn. All the same, she admitted her husband was right. He was a good, patient fellow with only one failing: he did not obey her father enough. She found that incomprehensible, and would rather have seen her husband knuckle under to her father. When all's said and done, a father is still a father. In the frequent quarrels she always took her father's part. But she had nothing to say against her husband,

and he was usually right in his protests, but even so one must stand by one's father.

Soon it began to seem to her that she had sinned against her father by marrying against his will, and she often felt, after one of these incessant wrangles, that her love for her husband had died. And since her father's death it was impossible to love him any more, for his disobedience had usually been the cause of her father's fits of raging and swearing. At one time the quarrelling had become too much for the husband, and he induced his wife to find a room for her father elsewhere, where he lived for two years. During this time husband and wife lived together peaceably and happily. But by degrees she began to reproach herself for letting her father live alone; in spite of everything he was her father. And in the end, despite her husband's protests, she fetched her father home again because, as she said, at bottom she loved her father better than her husband. Scarcely was the old man back in the house than the strife broke out again. And so it went on till the father's sudden death.

After this recital she broke into a string of lamentations: she must get a divorce from her husband, she would have done so long ago but for the children. She had committed a great wrong, a grievous sin, when she married her husband against her father's wishes. She ought to have taken the man her father wanted her to have; he, certainly, would have obeyed her father, and then everything would have been all right. Oh, she wailed, her husband was not nearly as nice as her father, she could do anything with her father, but not with her husband. Her father had given her everything she wanted. And now she wanted most of all to die, so that she could be with her father.

When this outburst was over, I asked curiously why she had refused the husband her father had proposed.

It seems that the father, a small peasant on a lean little holding, had taken on as a labourer, just at the time when his youngest daughter was born, a wretched little boy, a foundling. The boy developed in a most unpleasant fashion: he was so stupid that he could not learn to read or write, or even to speak properly. He was an absolute blockhead. As he approached manhood a series of ulcers developed on his neck, some of which opened and continually discharged pus, giving this dirty, ugly creature a truly horrible appearance. His intelligence did not grow with his years, so he stayed on as a farm-labourer without any recognized wage.

To this oaf the father wanted to marry his favourite daughter.

The girl, fortunately, had not been disposed to yield, but now she regretted it, for this idiot would unquestionably have been more obedient to her father than her good man had been.

Here, as in the foregoing case, it must be clearly understood that the patient was not at all feeble-minded. Both possessed normal intelligence, although the blinkers of the infantile constellation kept them from using it. That appears with quite remarkable clearness in this patient's life-story. The father's authority is never even questioned. It makes not the least difference to her that he was a quarrelsome old drunkard, the obvious cause of all the bickering and dissension; on the contrary, her husband must bow down before this bogey, and finally our patient even comes to regret that her father did not succeed in completely destroying her life's happiness. So now she sets about destroying it herself, through her neurosis, which forces on her the wish to die so that she may go to hell—whither, be it noted, her father has already betaken himself.

If ever we are disposed to see some demonic power at work controlling mortal destiny, surely we can see it here in these melancholy, silent tragedies working themselves out, slowly and agonizingly, in the sick souls of our neurotics. Some, step by step, continually struggling against the unseen powers, do free themselves from the clutches of the demon who drives his unsuspecting victims from one cruel fatality to another; others rise up and win to freedom, only to be dragged back later to the old paths, caught in the noose of the neurosis. You cannot even maintain that these unhappy people are always neurotics or 'degenerates'. If we normal people examine our lives, we too perceive how a mighty hand guides us without fail to our destiny, and not always is this hand a kindly one.[5] Often we call it the hand of God or of the devil, thereby expressing, unconsciously but correctly, a highly important psychological fact: that the power which shapes the life of the psyche has the character of an autonomous personality. At all events it is felt as such, so that today in common speech, just as in ancient times, the source of any such destiny appears as a daemon, as a good or evil spirit.

The personification of this source goes back in the first place to the father, for which reason Freud was of the opinion that all 'divine' figures have their roots in the father-imago. It can hardly be denied that they do derive from this imago, but what we are to say about the father-imago itself is another matter. For the parental imago is possessed of a quite extraordinary power; it influences the psychic life of the child so enormously that we must ask ourselves whether we may attribute such magical power to an ordinary human being at all. Obviously he possesses it, but we are bound to ask whether it is really his property. Man 'possesses' many things which he has never acquired but has inherited from his ancestors. He is not born as a *tabula rasa*, he is merely born unconscious. But he brings with him systems that are organized and ready to function in a specifically human way, and these he owes to millions of years of human development. Just as the migratory and nest-building instincts of birds were never learnt or acquired individually, man brings with him at birth the ground-plan of his nature, and not only of his individual nature but of his collective nature. These inherited systems correspond to the human situations that have existed since primeval times: youth and old age, birth and death, sons and daughters, fathers and mothers, mating, and so on. Only the individual consciousness experiences these things for the first time, but not the bodily system and the unconscious. For them they are only the habitual functioning of instincts that were preformed long ago. 'You were in bygone times my wife or sister,' says Goethe, clothing in words the dim feelings of many.

I have called this congenital and pre-existent instinctual model, or pattern of behaviour, the *archetype*. This is the imago that is charged with the dynamism we cannot attribute to an individual human being. Were this power really in our hands and subject to our will, we would be so crushed with responsibility that no one in his right senses would dare to have children. But the power of the archetype is not controlled by us; we ourselves are at its mercy to an unsuspected degree. There are many who resist its influence and its compulsion, but equally many who identify with the archetype, for instance with the *patris potestas* or with the queen ant. And because everyone is in some degree 'possessed' by his specifically human preformation, he is held fast and fascinated by it and exercises the same influence on others without being conscious of what he is doing. The danger is just this unconscious identity with the archetype: not only does it exert a dominating influence on the child by suggestion, it also causes the same unconsciousness in the child, so that it succumbs to the influence from outside and at the same time cannot oppose it from within. The more a father identifies with the archetype, the more unconscious and irresponsible, indeed psychotic, both he and his child will be. In the case we have discussed, it is almost a matter of *folie à deux*.

In our case, it is quite obvious what the father was doing, and why he wanted to marry his daughter to this brutish creature: he wanted to keep her with him and make her his slave for ever. What he did is but a crass exaggeration of what is done by thousands of so-called respectable, educated parents, who nevertheless pride themselves on their progressive views. The fathers who criticize every sign of emotional independence in their children, who fondle their daughters with ill-concealed eroticism and tyrannize over their feelings, who keep their sons on a leash or force them into a profession and finally into a 'suitable' marriage, the mothers who even in the cradle excite their children with unhealthy tenderness, who later make them into slavish puppets and then at last ruin their love-life out of jealousy: they all act no differently in principle from this stupid, boorish peasant. They do not know what they are doing, and they do not know that by succumbing to the compulsion they pass it on to their children and make them slaves of their parents and of the unconscious as well. Such children will long continue to live out the curse laid on them by their parents, even when the parents are long since dead. 'They know not what they do.' Unconsciousness is the original sin.

Case 4

An eight-year-old boy, intelligent, rather delicate-looking, brought to me by his mother on account of enuresis. During the consultation the child clung all the time to his mother, a pretty,

241

youthful woman. The marriage was a happy one, but the father was strict, and the boy (the eldest child) was rather afraid of him. The mother compensated for the father's strictness by a corresponding tenderness, to which the boy responded so much that he never got away from his mother's apron-strings. He never played with his schoolfellows, never went alone into the street unless he had to go to school. He feared the boys' roughness and violence and played thoughtful games at home or helped his mother with the housework. He was extremely jealous of his father, and could not bear it when the father showed tenderness to the mother.

I took the boy aside and asked him about his dreams. Very often he dreamt of a *black snake that wanted to bite his face*. Then he would cry out, and his mother had to come to him from the next room and stay by his bedside.

In the evening he would go quietly to bed. But when falling asleep it seemed to him that a *wicked black man with a sword or a gun was lying on his bed, a tall thin man who wanted to kill him*. The parents slept in the next room. The boy often dreamt that something dreadful was going on in there, as if there were *great black snakes or evil men who wanted to kill Mama*. Then he would cry out, and Mama came to comfort him. Every time he wet his bed he called his mother, who would then have to change the bedclothes.

The father was a tall thin man. Every morning he stood naked at the washstand in full view of the boy, to perform a thorough abution. The boy also told me that at night he often started up from sleep at the sound of strange noises in the next room; then he was always horribly afraid that something dreadful was going on in there, a struggle of some kind, but his mother would quiet him and say it was nothing.

It is not difficult to see what was happening in the next room. It is equally easy to understand the boy's aim in calling out for his mother: he was jealous and was separating her from the father. He did this also in the daytime whenever he saw his father caressing her. Thus far the boy was simply the father's rival for his mother's love.

But now comes the fact that the snake and the wicked man threaten him as well: the same thing happens to him as happens to his mother in the next room. To that extent he identifies with his mother and thus puts himself in a similar relationship to the father. This is due to his homosexual component, which feels feminine towards the father. The bed-wetting is in this case a substitute for sexuality. Pressure of urine in dreams and also in the waking state is often an expression of some other pressure, for instance of fear, expectation, suppressed excitement, inability to speak, the need to express an unconscious content, etc. In our case the substitute for sexuality has the significance of a premature masculinity which is meant to compensate the inferiority of the child.

Although I do not intend to go into the psychology of dreams in this connection, the motif of the black snake and of the black man should not pass unmentioned. Both these terrifying spectres threaten the dreamer as well as his mother. 'Black' indicates something dark, the unconscious. The dream shows that the mother-child relationship is menaced by unconsciousness. The threatening agency is represented by the mythological motif of the 'father animal'; in other words the father appears as threatening. This is in keeping with the tendency of the child to remain unconscious and infantile, which is decidedly dangerous. For the boy, the father is an anticipation of his own masculinity, conflicting with his wish to remain infantile. The snake's attack on the boy's face, the part that 'sees', represents the danger of consciousness (blinding).

This little example shows what goes on in the psyche of an eight-year-old child who is over-dependent on his parents, the blame for this lying partly on the too strict father and the too tender mother. The boy's identification with his mother and fear of his father are in this individual instance an infantile neurosis but they represent at the same time the original human situation, the clinging of primitive consciousness to the unconscious, and the compensating impulse which strives to tear consciousness away from the embrace of the darkness. Because man has a dim premonition of this original situation behind his individual experience, he has always tried to give it generally valid expression through the universal motif of the divine hero's fight with the mother dragon, whose purpose is to deliver man from the power of darkness. This myth has a 'saving', i.e. therapeutic significance, since it gives adequate expression to the dynamism underlying the individual entanglement. The myth is not to be causally explained as the consequence of a personal father-complex, but should be understood teleologically, as an attempt of the unconscious itself to rescue consciousness from the danger of regression. The ideas of 'salvation' are not subsequent rationalizations of a father-complex; they are, rather, archetypally preformed mechanisms for the development of consciousness.

What we see enacted on the stage of world-history happens also in the individual. The child is guided by the power of the parents as by a higher destiny. But as he grows up, the struggle between his infantile attitude and his increasing consciousness begins. The parental influence, dating from the early infantile period, is repressed and sinks into the unconscious, but is not eliminated; by invisible threads it directs the apparently individual workings of the maturing mind. Like everything that has fallen into the unconscious, the infantile situation still sends up dim, premonitory feelings, feelings of being secretly guided by other-worldly influences. Normally these feelings are not referred back to the father, but to a positive or negative deity. This change is accomplished partly under the influence of education, partly spontaneously. It is universal. Also, it resists conscious criticism with the force of an instinct, for which reason the soul (*anima*) may fittingly be described as *naturaliter religiosa*. The reason for this development, indeed its very possibility, is to be found in the fact that the child possesses an inherited system that anticipates the existence of parents and their influence upon him. In other words, behind the father stands the archetype of the father, and in this pre-existent archetype lies the secret of the father's power, just as the power which forces the bird to migrate is not produced by the bird itself but derives from its ancestors.

It will not have escaped the reader that the rôle which falls to the father-imago in our case is an ambiguous one. The threat it represents has a dual aspect: fear of the father may drive the boy out of his identification with the mother, but on the other hand it is possible that his fear will make him cling still more closely to her. A typically neurotic situation then arises: he wants and yet does not want, saying yes and no at the same time.

This double aspect of the father-imago is characteristic of the archetype in general: it is capable of diametrically opposite effects and acts on consciousness rather as Yahweh acted towards Job—ambivalently. And, as in the Book of Job, man is left to take the consequences. We cannot say with certainty that the archetype always acts in this way, for there are experiences which prove the contrary. But they do not appear to be the rule.

An instructive and well-known example of the ambivalent behaviour of the father-imago is the love-episode in the Book of Tobit. Sara, the daughter of Raguel, of Ecbatana, desires to marry. But her evil fate wills it that seven times, one after the other, she chooses a husband who dies on the wedding night. It is the evil spirit Asmodeus, by whom she is persecuted, that kills these men. She prays to Yahweh to let her die rather than suffer this shame again, for she is despised even by her father's maid-servants. The eighth bridegroom, her cousin Tobias, the son of Tobit, is sent to her by God. He too is led into the bridal chamber. Then old Raguel, who had only pretended to go to bed, goes out and thoughtfully digs his son-in-law's grave, and in the morning sends a maid to the bridal chamber to make sure that he is dead. But this time Asmodeus' rôle is played out, for Tobias is alive.

The story shows father Raguel in his two rôles, as the inconsolable father of the bride and the provident digger of his son-in-law's grave. Humanly speaking he seems beyond reproach, and it is highly probable that he was. But there is still the evil spirit Asmodeus and his presence needs explaining. If we suspect old Raguel personally of playing a double rôle, this malicious insinuation would apply only to his sentiments; there is no evidence that he committed murder. These wicked deeds transcend the old man's daughter-complex as well as Sara's father-complex, for which reason the legend fittingly ascribes them to a demon. Asmodeus plays the rôle of a jealous father who will not give up his beloved daughter and only relents when he remembers his own positive aspect, and in that capacity at last gives Sara a pleasing bridegroom. He, significantly enough, is the eighth: the last and highest stage.[6] Asmodeus stands for the negative aspect of the father archetype, for the archetype is the genius and daemon of the personal human being, 'the god of human nature, changeful of countenance, white and black'.[7]

The legend offers a psychologically correct explanation: it does not attribute superhuman evil to Raguel, it distinguishes between man and daemon, just as psychology must distinguish between what the human individual is and can do and what must be ascribed to the congenital, instinctual system, which the individual has not made but finds within him. We would be doing the gravest injustice to Raguel if we held him responsible for the fateful power of this system, that is, of the archetype.

The potentialities of the archetype, for good and evil alike, transcend our human capacities many times, and a man can appropriate its power only by identifying with the daemon, by letting himself be possessed by it, thus forfeiting his own humanity. The fateful power of the father complex comes from the archetype, and this is the real reason why the *consensus gentium* puts a divine or daemonic figure in place of the father. The personal father inevitably embodies the archetype, which is what endows his figure with its fascinating power. The archetype acts as an amplifier, enhancing beyond measure the effects that proceed from the father, so far as these conform to the inherited pattern.

Notes

1. I have discussed this question on two occasions: *Symbols of Transformation* (in regard to the son), and 'Psychological aspects of the mother archetype' (in regard to the daughter). [*CW* 5 and *CW* 9i respectively—Ed.]

2. Sommer, R. (1907). *Familienforschung und Vererbungslehre,* Leipzig. Jörger, J. (1905). 'Die Familie Zero', *Arch. Rass. u. GesBiol.* II, Leipzig and Berlin.
   Ziermer, M. (1908). 'Genealogische Studien über die Vererbung geistiger Eigenschaften', *Arch. Rass. u. GesBiol.* V.

3. Fürst, E. (1907). 'Statistical investigations on word-associations and on familial agreement in reaction-type among uneducated persons', in *Studies in Word-Association,* ed. Jung, C.G., trans. Eder, M., London, 1918; New York, 1919.

4. Vigouroux, A., Juquelier, P. (1904). *La Contagion Mentale*, Paris, Bibliothèque Internationale de Psychologie.

5. 'Throughout we believe ourselves to be masters of our deeds. But reviewing our lives, and chiefly taking our misfortunes and their consequences into consideration, we often cannot account for our

doing this act and omitting that, making it appear as if all our steps had been guided by a power foreign to us. Therefore Shakespeare says: "Fate show thy force: ourselves we do not owe:/What is decreed must be, and be this so!".' In Schopenhauer, A. (1877). *Transcendent Speculations on the Apparent Design in the Fate of the Individual*, trans. Irvine, D., London, 1913, p.26.

6. Cf. the axiom of Maria and the discussion of 3 and 4, 7 and 8 in *Psychology and Alchemy* (*CW* 12, paras 201 ff. and 209).

7. Horace, *Epistles*, II, 2, 187-9. trans. Fairclough, H., London and New York, Loeb, 1929.

Glossary

ANDREW SAMUELS
BANI SHORTER
FRED PLAUT

ANIMA AND ANIMUS. Terms used in analytical psychology to suggest a personification of the woman within the man and the man within the woman. The imagery stems from Jung's encounter with such personifications arising from his unconscious after the break with Freud. For Jung, as a man, the inner figure was female and he called this *anima* (from the Latin word for 'soul'). Later, Jung recognized the same phenomenon in women and he called that the *animus* (from the Latin word for 'mind' or 'intellect'). Anima and animus may appear as human figures, but they may more accurately be seen as representative of archetypal patterns. For example, anima speaks of imagination, fantasy and play, while animus refers to focused consciousness, authority and respect for facts. Nowadays, it is widely regarded as fallacious to link such psychological traits to sex. Anima and animus can be understood as representing alternative modes of perception, behaviour and evaluation. The fact that 'contrasexual' figures appear in dreams etc. suggests a symbolic process; a man will express symbolically that which is foreign to him in the form of a being with a 'foreign' body. And the same applies to a woman. It is the very strangeness of anima and animus images that gives them their psychological value as harbingers, and often as guides, of psychological change. Anima and animus are psychologically analogous to the biological recessives in the genes whereby a person carries that which does not correspond to his or her anatomical sex. As far as personal relationships are concerned, anima and animus spark attraction between the sexes. However, projection of anima or animus onto a partner is usually highly problematic as no humans can live up to the standards of archetypal images. The relation of anima and animus to parental imagos is much discussed in analytical psychology: as the parent of the opposite sex is the first such figure to be encountered, do experiences of parents colour anima and animus imagery, or do anima and animus affect early experiences of parents?

ARCHETYPE. An innate, inherited pattern of psychological performance, linked to instinct. If and when an archetype is activated, it manifests itself in behaviour and emotion. Jung's theory of the archetypes developed in three stages. In 1912 he

250

wrote of primordial images which he recognized in the unconscious life of his patients as well as by way of his self-analysis. These images were similar to cultural motifs represented everywhere and throughout history. Their main features were their power, depth and autonomy. Primordial imagery provided for Jung the empirical content for his theory of the collective unconscious. By 1917, he was writing of dominants, nodal points in the psyche which attract energy and hence influence a person's functioning. It was in 1919 that he first made use of the term 'archetype' and he did so to avoid any suggestion that it was the content and not the irrepresentable, fundamental structure that was inherited. References are made to the archetype-as-such, to be distinguished clearly from archetypal images, motifs, themes, patterns. The archetype is psychosomatic, linking instinct and image. Jung did not regard psychology and imagery as correlates or reflections of biological drives. His assertion that images evoke the aim of the instincts implies that they deserve equal place. All imagery partakes of the archetypal to some extent. But it may be erroneous to effect too rigid a divide between the personal and the collective unconscious, for the archetype, as a skeletal concept, requires ordinary experience to become fully fleshed out. Notions of innate structure exist in present day psychoanalysis, notably in the Kleinian school: Isaacs (unconscious phantasy), Bion (preconception), and Money-Kyrle. Jung may also be considered a pioneer of European structuralism.

COLLECTIVE UNCONSCIOUS. Like Freud, Jung used the term 'unconscious' both to describe mental contents which are inaccessible to the ego and also to posit a place in psychic structure with its own character, laws and functions. Jung did not regard the unconscious solely as a repository of repressed, usually infantile, personal experience but in addition as a form of psychological activity which transcended personal experience altogether, relating directly to the phylogenetic, instinctual bases of the human race. The contents of the collective unconscious have never been in consciousness and reflect the influence of archetypal processes. Jung, speaking metaphorically, assigns to the collective unconscious a form of 'knowledge', even of thought.

This may be expressed in the language of philosophy as the 'final cause' of a psychological tendency or line of development—the 'sake' for which it happens or is brought about. The final causes which operate in the unconscious may be experienced by a person as promoting the pattern and meaning of his or her life. This aspect of the unconscious is referred to as teleological (from the Greek *telos*, meaning 'end' or 'goal'). It should be noted that Jung is not saying that the unconscious goal causes things to happen in a totally predetermined way.

COMPLEX. Collection of imagos, images and ideas, clustered round a core derived from one or more archetypes, and characterized by a common emotional aura. When they come into play (become 'constellated'), complexes contribute to behaviour and affect whether a person is conscious of them or not. They are useful tools in the understanding of neurotic symptoms. At one time, the concept of complex was so important to Jung that he considered labelling his thought 'Complex Psychology'. Jung referred to the complex as the *via regia* to the unconscious and as 'the architect of dreams'. Contemporary analytical psychology has revised this assessment and the idea is now valued more for its capacity to link the personal and archetypal components of an individual's various experiences, particularly in infancy and childhood. Jung developed his theory via the use of the (now discontinued) Word Association Test. The use of a psychogalvanometer in the test suggests that complexes are rooted in the body and express themselves somatically. The discovery of complexes by Jung between 1904 and 1911 was valued by Freud as an empirical proof of his concept of the unconscious. Though few psychoanalysts use the term (save for Oedipus and castration complexes), it has been argued that the structural theory is itself a theory of complexes and that ego, super-ego and id are examples of complexes.

EXTRAVERSION. See *typology*.

IMAGO. Term introduced by Jung in 1911-12 and adopted in psychoanalysis. When 'imago' is used instead of 'image', this is to underline the fact that many images are generated subjectively, particularly those of other people. That is, the object is perceived according to the internal state and dynamics of the subject. There is the additional specific point that many images (e.g. of parents) do not arise out of actual personal experiences of parents of a particular character, but are based on unconscious fantasies, or derived from the activities of the archetypes. An imago which has operated in a person over time will develop to the point where it functions like an expectation, or rather a filter through which experiences of certain categories of people are perceived. Hence, an imago leads to feelings and behaviour towards others as well as to how they appear in the mind's eye. Complexes are composed of imagos. For example, the imago of the mother signifies the infant's innate tendency to organize his experiences of his early vulnerability round positive and negative poles. The positive pole draws together such qualities as 'maternal solicitude and sympathy; the magical authority of the female; the wisdom and spiritual exaltation that transcend reason; any helpful instinct or impulse; all that is benign, all that cherishes and sustains, that fosters growth and fertility'. The negative pole suggests 'anything secret, hidden, dark; the abyss, the world of the dead, anything that devours, seduces, and poisons, that is terrifying and inescapable like fate' (*CW* 9i, para. 158). From a developmental perspective, this refers to the splitting of the image of mother into her good and bad variants. Jung pointed out that such contrasting images are very widespread culturally so that mankind as a whole does not find it odd or unbearable that the mother imago should be split. However, an infant has eventually to come to terms with the indivisibility of his mother and bring these opposite perceptions of her together if he is to achieve the depressive position.

INDIVIDUATION. The term 'individuation' was taken up by Jung via the philosopher Schopenhauer but dates back to Gerard Dorn, a sixteenth century alchemist. Jung's first published definition emphasized that (1) the goal of the process is the development of the whole personality, (2) it presupposes and includes collective relationships, i.e. it does not occur in a state of isolation, (3) individuation involves a degree of opposition to social norms which have no absolute validity. The unifying aspect of individuation is highlighted by its etymology: a person becomes 'in-dividual', a separate indivisible unity or whole. Jung was at pains to distinguish his concept of individuation from personality integration or ego-consciousness. Rather, the essence is that the self should become divested of whatever is false in the persona and also struggle free from the suggestive power of the archetypes. Many of Jung's statements have contributed to the unfortunate impression that individuation is somehow only for an élite. On the other hand, it also is the case that individuation may proceed in an unobtrusive manner, or be facilitated in analysis. One danger of an intense involvement with the inner world is that its fascinating images may lead to a narcissistic preoccupation. Another danger would be to consider manifestations such as antisocial activity or psychotic breakdown as justifiable results of an individuation process. The symbolism of individuation is often approached via an understanding of the way in which conflicting opposites may reunite to produce a new synthesis in the personality. Mandalas (drawings of geometric figures with more or less regular sub-divisions, divided by four or multiples thereof) were said by Jung to express the totality of the psyche as this is apperceived and experienced in individuation. Though Jung felt that individuation proper was confined to the second half of life, contemporary analytical psychology tends to refer to individuation processes taking place over a lifetime. The main unanswered question concerning individuation is whether integration must of necessity precede individuation. Obviously it is better if there is a strong enough ego resulting from the former to withstand individuation phenomena when they erupt into consciousness, as they can at times.

INTROVERSION. See *typology*.

PERSONA. Term introduced by Jung, deriving from the Latin word for the mask worn by actors in classical times. Hence, persona refers to the social mask or face a person puts on to confront the world. Persona can refer to gender identity, a stage of development (such as adolescence) or a profession. Or a person may consciously or unconsciously highlight one aspect of their personality as a persona. Over a lifetime, many personae will be worn and several at any moment. Jung's conception is of an archetype, meaning in this context that persona is inevitable.

In any society a means of facilitating relationship and exhange is required; this function is partly carried out by the persona. It follows that persona is not to be thought of as inherently pathological or false. There is a risk of pathology if a person identifies too closely with his/her persona. This would imply a lack of awareness of much beyond social rôle (lawyer, analyst, labourer), or too rigid a conception of gender rôle, or a failure to take into account the changing requirements of life at different stages of development. Persona occupies a specific place in Jung's model of the structure of the psyche. That is as the mediator between the ego and the external world. The anima and animus perform the same mediating function between the ego and the internal world.

SELF. Used in analytical psychology from 1916 on with certain distinct meanings: (1) the totality of the the psyche; (2) the tendency of the psyche to function in an ordered and patterned manner, leading to intimations of purpose and order; (3) the tendency of the psyche to produce images and symbols of something 'beyond' the ego—images of God or of heroic personages fulfil this role, referring man to the need and possibility of growth and development; (4) the psychological unity of the human infant at birth. This unity gradually breaks up as life experiences accumulate but serves as the template or blueprint for later experiences of feeling whole and integrated. Sometimes the mother is referred to as 'carrying' the infant's self. By this is meant something akin to the process called by psychoanalysis 'mirroring'.

SHADOW. Used by Jung to refer to the negative side of the personality, the sum of all unpleasant qualities one wants to hide, the inferior, worthless and primitive side of man's nature, the dark side of oneself—'the thing a person has no wish to be'. Jung emphasized that the ego is to shadow as light is to shade, that it is the shadow which makes us human. Jung gave Freud the credit for calling the attention of modern man to this aspect of himself. As the shadow cannot be eradicated (and that should not even be attempted), the best that can be hoped for is a coming to terms with it. This is one of the stated purposes of Jungian analysis: to facilitate the patient's reaching a non-judgemental position in relation to his instinctual side so that he can extract

255

what is of worth therein. It is possible to develop a consciousness concerning those people and situations most likely to call forth the shadow side.

TYPOLOGY. System developed by Jung to demonstrate and ascertain different modes of psychological functioning in terms of 'psychological types'. Some individuals are more excited or energized by the internal world and others by the external world: these are *introverts* and *extraverts* respectively. But, in addition to these basic *attitudes* to the world, there are also certain properties or *functions* of mental life. Jung identified these as *thinking*—by which he meant knowing what a thing is, naming it and linking it to other things; *feeling*—which for Jung means something other than affect or emotion, a consideration of the value of something or having a viewpoint or perspective on something; *sensation*—which represents all facts available to the senses, telling us that something is, but not what it is; and, finally, *intuition*, which Jung uses to mean a sense of where something is going, of what the possibilities are. A person will have a primary or *superior* function; this will be the most developed and refined of the four. The other three functions fall into a typical pattern. One will be only slightly less developed than the superior function and this is called the *auxiliary* function. One will be the least developed of all. Because this is the most unconscious, least accessible and most problematic function, it is referred to as the *inferior* function. Using the two attitudes and the superior and auxiliary functions, it is possible to produce a list of sixteen basic types. Several psychological tests exist, based on Jung's hypotheses. These are used by some analytical psychologists clinically and also have educational and industrial application. There is a difference of emphasis in analytical psychology between those who welcome the scientific tenor of typology and those who use it as a rule-of-thumb approach, the value of which lies in providing an overall assessment of a person's functioning. Jung worked on his typology as a means of understanding the differences between himself and Freud (to put it concisely, he felt he was introverted and Freud extraverted). It seems to be the case that interpersonal dysfunction can be understood in terms of typological difference.

256

INDEX

Compiled by Albert Dickson

257

THE FATHER

260